INSIDE
RED BULL RACING

A season with F1's most thrilling team

MATT MAJENDIE

First published in the UK in 2026 by Blink Publishing
An imprint of Bonnier Books UK
5th Floor, HYLO, 105 Bunhill Row,
London, EC1Y 8LZ

Copyright © Matt Majendie, 2026

All rights reserved.

No part of this publication may be reproduced, stored or transmitted in any form
or by any means, electronic, mechanical, photocopying or otherwise, or used or
reproduced for the training or development of artificial intelligence technologies or
systems, without the prior written permission of the publisher.

The right of Matt Majendie to be identified as Author of this work
has been asserted by him in accordance with the Copyright, Designs and
Patents Act, 1988.

A CIP catalogue record for this book is available from the British Library.

Hardback ISBN: 978-1-78512-813-4
Trade Paperback ISBN: 978-1-78512-814-1

Also available as an ebook and an audiobook

1 3 5 7 9 10 8 6 4 2

Designed and Typeset by Envy Design Ltd
Printed and bound in Great Britain by CPI (UK) Ltd, Croydon CR0 4YY

At Bonnier Books UK, we are committed to publishing sustainably.
Find out more here: bonnierbooks.co.uk/sustainability

Every reasonable effort has been made to trace copyright holders of
material reproduced in this book, but if any have been inadvertently
overlooked the publishers would be glad to hear from them.

The authorised representative in the EEA is
Bonnier Books UK (Ireland) Limited.
Registered office address:
Block B, The Crescent Building
Northwood, Santry
Dublin 9, D09 C6X8
Ireland
compliance@bonnierbooks.ie

www.bonnierbooks.co.uk

CONTENTS

Prologue: *THE FINAL RECKONING*   1

Part One: The First Act   5

1. *TITLE NUMBER FOUR*   7
2. *OPEN-DOOR POLICY*   12
3. *HOME SWEET HOME*   16
4. *BEHIND THE CURTAIN*   24
5. *ALL CHANGE*   31
6. *NEW KID ON THE BLOCK*   39
7. *DESERT BEGINNINGS*   48
8. *CRUNCH TIME*   60
9. *LIGHTS OUT*   64
10. *THE AXE*   71
11. *RACER TURNED LEADER*   80
12. *HIGH-SPEED CHESS*   94
13. *THE MAX FACTOR*   104
14. *IN THE PITS*   118

15. *THE DIVA*   128

16. *IN THE BARRIERS*   135

17. *WELCOME TO MONACO*   145

18. *PAIN IN SPAIN*   160

19. *BAN LOOMING*   166

20. *WILL HE STAY OR WILL HE GO?*   177

21. *END OF AN ERA*   183

Part Two: The Resurgence   199

22. *THE NEW REGIME*   201

23. *MEET THE BOSS*   208

24. *WHO'S IN THE HOT SEAT?*   217

25. *THE TURNAROUND*   228

26. *A NEW POWER*   243

27. *YOU WIN SOME, YOU LOSE SOME*   251

28. *THE KING OF GRAZ*   263

29. *BACK IN THE FIGHT*   273

30. *MEXICO MAYHEM*   284

31. *ENGINEERING A MOVE*   293

32. *THE WONDER DRIVE*   302

33. *WINNING BIG IN VEGAS*   309

34. *CALL ME CHUCKY*   320

35. *THE TITLE SHOWDOWN*   328

36. *ON THE WAY OUT*   341

Acknowledgements   351

Index   353

THE FINAL RECKONING

7th December, 2025, Abu Dhabi Grand Prix

The RB21 comes to rest in its grid box. Its driver has parked it angled slightly to the left, as if to signal the direction of attack for the start of the Abu Dhabi Grand Prix. Max Verstappen sits inside the cockpit, the voice of his race engineer now fallen silent. Verstappen, those on the pit wall, his mechanics watching the big screens nervously in the garage, those in the operations room in Milton Keynes and hundreds of other team members glued to their televisions at home are all aligned in the same goal: victory is everything. But with Verstappen, winning is almost the easy part. To seal a record-equalling fifth consecutive title, he needs championship leader Lando Norris to also finish fourth place or lower.

Moments before, the grid had been full, the final vestiges of the early Sunday-evening sun glinting off the cars and the sunglasses of a conveyor belt of celebrities crammed onto the grid. The Hollywood star Ana de Armas is guided past the two McLarens, a trio of former footballers are leaning against an advertising hoarding in light-hearted conversation, while the American actor Terry Crews, a Formula 1 regular all season long, is his usual all-smiles muscle-popping ebullient self. Overhead, an Airbus A380 performs a fly-past accompanied by an aerobatic team, with trails of red, green, white and black smoke to signify the colours of the United Arab Emirates flag. The list of former F1 world champions in attendance to applaud the latest incumbent is lengthy and prestigious. Will they welcome a 35th new champion to their exclusive club or will that number stay at 34 for now?

Verstappen sits motionless as his trainer Rupert Manwaring pumps cold air into his seating area to counter the track temperature, which hovers in the low 30s even as day turns to a cooler night. For weeks now, all the talk has been of whether he can pull off the impossible, then improbable and now perfectly plausible, thanks to his and his team's refusal to give up, and the calamitous recent weekends of rivals McLaren. As it stands, Norris leads Verstappen by 12 points while Norris's McLaren teammate Oscar Piastri sits four points further back. All the permutations have been pored over by each team, via billions of race simulations, and then dissected through countless in-house meetings.

Somehow, a marathon 24-race season has again come down to the final race, as it did in Abu Dhabi most recently in 2021, the scene of the first of Verstappen's four consecutive world titles. It was also here in 2010 that Sebastian Vettel won Red Bull a first driver's title having started the day third in the championship race. That day, Vettel's cause was aided by a Ferrari error on the timing of pitting championship leader Fernando Alonso. Alonso's race engineer all those years ago, Andrea Stella, is now calling the shots at McLaren as their team principal. And in a further quirk, the other key driver battling for the world title 15 years ago in Abu Dhabi, Mark Webber, is Piastri's manager. Such history is probably meaningless but, at the same time, it adds intrigue to the pre-race build-up.

As championship leader, a first world title is within the grasp of Norris, and yet there is still the great unknown of what Verstappen might do off the line. In 2016, Lewis Hamilton tried to back up the field in the hope it could put teammate and title rival Nico Rosberg under threat from the chasing pack. In the end, it proved to no avail. Verstappen has been asked about employing the same tactic and, despite claiming the track configuration changes since 2016 negate that, it is a ploy that has been actively discussed in Red Bull team briefings. But the two McLarens are equipped with different tyres and different strategies. Even the best driver on the grid will be hard pressed to snub out both at once.

It has been another season of turmoil and triumph for Verstappen. First, his teammate Liam Lawson was brutally axed after just two Grands Prix, then his team boss, Christian Horner, was sacked following the British Grand Prix. The car, described by the removed Horner as a diva, has blown hot and cold, a race winner one weekend, making up the numbers the next. Verstappen, the dominant driver of his era, has become the underdog. Where familiarity has bred boredom over recent seasons, Verstappen's popularity is now seemingly on the rise, even in the UK where he has often been portrayed as the villain of the track.

McLaren have played a part in aiding the turnaround of their rivals. In their team villa in the Abu Dhabi paddock the nerves are understandably far greater than a few doors down at Red Bull. Stella and team CEO Zak Brown have stuck steadfastly to their principle of backing both drivers equally. Should neither of their drivers win the title, the critics will be lining up with the post-season vilification. From one week to the next, Verstappen has begun to breathe more heavily down their necks to take the title fight down to the wire. In 2021, it went to the final lap of the final race of the season. This time, so many eventualities seem possible; car reliability could play its part, a crash, an untimely safety car . . . all have been spoken of and their potential impact. Central to navigating each and every eventuality is Red Bull's strategist Hannah Schmitz, who has arrived at Yas Marina Circuit long before most on this final day, having woken up early feeling nervous, to pore over her calculations and her pre-race report to ensure every single distinct possibility in the upcoming race has been thought through.

As the first light glows red, Red Bull's collective hearts are pounding, as the second illuminates even the usually nerveless Verstappen feels the enormity of the occasion, light three comes on moments later and team principal Laurent Mekies shifts a fraction on his high stool, a fourth red flickers and Verstappen stares intently forwards, waiting for the fifth. As quickly as it illuminates, the five lights extinguish and the engines erupt as the cars scream forwards. Verstappen cuts across from right to left to fend off the challenge of Norris. Verstappen has the lead into turn one of the 58-lap race.

It is the perfect start.

PART ONE

THE FIRST ACT

1

TITLE NUMBER FOUR

Cardboard boxes sit stacked one upon another in a side room of the Red Bull operation in Las Vegas, unopened for fear of jinxing the outcome. Inside is a pile of neatly folded navy-blue T-shirts with M4X emblazoned across the front of them. It is a simple three-lettered logo that says so much: four consecutive world titles, the driver that bit more capable and complete with each passing one. The first was decided in Verstappen's favour following a thrilling season-long tussle with Lewis Hamilton. Number two had started as a close fight – this time with the Ferraris of Charles Leclerc and Carlos Sainz, who had begun the year as the ones to beat – and was eventually captured and celebrated in Suzuka, the home of the team's engine supplier Honda. And then there was Qatar in 2023, where Verstappen won 19 of 22 races, dominating the sport as never before seen and sewing up the title with five races remaining.

Now on the Las Vegas Strip in late November, 2024, title number four is achieved, but not in a manner that Verstappen's early-season form suggested, eschewing his normally agg-ressive approach for a relatively conservative race, with Red Bull off the pace to finish fifth. However, it is enough for those packed boxes of celebratory T-shirts to be ripped open.

Seconds after Verstappen crosses the line, Christian Horner comes on the race radio: 'Max Verstappen, you are a four-time world champion, that is a phenomenal, phenomenal achievement.' In response, his lead driver says: 'Oh my God, man, what a season. Four times, ha! It was a little bit more difficult than last year but we pulled through and we gave it all.'

That understatement belies Verstappen and Red Bull's historic achievement. Before Verstappen, only four men have pulled off the feat of four drivers' titles in a row: Juan Manuel Fangio, Michael Schumacher, Sebastian Vettel and Lewis Hamilton. And only three have more world titles: Fangio, Hamilton and Schumacher. Already the quest has begun back at Red Bull Racing headquarters near Milton Keynes for 2025 with Verstappen in hot pursuit of that lauded triumvirate.

Rarely has a fifth place been more celebrated. The team spray cans of Red Bull, the fizzing sound quickly replaced by that of champagne corks popping. Fireworks fill the Las Vegas night sky and team members don their Max T-shirts, the 'A' replaced by a quirky '4'. Verstappen, giddy with smiles, is held aloft on the shoulders of the mechanics who have shared every second of the season with him. It is a title won in what has become the third-fastest car on the grid in the latter part of the season, one conceding on average more than a tenth of a second per lap to the McLarens of Lando Norris and Oscar Piastri. In a dig at his vanquishers, he tells the Dutch newspaper *De Telegraaf*, 'Would I have become champion in the McLaren? Yes, and much sooner.' It's hard to argue with this statement, such has been the faultlessness of his driving. He has barely put a foot wrong.

Horner will later admit that Verstappen outperformed the car at almost every race. The fourth, fifth and sixth placings were no less important than the wins as the season ticked on and the opportunities for Norris to wrestle back points petered out. But the four-time world champion's cause was also aided by McLaren giving equal billing to their two drivers rather than shifting their full backing to Norris, the better placed of the pair.

Norris, who will end up 63 points adrift in the title race following the season finale in Abu Dhabi, has nothing but praise for his rival. He tells reporters gathered for Verstappen's crowning glory: 'He has no downsides, no negatives. When he's had the quickest car, he's dominated races. When he's not had the quickest car, he's still been just behind us and almost winning the races anyway. He has not had any bad races all year. He has just driven as Max has always driven, which is perfectly and you can't fault him anywhere.' Despite the rivalries and on- and off-track clashes, the pair remain friends, going all the way back to their karting days. And despite being denied a maiden title win, Norris seems genuinely pleased for his old pal. Norris's team principal Andrea Stella, formerly a race engineer for Schumacher and latterly Alonso, says simply that 'we are in the era of Max Verstappen'.

It was in Las Vegas where Verstappen finally put the title out of the reach of Norris. But the deal had been all but sealed the previous race weekend in Brazil. When Verstappen started the São Paulo Grand Prix in 17th – in part down to a poor qualifying session and a five-place grid penalty for a new power unit for the race above his allocated amount — Norris and McLaren sniffed their chance of closing the gap in the title battle. That's not how it transpired. On the first lap alone, Verstappen made up six places in damp conditions, finding himself just outside the points, the audacity of his moves earning comparisons to Ayrton Senna's infamous start at the European Grand Prix back in 1993. By lap two, he was into the points, eventually climbing up to fifth before the likes of Norris and Russell pitted for new tyres. Red Bull took the gamble to delay Verstappen's stop despite others careering off the track in the hope of a safety car being deployed. That came on lap 31, a lap later turning into a red flag when Franco Colapinto crashed heavily in abhorrent weather. By that point, Verstappen was up to second behind only Esteban Ocon for the subsequent restart. By lap 43, he had scythed his way into the lead, eventually winning by 20 seconds. It was a drive that highlighted the supremacy of his car-handling skills.

While there are two more races to come after Vegas, in Qatar and Abu Dhabi, they are little more than glorified victory laps, although Verstappen still wins one and picks up another fifth place in the other to round off the 24-race season. Reflecting on title number four, he says: 'This year we had a car running well but we had a lot of tough races and that is something I am very proud of. The races where we were not the fastest car, we kept it together as a team, worked very hard, remained calm most of the time and barely made any mistakes. We really maximised and maybe over-performed in some places, plus our opposition in a few places definitely didn't grab the points they should have, and all of those things matter when you are fighting for a championship.'

It leaves McLaren scratching their heads at an opportunity

gone begging, and yet going into the new season in 2025, Norris and Piastri will be confident of having the quickest car on the grid. Whether that's enough is another matter. As Norris puts it: 'If you want to beat Max, you have to be close to perfect.'

But Verstappen knows perfection is likely to be required on his part too. The RB20 has been a handful for him and Red Bull's myriad engineers. Then there are the unresolved tensions between Verstappen and the management. Has Verstappen's number-four title merely papered over the cracks in the relationships within the Red Bull hierarchy? Or will the new season bring fresh tensions? Only time will tell.

2

OPEN-DOOR POLICY

Red Bull are unlike any other team on the grid. They were the fizzy drinks company trying to unsettle, take on and beat the established order, and successful in all three ventures. And despite the eight drivers' titles and six constructors' championships courtesy of two very clear periods of dominance, in the years that have followed it has kept that same upstart mentality to a certain degree of an 'us against the established order'. They can be pugnacious and act almost like they are unloved. However, a recent survey carried out by Nielsen and Motorsport Network found Red Bull only second to McLaren in the popularity stakes.

Each team has their own idiosyncrasies. Ferrari long ago earned a reputation for chaos; Mercedes are precise, methodical, with everything planned to perfection. In contrast, Red Bull aren't afraid to hang on until the last minute, new or spare parts often arriving in the nick of time. This flexibility makes them the best at altering course during a race weekend or a full season, and it has consistently made them the best operationally. There may have been slicker and smoother ways to do it – and it doesn't suit every personality on the grid (at Red Bull or otherwise) – but one only has to look at their trophy cabinet to see the success of it.

Another great strength up until the 2025 season has been the two people at the very helm of the team: Adrian Newey and Christian Horner. Arguably the greatest F1 teams have shone with one or two puppet masters pulling the strings. There was Frank Williams at his eponymous team, which he established in 1977 with Patrick Head. By 1980, it had fought off the big names to win both the drivers' and constructors' championships with the bullish Australian driver Alan Jones. There was Ron Dennis at McLaren, the other top team of that decade; Jean Todt in partnership with Ross Brawn for the Ferrari years; and Mercedes' Toto Wolff for Lewis Hamilton's period of dominance. The philosophy is straightforward enough: give an overall head the chance to do as they see fit. Red Bull founder Dietrich Mateschitz and his motorsport right-hand man Helmut Marko were bold enough to put their trust in thirty-something Christian Horner when they first appointed him two decades ago, and, within six years, the team had the first of his cavalcade of titles. The trophies have kept on coming thick and fast ever since.

Alongside Verstappen and Liam Lawson, his two drivers for 2025, the Netflix documentary series *Formula 1: Drive to Survive* has made Horner a star, fans clamouring for his autograph or a selfie. That trio bear the spotlight for Red Bull. But Horner always points out that the team are the sum of their parts. While Verstappen and, to a lesser degree, he are the biggest stars, away from the cameras there is a galaxy of others shining brightly at the racetrack and back at the factory.

Some are known to the wider public, such as Pierre Waché, the French technical director trying to jump out of the shadow of Newey, or Marko, the octogenarian racing director who was once the mouthpiece for owner Mateschitz in Formula 1. But there are all manner of lesser lights, few of whom get the spotlight on them outside the wider team. There are the Caller brothers, the identical twins Matt and Jon, as number-one mechanics for the drivers on either side of the garage. There are the Red Bull lifers such as Will Courtenay, the head of race strategy into his last full season in the team before moving to rivals McLaren to become their sporting director. There is Hannah Schmitz, the strategist, who had no idea such a role even existed in F1 when she first joined Red Bull. Or there is Paul 'Pedals' Monaghan, another long-term mainstay of the team as chief engineer, originally joining at the end of their first season as Red Bull and an integral part of everything they have done since.

There are the race engineers for both drivers. First, Gianpiero Lambiase, the Anglo-Italian race engineer for the entirety of Verstappen's tenure at the team and promoted to head of racing for the upcoming season as a reward for his ability to balance Verstappen's race temperament to a tee. He acts like the older brother to Verstappen, admonishing him over the race radio if he feels he is getting out of line and receiving his own tongue lashings in return from the star driver. They are every bit the team's odd couple, on paper too hot-headed to gel, and yet it works and they have been astonishingly successful together. It is hard to think of them ever not being a driver–engineer partnership. On the other side of the Red Bull garage heading up the engineering for Lawson is a newcomer to the role this year, Richard 'Woody' Wood, the softly spoken

Scottish engineer having been part of Sergio 'Checo' Pérez's trackside engineering team in seasons past.

There are other key figures like Steve Knowles, the new head of sporting who acts as the team's conduit with F1 governing body, the FIA. He also liaises with race control – the arbiter of in-race indiscretions – during the course of a Grand Prix weekend. A wrong call can mean the difference between winning a Grand Prix and being among the also-rans. And then there's the photographers, notably Mark 'Tommo' Thompson and Vladimir Rys, who capture everything on and off track throughout the season. There are those at the racetrack and those back at base – too many to mention, a remarkable number of people – 2,000 in all – required to get two racing cars on track and towards the front of the grid.

It is the perfect season to have a front-row seat. McLaren are breathing down their necks, Ferrari have been boosted by the arrival of Lewis Hamilton and George Russell is the new leader of Mercedes, confident he can bring the team back to winning ways with the sport's newest star, Kimi Antonelli, alongside him. Verstappen is the driver with the target on his back. His team make for compelling viewing, not just because of their recent dominance making them the benchmark for the sport but also the controversy that goes on behind the scenes. Red Bull Racing can be like a goldfish bowl of a team, no other outfit airing their dirty laundry quite so publicly. It makes them a fascinating team to go behind closed doors with for the season ahead, a surprisingly transparent collective in such a secretive world as Formula 1 willing to let an outsider in. Inside the four walls of the factory or at a race weekend, there is a real family feel, albeit an occasionally dysfunctional family that does not always see eye to eye.

3

HOME SWEET HOME

It is Monday at an innocuous industrial estate on the outskirts of Milton Keynes. Here, there is no sense of dread for the start of the working week. But then at Red Bull Racing, as team principal Christian Horner likes to put it, this isn't nine to five. Instead, the hundreds of men and women on the payroll toil around the clock to stay ahead of the chasing pack as Formula 1's most recent front-runners. On the eve of the 2025 season, one more trophy – Max Verstappen's hard-fought drivers' title from the previous season – has been added to the already bulging cabinet in the reception of the team's headquarters. The trophy-winning began with a first podium from David Coulthard, who was third at the 2006 Monaco Grand Prix, a first victory coming courtesy of Coulthard's replacement, Sebastian Vettel, in China three years later. In short, it is a metallic homage to unrelenting success – floor to ceiling spanning 12 levels of trophies for 122 Grand Prix victories, as well as eight drivers' titles and six constructors' championships. Much more success and an extension will be required.

Milton Keynes, a town just 50 miles north of London that only came into being in 1967 in a bid to provide a partial solution to London's housing crisis, is the unlikely backdrop to this British sporting success story. While bankrolled by Austrian-Thai billionaires, this is a team on British soil made up of a largely British workforce – and yet not always celebrated in the UK as it perhaps should be. Arguably its most famous inhabitants have a far more recent history than one of the UK's newest towns, this particular F1 operation having only come into being ahead of the 2005 F1 season when Dietrich Mateschitz and his energy drinks company bought the Jaguar racing team.

There is still a nod to Sir Jackie Stewart at Red Bull Racing's Milton Keynes campus. The main structure bears the name the Stewart Building, a curved glass-fronted building with big bulls either side, head down and horns bowed. The name is a hat tip to the octogenarian three-time world champion Scot who founded his eponymous team for the 1997 season, a predecessor of what would become Red Bull Racing. Undone by what seemed like two seasons full of race retirements – Rubens Barrichello's excellent second place at the 1997 Monaco Grand Prix aside – its fortunes turned in 1999 following a brief stint with Jos Verstappen in one of its race seats just nine months after son Max was born. Barrichello was consistently in the points while new teammate Johnny Herbert won that year's European Grand Prix, the third and final Grand Prix victory of the British driver's career. But with Stewart struggling financially and the team wanting major investment to take on the sport's behemoths like McLaren and Williams, manufacturer Ford stepped in to buy it for the 2000 season. Speaking at the time of the buyout, Ford chief executive officer and president Jac Nasser said: 'Ford Motor Company has a long and very successful record in auto racing. Our latest move will allow us to take our performance to the next level.'

Under the Jaguar Racing name, Ford ploughed something in the region of half a billion pounds into the team for its 85-Grand Prix history, which equated to two podium finishes and 49 championship points in total, more than £10 million per point. It would later be referred to as one of the most high-profile failures in F1 history. With the team haemorrhaging money and Ford head office in the United States deciding to pull the plug, it was announced in September, 2004 that the team was being put up for sale with a mid-November deadline for any deal to go through. Suitors were hardly queuing up to step in, but just before the deadline was reached, Red Bull founder Mateschitz bought Jaguar for a nominal $1 fee with the promise of ploughing in something in the region of £100 million per season for the next three seasons. In the process some 350 jobs were saved – a workforce a sixth of what it is now.

Mateschitz and the brand had been involved in Formula 1 previously as a 60 per cent owner of another team on the grid, Sauber, a stake he had sold in 2002. Now as a full team owner, Mateschitz, on the advice of his motorsport consultant and close friend Helmut Marko, raised further eyebrows in signing Horner as team principal over a more established figurehead. Two months previously, the Austrian had publicly indicated Tony Purnell would remain as team principal. By January, Purnell was out. Horner recalls sitting in the car park at Red

Bull sheepishly watching Purnell be escorted off the premises, a fate that would befall Horner himself two decades later. Horner had shone as team boss in F3000 – then the leading feeder series for F1 – and was looking for a way into F1. Aged 31, he was comfortably the youngest team boss on the grid, two years the junior of one of the team's drivers, Coulthard.

Looking back on that first season years later, Marko recalls wistfully: 'When the decision was done that we will buy Jaguar, Mr Mateschitz said, "OK, we will try it." We thought maybe we can win a Grand Prix once. I don't know the number exactly we've won but I know the championships. We had eight drivers' championships and six constructors' championships. That's very impressive and it was a big surprise, our first win – I think it was in China in the rain. Now we are fighting for a fifth title with Max.'

Horner and the team went on a recruitment drive, bringing in the likes of Guenther Steiner, who would later go on to become Haas team principal and, for a period, one of the stars of *Drive to Survive*. Mark Smith, previously of Jordan and Renault, was signed as technical director tasked with creating a competitive car, something predecessors Jaguar had never really achieved. Remarkably, the team did not flop in their debut season. At their first race, the 2005 Australian Grand Prix, Coulthard was fourth with teammate Christian Klien seventh, a result that led to raucous celebrations. In one race, the pair had scored just one point fewer than predecessors Jaguar had the entire previous season. Between them, the drivers scored points in the opening five races.

Horner talked from the outset of a work-hard play-hard philosophy, and he and the team stuck to that throughout. A few races into season one came the birth of the Energy Station, the team's hospitality suite in the paddock at Grand Prix weekends. In the secretive world of F1, theirs was an open-door policy, a DJ playing to a packed house every Thursday evening while those through the doors drank all manner of sundowners. Inevitably, it led to a reputation as a party team. Many assumed its time on the grid would be short-lived, a flash in the pan.

Klien recalls two decades on: 'They were good days, the beginning of Red Bull. I knew the team very well because it was the same people as Jaguar, although the people at the top had changed. The basics were still the same but Red Bull wanted to have a totally different approach. It started with the Energy Station. They wanted to be a very open team who invited everybody in. They broke up the approach of Formula 1 a bit in the paddock. Before every Grand Prix and after every Grand Prix there were big parties. And all the other teams were always seen there, especially on the Sunday night! But of course you couldn't have that reputation for years two, three, four, because in the end Red Bull didn't want to be there just to be a number. They also wanted to be successful. So after two years the approach of having a party team changed.'

Klien would be replaced after two seasons by his former teammate Mark Webber, who broke the news to his friend himself that he would be taking the seat as part of a new engine deal with Renault. In his time at the team Webber would come agonisingly close to winning the world title in 2010 and admits the early celebrations were a bit over the top. 'Some of the parties were absolutely legendary, going to sunrise often,' he says of the aftermath of a win. 'And I think everyone loved that, it was great. Early on maybe they overcooked it a bit.'

Red Bull also flipped the traditional marketing approach on

its head thanks to Mateschitz, who in many ways changed the face of how a brand could market itself. Central to his approach was always selling the can, a mantra that continues across Red Bull as a whole today, but with it he sold a sense of adventure and adrenaline. At a memorable Monaco Grand Prix that first year, the team partnered with the latest Star Wars film, *Revenge of the Sith*. The two cars bore Star Wars livery, its pit crew dressed as Stormtroopers, and the likes of Darth Vader and Chewbacca were even in attendance in a paddock that was more accustomed to billionaires and a conveyor belt of celebrities. To prove it wasn't just a publicity stunt, Coulthard also picked up the team's first podium that weekend.

But Monaco was only the beginning. Undeniably the biggest play in Horner's entire F1 tenure would come next in luring technical whizz Adrian Newey, who had created dominant cars at Williams and McLaren and is generally regarded across the grid as the greatest designer in F1's 75-year history. Coulthard organised dinner between the relevant parties at Bluebird restaurant in London, the Scot's plan being for him to sweet-talk Newey's then wife Marigold while Horner set about persuading the McLaren man to take a risk and switch teams. The pair hit it off almost immediately. They'd grown up in a similar part of the UK, their outlook was not dissimilar and Newey liked the Red Bull approach of going all in, effectively starting from scratch to build a championship-winning car. Newey then flew to Austria, where Mateschitz pushed the wider virtues of Red Bull as a brand, its philosophy and its vision for growth both in F1 and as an entire commodity.

Newey was convinced by the project even in its relative infancy, although Mateschitz took some persuading to spend the sort of cash usually reserved for a top racing driver on a technical boss. On 8th November, just three weeks after the end of their first F1 season, the eye-raising Newey deal was finalised. With Newey in place and able to recruit others around him, Red Bull had properly arrived. When I ask Marko two decades on if it was the best signing ever, even beyond that of Verstappen, who he brought into the team, he says: 'Yes, because he was the only one who had won championships and who knew what was necessary. In the end, that was where the big change came.'

Newey initially leaned heavily on Coulthard and Klien. As the Austrian driver recalls: 'He's an engineer who understands the driver part as well as driving and racing – it was very beneficial and a positive that he had the experience of what it's like to be behind the wheel of other racing cars.' On Horner, Klien adds: 'He was very young, younger than David Coulthard, but with Christian it was great, to be honest. He was at the same level as us because he used to be a race-car driver, so he understood the driver's side even better. He was always a very approachable guy and did a really good job because he did all the day-to-day work in Milton Keynes with a lot of help from Adrian and learned a lot from his work style and leadership. That developed into a really good combination.'

On Newey's first lunch with his engineers, he recalls being told that he had to adhere to the Jaguar way of doing things and simply fit in. That has never been his style. Initially, he threw himself into designing his first car, the RB3, and gradually instilled the belief that this team could be race winners rather than a midfield outfit. He unapologetically cut anyone who didn't fit within the engineering department and recruited the right people to change the culture.

In addition, Mateschitz stepped in before the start of the

2006 season to buy a second F1 team, Minardi, which was rebranded Toro Rosso, now Racing Bulls or VCARB. It became a hotbed, giving drivers from Red Bull's junior programme a first taste of F1, most compellingly early on with Sebastian Vettel in 2008, a year before he stepped up to the A team. Verstappen would also make his debut on the F1 grid with the team nearly a decade later.

4

BEHIND THE CURTAIN

It is a grey January afternoon. A recent downpour means there is limited footfall along Bradbourne Drive, with its neatly cut lawns and smattering of trees giving little indication of the operation going on behind closed doors. A forklift truck trundles past quietly beeping, with its driver head-to-toe in Red Bull kit. The location is just three miles away from Bletchley Park, which became the central hub for the Allies code-breaking during the Second World War. A newer generation of mathematical and engineering brains are now trying to unlock something rather more fanciful: how to extract more speed from a car travelling on mostly clockwise circuits at breakneck speed. Alan Turing, who at Bletchley Park was among those who cracked intercepted Germany messages, once said: 'Machines take me by surprise with great frequency.' Red Bull are once again hoping to do the same to their rivals after having their hegemony threatened last season, losing the constructors' championship to rivals McLaren but still guiding Verstappen to the drivers' title.

This location stands itself apart from many of its rivals on the grid in that the campus is open to the public. There were calls to tighten security when a gang of four ram-raided the trophy-laden reception in the middle of the night back in 2014 and stole 60 trophies, a third of which were later recovered from a lake some 70 miles away. The quartet were sentenced to between two and seven years each in prison for the crime and, in the aftermath, some suggested beefing up security or even closing the site to the public. Horner insisted it was important to keep it open to curious fans and today, despite barriers at either end of the campus, there remains an open feel to the site, with many fans wandering around, some having paid for tours inside the state-of-the art facilities.

On the first floor is Horner's office where, when not at a race weekend, he sits behind an unassuming desk surrounded by miniature helmets, cars and Red Bull Racing pictures, the few items of Formula 1 memorabilia dotted around the room. Across from it is a communal office where Newey once sat, the technical mastermind having taken his drawing board to rivals Aston Martin for the coming season.

Elsewhere, there is the operations room where engineers feed live information to the track team during the course of a Grand Prix weekend. There is another vast open-plan office filled with designers glued to their computer screens, each showing a different part of the RB21, the team's car for the upcoming season. Elsewhere, a Red Bull F1 car is pushed into a makeshift parking spot as the pit crew practise their pit stops, aiming to duck under the two-second barrier for changing all four tyres. Some corridors are hospital-like, spotless, to avoid even a speck of dust falling on the complex machinery that's housed behind its various doors.

It is like a white-walled maze, too easy to get lost within its confines. No quarter of it is the same, a peer through each door giving a sense that this winning machine is way beyond what one might see watching on television at a Grand Prix weekend or up close and personal for those lucky enough to get trackside. In one, Verstappen's gearbox is being put through its paces, stress-tested to assess its durability. Inputted in a computer is every single gear change from Verstappen at a race weekend. From the other side of the perspex glass, a research-and-development engineer watches and listens out for any issues as it roars from first up to eighth gear and back again. Across the way, Verstappen's start from the last United States Grand Prix is being played out on repeat. A technician is observing the moment when the five red lights go out, Verstappen engages first gear and is off the line, all aimed at assessing the durability of the clutch. British Cycling boss Dave Brailsford liked to talk about marginal gains in the British team's pomp. This takes it to the nth degree, some of the advances seem astonishingly minuscule and all are aimed at fractional improvements.

There are so many nooks and crannies at Red Bull – each one needing accessing with fingerprint recognition – it is hard to keep up with everything that is happening. Walk further down Bradbourne Drive and there is an adult playground complete with a gym and a padel court on which two members of staff are playing. There is an inter-team tournament each year which is hotly contested. To one side of the court sits a golf simulator in front of a giant screen with golf clubs at the ready. For now, it is idle, while in another corner six staff, also in their Red Bull team kit, loudly play table football. Competition oozes from every pore at this place.

Next to it is Powertrains, where for the first time in their history Red Bull are building their own engine in-house for next season, headed up by former Mercedes man Ben Hodgkinson and in partnership with Ford. The main facility bears the metallic structure of an F1 car – presumably a Red Bull – as the gateway to its entrance. Across the way, Red Bull Advanced Technologies is perhaps a less well-known facet of the operation, detached from its F1 team. Its staff are behind the RB17 hypercar created by Newey as his pet project for his last full year with the team. It also has a hand in many other creations outside this sport, applying F1 tools and technology to differing engineering challenges, be that America's Cup sailing, hydrogen racing cars, hot-air balloons or electric bicycles.

As if to sum up the ever-expanding nature of the campus, a giant crane hovers above where a new wind tunnel is being built that's expected to be fully operational some time in 2026. Horner looks proudly at what has effectively become his domain and what, with others, he built from the ashes of Jaguar Racing to become the benchmark for the sport. 'When I first came here there were 350 people, we're now 2,000 across the entire group of Red Bull Racing, Powertrains, Advance Technologies, across the marketing group,' he says. 'It means there's always something going on. The most rewarding thing is seeing and working with some tremendously talented people.'

In the opposite building to where he sits is MK-7, which opened its doors in 2019. Out front, an electronic billboard shows on loop M4X and 2024, reliving that fourth straight drivers' championship for Verstappen. That season only ended a few weeks previously, giving team members barely enough time to catch their breath before the build-up to another begins. At the entrance sits a shop selling Red Bull Racing merchandise and on the wall is a giant picture of Red Bull celebrations from another time with Mateschitz front and centre, all smiles, and the likes of Horner and other team members looking infinitely younger, all in thrall to another win. In the foyer is parked an F1 car acting as a precursor to the auditorium that lies behind double doors.

MK-7 is a 1,000-square-metre space and below a state-of-the-art LED video wall sit 15 former Red Bull F1 cars in chronological order, each telling a different story and highlighting how Red Bull have evolved, and so too the sport, with various facelifts and regulation changes. On one wall, stencils spell out the names and numbers of the drivers' and constructors' championships. Such is the speed of success, Verstappen's crown from 2024 has yet to be added. Beside it stands a picture of Sebastian Vettel with four fingers raised, the German being the team's other four-time world champion. Beneath are five different Pirelli tyres with the five compounds for the past season, while above is a raised platform with tables and chairs, as well as side rooms sporting different names, all a nod to Red Bull's past. Inside 'Coulthard' sits a boardroom table with a fridge full of Red Bull and helmets littered around the room, one bearing Coulthard's name, others belonging to Verstappen, Vettel and Daniel Ricciardo. You can rent the space for a not insubstantial fee and it is here where staff gather for team briefings, usually delivered by Horner, and typically after a Grand Prix weekend, immaterial of the result. MK-7 is also home to the massive marketing operation – a central part of the wider Red Bull success story. It's worth remembering the team exists to sell the can. Red Bull have

30-something main partners for the coming season, from title sponsor Oracle to Heineken, who have all paid millions for the privilege. Others include watchmaker TAG Heuer, engine supplier Honda, clothes manufacturer Castore, Visa, AT&T and Siemens to name but a few.

Verstappen has driven a Red Bull car across campus in the past in title celebration, so too down the most notorious downhill ski slope in alpine skiing, the Hahnenkamm in Austria; while Coulthard has performed doughnuts on the helipad of the seven-star Burj Al Arab hotel in the United Arab Emirates. A Red Bull F1 car has been driven down a beach in the Dominican Republic and created road closures in city centres, including the Bay Bridge in San Francisco to allow a pit stop to be carried out on it, much to the bemusement of Americans held up in their cars behind.

Red Bull have a penchant for doing things differently to their F1 rivals and the Heritage team is a case in point. Set up some 15 years ago, it resides in a small corner of a car park behind MK-7 and to the side of Red Bull Advanced Technologies. The Heritage team's job is to keep its former cars running long after their racing retirement and ensure they are in good working order. It also takes the RB7 and RB8, cars for the 2011 and 2012 seasons, to showcase around the world. The thinking is to introduce Red Bull Racing and Formula 1 to both places and audiences that might not ordinarily get to see it. Much like its F1 team, it is a full-on marketing operation aimed at spreading awareness. And those coming to the show runs, as they are called, can get infinitely closer to an F1 car than they might do from the grandstands at a Grand Prix weekend.

Like most rooms inside Red Bull Racing, this one is virtually spotless. On the wall hang the race suits of drivers past and present behind glass frames. To one side of the room rests the Valkyrie, the sports car created by Newey in conjunction with Aston Martin. In another corner sit two past Red Bull F1 cars, but not as you might know them – they are raised up, without tyres, and stripped bare to expose much of the complex inner workings.

Such are the complexities of an F1 engine, a team of engineers from France has been flown in from Renault (who supplied the power units to Red Bull from 2007 to 2018) to start them. As they ignite, the roar inside the four walls of the white-painted room is deafening – a throwback to an entirely different and noisier time in F1. The current engines are hybrid V6s, these are V8s and are much missed by the sport's traditionalists – less so by the greener-minded, as F1 heads towards its net-zero carbon emissions target by 2030. There is a genuine excitement by those from Renault and Red Bull around the RB6 in particular, the car having been rebuilt in recent months. This is effectively a systems check on the car where the success story began.

It was at the wheel of the RB6 that Vettel edged a thrilling season-long battle to become world champion in 2010, usurping teammate Webber in the drivers' standings, then McLaren driver Lewis Hamilton and then Fernando Alonso, who at that point headed up Ferrari's race ambitions. It was the catalyst for Red Bull's first period of dominance and what would turn into four consecutive drivers' championships and a quartet of constructor titles. Within this sprawling site, everything is geared towards a battle for title number five for Verstappen and to wrestle back the constructors' championship from McLaren.

5

ALL CHANGE

In the early days of Red Bull Racing, Newey and Horner would sit down to lunch every day in the factory canteen. Talk would centre on how to turn the nascent team into the sort of sporting behemoths that Newey had helped create at Williams and McLaren. How to turn a fizzy drinks company into a racing entity with a winning mentality?

Sixty-six-year-old Newey is the greatest designer in Formula 1 history, the brains behind winning cars for the likes of Ayrton Senna, Nigel Mansell, Damon Hill, Mika Häkkinen, Sebastian Vettel and, of course, Max Verstappen. In all, 11 drivers' titles and 10 constructors' crowns have been won in cars masterminded by Newey. If he were a team, Newey would rank behind only Ferrari on the all-time constructors' standings in F1's history.

It was only a few years ago that Newey thought his career was over. Pedalling along a cycle path at night on holiday in Croatia with his wife Amanda, the pair edged out of the way of a group of children sharing the same path only for Newey to fall six feet and fracture his skull. After being rushed to hospital, Newey was told by his neurosurgeon that he had a 10 per cent chance of suffering brain damage. 'At that point,' he says, 'I told my wife to get me out of there.' Bernie Ecclestone, with whom he had been holidaying just days before, found him a top neurosurgeon in London while Horner joined forces with another friend to fly him back to the UK to be operated on immediately. He made a full recovery. Within a month, he was back on the Red Bull pit wall at a Grand Prix weekend and from then was fully hands-on for the climax to Verstappen's maiden title in 2021 as he went wheel to wheel with Lewis Hamilton.

Newey was once described by Frank Williams as the most competitive person he had ever met. It is a sentiment shared by many of those who have worked with him at Red Bull, along with former employers and rivals. Initially, his move to Red Bull Racing had a number of industry insiders scratching their heads. 'When I joined Red Bull, people thought it was career suicide,' he recalls. 'It's been the most satisfying because, along with Christian, we took it from the ashes of Jaguar to exactly how we wanted it.'

Such is his competitive nature that he would pack up on the Sunday of a race weekend in a foul mood if events had not played out as he had hoped. But by the time he arrived in the office he had shaken off any post-race grumpiness to bring as much positivity as he could muster. His thinking was that those around him were also acutely aware of a tough weekend and needed both motivation and a lift to ready themselves for the next fight. Mark Webber recalls Newey, usually one of the most softly spoken figures on the grid, not being afraid to let rip if the need required. Webber saw Newey as a Goliath in the team, his presence a huge factor in luring him there in the first place. 'Adrian had the most hay in the barn when it came to winning,' he says. 'It was never in an arrogant way, but he knew what it took to win and people fed off that.' His CV enabled him to recruit some of the best people on the grid and, in turn, Red Bull transformed into the benchmark.

For the past season – in part a reaction to his biking accident but also because of the gnawing need for a fresher challenge – he took a step back from day-to-day operations. He was released from focusing solely on F1 to additionally work on the RB17 hypercar, each of the 50 made costing in excess of £5 million. As Red Bull continued to dominate in 2024 without Newey's hand fully on the design tiller, the story was that the cars were now less Newey creations and more the sum of their parts under Pierre Waché and the technical team the pair had built around them. Bit by bit that began to grate on Newey, so too the infighting at the helm of the team. Then there was the simple matter of wanting another mental challenge in F1. A man who still sketches his car designs with pen and paper on a drawing board, he also peruses the paddock with a red notebook in hand to jot down any observations of his rivals. He would also have pen and paper on his bedside table should an idea or a solution to a problem crop up in his head in the middle of the night. That desire to wake up and sketch ideas had gone, he no longer felt challenged, the reality being he had achieved everything possible at Red Bull and much beyond.

While Newey's exit has been gradual, the departure of such an influential figure cannot help but be keenly felt. His replacement as technical director, Waché, is very much a Newey disciple, brought into the team by him from Sauber, and the Frenchman readily admits he will miss working with him first-hand, no longer able to lean on his vast experience and knowledge. 'I'm sure I can see him in the paddock soon, but we have to move on without him,' he says on the eve of the new season. 'It's how life is.'

Newey has been signed by Aston Martin to work on the 2026 car when the sport undergoes its latest set of regulation changes, so it doesn't bring him and his former employers into direct competition immediately. The team's owner Lawrence Stroll, who beat original suitors Ferrari to Newey's signature, has paid handsomely for his services. His contract means he can earn as much as £30 million a year, including bonuses and add-ons, putting him behind only a small handful of drivers on the grid in terms of annual salary. In addition, Stroll has given Newey a small stake in the Aston Martin business.

Red Bull Racing continue to say it's business as usual, but there can't help but be an impact from the exit of the architect behind some of the most iconic and dominant cars to have made it onto the F1 grid. But already, the focus is on moving forwards and not dwelling on the successes Newey helped create. Horner does at least concede: 'From a personal point of view, it is different.' But he also downplays its significance, understandably not wanting to show signs of weakness to his rivals. 'Adrian's not been there since May but we still have lunch together occasionally. We still retain a great friendship – he's godfather to my daughter, and outside of racing that friendship will remain. Everything evolves and moves on. What excites me is the talent and strength in depth we've got within the business and seeing them have that chance to rise to the surface.'

F1 teams inevitably go through cycles of change, but this

time it's more pronounced than usual for Red Bull at the top, with Newey not being the sole exodus of note. Jonathan Wheatley was the team's sporting director until Kick Sauber offered him the role as their new team principal and persuaded him and his wife Emma to relocate to Zug, Switzerland. It's a far cry from Milton Keynes, the Swiss town a picture postcard of a place hugging a stunning lake and providing hot summers and snow-capped mountain winters. It is also a financial metropolis, tax haven and home to some 30,000 registered companies as well as the Kick Sauber operation, which will become the Audi works team for 2026. As integral as Wheatley has been to the team, Red Bull cannot compete with the salary on offer in the cost-cap era; nor the position of team principal, with Horner in charge.

Wheatley began his career in F1 as a mechanic for Benetton before its rebranding as Renault, rising up to the role of chief mechanic. He was lured to Red Bull for the 2006 season and climbed up the ranks to become one of the team's most influential figures as sporting director and team manager. Wheatley is perhaps best known within the sport for his role in the season-ending championship-deciding Abu Dhabi Grand Prix back in 2021. As sporting director, part of his role was as the team's eyes and ears to the FIA and race control. He successfully persuaded then race director Michael Masi to restart the race with one lap remaining, a controversial decision that effectively helped pave the way for Verstappen to win a maiden title and deny Hamilton a record eighth after a captivating season-long battle.

Newey's exit in particular piles massive pressure on Waché as the technical director, but Horner likes to push the message that Red Bull is all about the collective from top to bottom.

As he puts it: 'Everybody matters and everybody counts. The spirit created here, you feel it, it's self-perpetuating and emanates around the business. It's all about the team. To achieve the results we have, you need every one of those members of the team and each of their departments to be doing their bit.'

Horner describes himself as the boss of a sports team for 22 weekends of the year and the CEO of a technology company for 365 days of the year. Like Newey, immensely competitive, he says that attitude permeates throughout the whole organisation. As a leader he is quick to point out he is 'not in the Alex Ferguson mould' of screaming and shouting, the Scot's so-called 'hairdryer treatment'. Instead, he prefers to give those around him the autonomy to shine. 'I've always believed in employing the right people for the right roles,' he said. 'There's no point employing Adrian Newey and telling him how to design a car – he's a creative guy and you've got to give him creative freedom.'

Horner's own position at the helm of a team he has run for two decades had also looked under threat for great chunks of the previous season after being accused of controlling and coercive behaviour by a female member of staff in December, 2023, the details of which were made public in February, 2024. A whole raft of WhatsApp messages allegedly involving Horner were leaked to the entire F1 paddock in graphic detail on the eve of last season, which Horner dismissed as 'anonymous, speculative messages from an unknown source'. He has always denied any wrongdoing and was cleared following a subsequent investigation led by an external lawyer. He still holds the reins at the team he joined but, for weeks afterwards, there had been some very public infighting between Horner and Verstappen's father, Jos. In one particularly explosive interview, Verstappen Snr told the *Daily Mail*: 'The team is [in] danger of being torn apart. It can't go on the way it is. It will explode. He is playing the victim when he is the one causing the problems.' But an uneasy peace settled in, brokered partly in somewhat unlikely fashion by the team's lead driver, and thanks primarily to him winning title number four. It's hard to stay mad when you're beating everyone else.

With change at the top of the team and rivals breathing down his neck, never has Verstappen and Red Bull's winning run felt more threatened and, even before the title-number-four celebrations, attention has long since turned to next season and beyond that.

Horner, a far more genial personality than he might at times appear on camera, makes the point that it is incredibly hard to make the dominance look easy and emphasises there is no one secret ingredient to the current success. 'Everyone else is searching for a magic bullet. The reality is there isn't a magic bullet but a combination of things coming together.' And his warning for rivals, despite them having closed the gap in the past 20-plus races, is that they still have not mastered their current car, with more pace yet to be extracted from it. 'We're still learning,' he says with his eyes already on the coming season.

But for much of the 2024 season, Verstappen and Red Bull have been threatened primarily by the McLarens of Lando Norris and Oscar Piastri, arguably the best driver partnership on the grid. Meanwhile, Ferrari are hoping for a title boost by the arrival of seven-time world champion Lewis Hamilton, and Mercedes, F1's dominant force prior to Red Bull, insist they are clawing their way back into contention despite a difficult 2024 campaign. After a period of procession by Verstappen and Red Bull, the dominance has been turned on its head, the Dutchman doing well to hold on last time, and rarely has a season been more eagerly awaited than 2025. Verstappen and Red Bull know they have major targets on their backs and the events of the past season leave the build-up to 2025 finely balanced with four teams having title aspirations. It leaves huge question marks hanging over whether Verstappen can battle for a fifth straight world title when racing gets under way again in March in Melbourne, Australia. The Red Bull winning machine that has looked so unstoppable is finally in danger of being derailed.

6

NEW KID ON
THE BLOCK

How each team approaches its driver line-up is entirely different. McLaren have made it clear they give equal billing to Norris and Piastri, while Verstappen has long established himself as the number one both at Red Bull Racing and on the wider grid, and hence the team's focal point. The second seat alongside him has often proved something of a poisoned chalice. A who's who of star drivers have fallen by the wayside. Pierre Gasly lasted just 12 races before he was demoted to the sister team Racing Bulls; his replacement Alex Albon fared a little better, racing 26 Grands Prix as Verstappen's teammate before the axe came down on him too. Sergio Pérez was one of the few to handle that position for any length of time before the results highlighted the ever-widening gulf to the Dutchman. He too was eventually for the chop not long after signing a contract extension for 2025 and beyond.

Ironically, each of the trio's stock has risen since their sacking: Gasly shining despite a largely uncompetitive Alpine at his disposal; Albon spearheading the renaissance of Williams; and Pérez, it will later transpire as his successors struggle, just by sitting out the 2025 season altogether. Pérez will later say on a Mexican podcast: 'I think it has been my best year in Formula 1, the one I didn't race and the one where everyone realised how successful I was.' In another interview, he will insist 'there is no driver who can survive there', arguing even established figures like Lewis Hamilton and Charles Leclerc would struggle alongside Verstappen. Pérez aside, who joined from Racing Point (since rebranded to Aston Martin), the Red Bull philosophy has been to promote from within, habitually taking drivers from their sister team. These drivers in turn have come through the junior programme, where millions have been spent trying to discover Formula 1's next star, and has included the resounding success stories of Vettel and Verstappen. But even with that pedigree, taking the second seat alongside Verstappen has been a case of 'be careful what you wish for'.

Liam Lawson's stock is already high following two stints with the sister team Racing Bulls: first for five races in 2023 for an injured Daniel Ricciardo after the Australian broke his hand in practice for the Dutch Grand Prix, and again in 2024 from the United States Grand Prix to the season's end for a by-then-discarded Ricciardo. The drive that initially won Lawson plaudits was his one-lap effort at Marina Bay, knocking out Verstappen in qualifying at the 2023 Singapore Grand Prix – perhaps a high-risk strategy towards his employers – and then going wheel-to-wheel with him for a stage in the race. It is this elbows-out racing that has caught the eye of both Christian Horner and Helmut Marko. With Pérez bought out of the remaining two years of his contract to the tune of £10 million – on reflection a costly move to have given him a contract extension in the first place – it was a straight shoot-out between Lawson and Yuki Tsunoda for the second seat at Red Bull Racing.

On one side, Tsunoda had the experience of four years in an F1 car while Lawson had just 11 races. On the other, while Red Bull's hierarchy admired Tsunoda's outright pace, there was concern over a lack of maturity, highlighted by his often four-letter outbursts over the race radio. Lawson, it was considered, was worth the risk on his raw pace alone despite such inexperience. Shortly before Christmas, 2024, the New Zealander was unveiled in the second seat.

The Kiwi's initiation in the team's new colours comes a few weeks before the start of the 2025 season in unlikely surroundings. Smoke billows out from a tall chimney at the Tate & Lyle factory in the East End of London, the largest sugar refinery in Europe. Docklands Light Railway trains pass back and forth on the neighbouring tracks while others are on foot for their morning commute or else on the school run, scooters, bikes and prams passing each other along the other pavement.

The traffic on the roads is relatively minor as, somewhat ironically considering the inter-team rivalry, a Mercedes with blacked-out windows pulls up at a large set of white metal-grilled double gates. A brief interaction between the security guard on duty and the car's driver and the gates swing open. In the back seat sits Verstappen, the star attraction, set against an unlikely backdrop for such a cutting-edge F1 operation. Lawson is already inside what is a giant warehouse that feels like a disused car park in places, held up by giant steel pillars. Light pours through the side windows onto an array of cars on an occasionally sunny February day, large lights stepping in to recreate that sunshine behind the lens as it ducks behind the clouds in this pocket of south-east London.

Music blares from speakers, the tunes reminiscent of the team's garage during a Grand Prix weekend. Four main rooms have been put aside for a brand shoot for Red Bull Racing, its sister team Racing Bulls and their line-up in F1 Academy, the all-female racing series and an attempt by the sport to bring in more women both as drivers and engineers. There are various backdrops, a green screen, a collection of makeshift studios. Photos, films and interviews are created for the sponsors and Formula 1 as a whole. On a noticeboard sits a timetable showing where each driver needs to be and when for a conveyor of commitments over the course of the next 12 hours. The neighbouring props are a nod to Red Bull's various backers. There are bottles of the team and Verstappen's sponsor Heineken – non-alcoholic – for drivers to hold in some shots, along with trainers, suntan lotion, even an electric guitar. Some 100 people race around the two-floor maze of a building: photographers, sound engineers, catering staff, hairdressers on hand to keep Verstappen's side parting in place. There is a constant flash of cameras, clothes being steam-ironed upright to remove any slight imperfections pre-shot, a dry-ice machine billowing out smoke with one person wafting a giant piece of cardboard to create exactly the right effect.

There's the first viewing of the sleek 2025-liveried car – not officially unveiled to the public for another two weeks – as well as a Ford Mustang and Honda sports cars, a nod to engine supplier Honda and also Ford, who are partnering Red Bull in their quest to create their own engine in-house for the first time for 2026. Amid the smoke, Verstappen sits side by side

Lawson, the Kiwi youngster looking inherently at ease despite the impossible mission he faces. For the past eight seasons, most of Verstappen's teammates – Gasly, Albon and Pérez – have not got remotely close to him. Admittedly, before that, both Ricciardo and Carlos Sainz had been a match for the now four-time world champion, but that was when he was in the relative infancy of his career. Pérez had his moments where he shone on track – eclipsing Verstappen at times, particularly at street circuits – and yet Verstappen is Formula 1's driver yardstick. He is a generational talent, the son of two former racing drivers and, in the words of former world champion Jenson Button, naturally the quickest driver ever to take to an F1 grid. Plenty of others concur.

A racing driver's instinct throughout the feeder series leading to F1 is to aspire to be the fastest in any given championship and, for Red Bull's junior drivers, to arrive at the A team with the aim of being the best driver both within the team and on the wider grid. While daunting, the challenge of trying to take on Verstappen is too tantalisingly tempting to resist for any racing driver's ego, but that can quickly unravel both in terms of pace and then mental fortitude. Once his superior pace and handling of the car gets into a teammate's head, it is hard to wrestle that back. Some would pore over the data to see how it was possible to go faster in certain sectors or corners in what they believed to be perfect laps by them only to be shy of Verstappen's time. Others might look to conspiracy theories around Verstappen's preferential treatment from Red Bull's engineers. But Albon readily admits Verstappen can do things in an F1 car others can't. The Thai-British driver once likened it to turning up the sensitivity on a computer game to the highest level imaginable, making it nigh-on impossible to control. Verstappen could do it, no one else has managed to do so consistently.

Last season's car, the RB20, boasted a heavy front end, which in turn created instability in the rear of the car, and Red Bull often struggled to get the balance right through a corner. In such instances, Verstappen might master its tricky handling sufficiently well to finish fourth rather than first, while for Pérez that could perhaps manifest itself in a lowly 14th, more a testament to Verstappen's ability than Pérez's lack thereof. Interestingly, Verstappen, for all his competitive nature, has perhaps surprisingly been known to fight behind closed doors on his teammate's behalf. Despite a superior finish and in contrast to his image solely as a cold-blooded racer, he would make the case the car was a nightmare to drive for lesser mortals. Somehow, he could simply make it work, such were his car-handling skills.

The latest incumbent, Lawson, signed to the Red Bull Junior Team development programme from an early age. He won on debut in the first five categories in which he raced: Formula First, Formula Ford, Formula 4, Formula 3 Asia and the Toyota Racing Series, all before the age of 17. Repeating the feat in F1 is nigh-on impossible – only one driver has ever achieved it, Italian Giancarlo Baghetti back in 1961. He wouldn't win another F1 race, though.

Sitting in a side room of this warehouse in London, he is surrounded by make-up and hair products in what has become a makeshift green room for the day. The warehouse sits not far from the home where he currently lives, before relocating to join most of the grid to set up home in Monaco. Speaking in his Kiwi accent – shaped from his upbringing on New Zealand's North Island in Pukekohe, just 40 miles south of Auckland – has not diminished despite the time spent racing in Europe, Lawson admits to a sprinkling of butterflies just a few weeks from the start of the season. There are excited murmurs within the team about his potential, that he likes the car set up similar to Verstappen, while Horner jokes he's been struggling to keep the young charge out of the team's cutting-edge simulator – where drivers can 'drive' any circuit on the calendar – such is his eagerness. For now, the target is simple: not to beat Verstappen but to consistently score points in the constructors' championship, with the team having relied on their four-time champion too often in that regard in recent years. Last season, he scored 75 per cent of the team's points, showing its reliance on his obvious talents. 'I need to drive the car as fast as I can and, if I score enough points for us to achieve that, then I think I'm doing my job,' says Lawson.

Today is a first chance to see the pair interact, although Lawson argues having spent time alongside him as a junior driver Verstappen has always been open to sharing any information. Such is his generosity, he will, in due course, be branded on social media by some as 'Mother Goose' for his dealings with the rookies ('ducklings' of F1). For all the bullishness of any racing driver, Lawson admits: 'It's not even so much testing myself against him but just being able to have access to everything that he's doing. If I want to win that's what I'm going to have to do [beat him] but to start off it's more a learning process and to basically learn off him inside the garage.'

Lawson is on a fast-track learning curve to the opening two race circuits – Melbourne and Shanghai – where he has never driven any car before, let alone a Formula 1 machine. Then there is the issue of pressure. F1 is an unrelenting world, the Red Bull seat far from a forgiving one, and Lawson is all too aware of drivers who have come and gone after just a short stint. 'That pressure has been there since [I was] very, very young in the junior programme. I don't think it's anything new. I'm in a new team but the principles and everything I'm doing are going to be the same. I'm still driving the car as fast as I can. From that side, if I look at it the right way it's all very similar to what I've been doing.'

And yet in F1, the glare is that much brighter, any mistakes far more amplified than they might ordinarily be. In an era of constant cameras, no move goes unnoticed . . . good or bad. At times, drivers can be forgiven for feeling like commodities but they understand the nature of F1, the fact that much of the budget comes from the many sponsors. At one point during the day's filming and photographing, Verstappen feigns headbutting a metal pillar in frustration at an umpteenth take but he remains at ease and good-humoured throughout a largely repetitive day. He stands on a green carousel for nigh on an hour slowly turning 360 degrees, sometimes with his hands on his hips, sometimes with his racing helmet in hand, all the while looking at a moving camera constantly thrust in his face. He is sporting a slight moustache and a little hair on his chin, his parting to the right constantly coiffured by a hairdresser waiting in the wings throughout, and he sips on a can of Red Bull between takes. There is none of the superstar ego or prima donna one might expect from the team's biggest asset.

Between takes he talks with his manager Raymond Vermeulen, who has flown in with him to City Airport by private jet, or else scrolls through his phone. He strikes up conversations with those around him, some in Dutch with the

Amsterdam-based Magenta firm heading up today's filming operation, or in English with others. One compares notes on impending parenthood: Verstappen will become a father for the first time in May with his partner Kelly. 'It's exciting,' he says with a warm smile, before joking he will approach Horner about taking two weeks' paternity leave at a time when he's likely to be racing in Miami. By that point, Verstappen will have a clearer indication whether title number five is a realistic ambition. Lawson's future will prove to be far less predictable.

7

DESERT BEGINNINGS

An eerie silence hangs over Bahrain International Circuit, home to an annual Grand Prix since 2004. With its generally milder, drier weather in February it's become the habitual base for winter testing. The circuit protrudes along the Gulf of Bahrain Road not far from the country's university and Sakhir Airbase in an otherwise uncrowded vista. In the car park, the teams disembark from their minibuses: flashes of red for Ferrari staff, papaya for McLaren and the navy jerseys of Red Bull make their way to entrance six at the circuit. Year on year, the colours remain the same, but the kits are new for 2025, such is the zest of fans globally to be seen in the latest garb of their favourite team. A big wheel, where fans will queue in their droves for the race weekend later in the year, stands idle, gathering dust. The only real noise is the occasional beep as team members pass through the security checks to enter the circuit.

Today, Formula 1 is behind closed doors, a shakedown before testing begins the following morning. In Formula 1, a shakedown is a private session where teams put their new cars through their paces to ensure everything is running as expected, and also to garner footage for sponsors. A member of Red Bull staff hands me a team pass as I make my way through an underground tunnel, the gateway to the F1 paddock for the pre-start to another season. Despite the choice of locale, the weather is cold, the sun popping out but a chilly breeze causing the palm trees to sway. This climate is not typical of this track, which has been used as a desert winter test since its first race 21 years ago. Where once testing took place at Spanish circuits like Jerez, Valencia or Barcelona, now it is the wealthy Middle East, which has an increasingly ever-present feature on the F1 calendar with races scheduled not just in Bahrain but in Saudi Arabia and Qatar too.

In the team, 24 hours before official testing begins, there is all the excitement and nervous anticipation of Christmas. Today is a chance for Red Bull Racing to record this year's car for themselves and their sponsors, away from the spotlight. It has been only a few weeks since the curtain came down on Max Verstappen's fourth world title and now he is aiming to become only the second driver in F1 history after Michael Schumacher to win five consecutive drivers' world championships. For all his past dominance, 2025 is his toughest test. It is only now that the Dutchman will truly know whether he has the machinery to pull off such a feat.

Anticipation within the camp is at a fever pitch. In attendance are his father Jos, Christian Horner and Helmut Marko. After the events of last season, there appears to be a level of conviviality among previously warring parties, smiles even, before the Dutchman takes to the track.

Prior to the fire-up, the engine is heated to the required temperature, which is then monitored by race engineers.

Then one of the mechanics places a large metal rod into the back of the car to give it a kick-start and the engine is duly started by the driver from a button on his steering wheel. Just before this process begins in a place where the noise ebbs and flows, briefly the garage falls silent as mechanics hover over the RB21, four of them crouched down on one knee holding tyre covers over the Pirelli rubber to ensure the perfect temperatures for their lead driver to take the car out on track for the very first time. Matt Caller, Verstappen's number-one mechanic, steps backwards out into the pit lane, checks to his right for no traffic and then ushers his driver forwards to begin his time on track.

Months of consideration, design work, construction and fretting have gone into this moment, countless simulations run and wind-tunnel time deployed. For all the number crunching, there is no certainty the car will perform as anticipated or that Verstappen will be able to hold off rivals breathing down his neck. Verstappen's stint is short-lived — barely a few laps – with reports of a slight issue with the floor of the car. He steps out of the cockpit while tweaks are made. He seems more interested in the testing that follows rather than protracted showboating for sponsors, leaving the brunt of the shakedown running to Liam Lawson.

On F1's pre-school start day, the New Zealander looks every bit the new kid. He has put on baggy jeans for his arrival on track, eighties-style sunglasses and his fair hair is carefully styled. Around his engineers he takes in every piece of information possible between now and the season start in Australia in less than three weeks' time. His trainer Declan Foley, a man mountain of muscle, is never far behind him with race helmet in hand, a water bottle with which to rehydrate him or a fan to cool him as he sits in the cockpit between sessions, which is warm despite the cooler-than-usual Bahrain temperatures.

The pressure is on Lawson but perhaps even more so on technical director Pierre Waché, and his expression does not hide it. He regularly vapes – having made the transition from cigarettes – and sips coffee from a paper cup. The crow's feet show at the sides of his eyes. After all, this is the first fully non-Adrian Newey car for Red Bull in 20 years. Is it sleepless nights before the first running? 'I sleep the same. I don't sleep a lot normally but it doesn't change,' he says over an espresso outside his makeshift office. But the expectation is monstrous on a man taking over from the greatest designer in Formula 1's rich history. 'For the team, it's a big change to not have Adrian there,' Waché says. 'For outside, maybe it's a big thing. For me, maybe less. I try to do the same job as before, work with the team to try to do the best car and fix problems because it's exactly what we're here for. I don't think it's changed a lot but maybe we miss Adrian a little bit, his presence and his view. But he's [been] a person in the team for so long, it's a big role to fill.'

The shakedown is akin to the calm before the storm, the first fire-up of the car gives the team the opportunity to pore over the data and get an understanding of its characteristics, to see how closely the simulation models that have been run ad infinitum in the factory equate to the reality. And yet for Waché there is still a sense of excitement. 'It's quite an impatience of seeing what the car is able to do and what the driver feels about it,' he says. 'The filming day is not really good feedback because the tyres that we run and how we run the car is not the proper conditions. But it's quite an excitement to have the first running of the car because, while it's clearly not an assessment of the competitiveness, we understand what we've done and what we've achieved during the full year to develop this car, what correlation we have, what direction we have to go for the next step based on the feedback. That's very interesting as a technical aspect.'

Unlike much of the paddock, Waché never had any intention of making his way onto the Formula 1 grid. Hailing from a family of doctors and vets, and himself a grade-A student, he eventually ended up with a PhD in biomechanics engineering. From there, he had every intention of going down the avenue of research and eventually taking up the post of a university professor. As he puts it, 'It was decided differently at the time. It was more by opportunity, lucky or unlucky depending on how you see it,' and he trails off into a gravelly laugh indicative of life as a long-time smoker.

Most of the workforce tend to be petrolheads with a lifelong fascination and remember with alacrity their first race in person as though it were just yesterday. In contrast, Waché's maiden race was in a working capacity in his first job – he was a sailing and rugby fan with a passing interest in F1. It was after he finished his PhD and started working for Michelin when he first became immersed in the sport. Back then, the French company was one of two tyre suppliers to F1, the other being Bridgestone. Nowadays there is just Pirelli. With Michelin, the role was trying to improve the understanding of the grip interaction between the rubber and the ground. But when Michelin's contract with F1 ended in 2006 he was forced to look for employment elsewhere. His work was of sufficiently high quality to catch the eye of one of the teams, BMW Sauber, who asked him to work on pneumatics and suspension. And then in 2012, Newey, clearly impressed by what he'd seen, got in touch to offer him a job.

The contrast from Sauber to Red Bull – already three-time world champions – was stark. 'Adrian called me and I accepted the challenge,' he recalls. 'There was excitement to work with him and see how to be a world champion. Where we were with Sauber, it was not realistic to be world champion at the time, we were just struggling to make the team survive and fight for the best we could do. Maybe he can be wrong to pick me but I think it was very nice of him to pick me up. And the main aspect for me was to work with him and this type of team with their level of experience and results. There's no excuse not to achieve the best and this is what I was looking for. We achieved something nice in my first season in 2013 with another world title as well as the last four years.'

Over the course of a decade he has steadily climbed up the ranks to be the team's technical director, in effect the new Newey. And during that time he readily admits to feeding off the knowledge base of his more experienced boss. 'I think it's two aspects that I retain from him the most,' he tells me. 'One is competitiveness – it's crazy how he's so competitive. And also being technically open-minded. That's why he's stayed so long in the business and he's been able to survive and learn things from the young ones coming in.

'Winning races and competing is one aspect of the job and it's the most exciting aspect and the most stressful,' he adds. 'But what is more interesting for me is when you have an issue and you try to understand where it's coming from and you try to solve it or improve the situation. That is what I prefer. The most difficult is when you can't solve the problem and find a solution.'

First and foremost, he is an engineer, obsessed with finding solutions to complex problems and trying to create the quickest car possible on the grid. 'I love that the pace of development in this business is very high, the technical challenge is very high, it's the only sport in the world with this engineering competition. It's why I'm here and I love it. You take opportunity when you have it and enjoy everything you're doing. When you're an engineer, this is the place to be, even when you compare it to the space industry or other competitions like the America's Cup. It's fantastic. You're able to explore and go to levels of detail you cannot find somewhere else and you meet some very talented engineers you don't meet in some other areas of the industry.' The America's Cup is not something that appeals, Waché preferring to keep his passion for sailing as a mere hobby. So instead he envisages seeing out his working days in F1, by which time he might be joined on the grid by his three engineering-minded children.

That trio – all boys, two of whom are twins – were young when he moved out to set up home near Red Bull Racing's Milton Keynes base, and now they're all at university. All sport English accents and, he says with a fond smile, they feel the accent he has is 'crazy'. Two of the three look like they're heading for a future career in F1 – one is focused on aerodynamics, another ensconced in vehicle dynamics. Despite readily admitting that F1 has resulted in him making sacrifices to the detriment of his family, Waché would willingly back them should they choose to join him on the grid, be that at Red Bull or a rival team. He has taught his children – an ethos he tries to stick to himself – to understand there are always people smarter than them which, in turn, will push them on to improve. 'When you don't think you're the best it's very important and pushes you to be better,' he says, acknowledging he is still striving to improve and learn in the sport nearly 20 years on from his arrival.

It's amusing to think of Waché as a professor in a university rather than nervously vaping the evening before testing gets formally underway. However, it is an alternative life that he wonders about, the sliding-doors moment had the Michelin opportunity in F1 not arisen. But this is the road he has chosen and he relishes the competition, the challenge, the perpetual search for knowledge and solutions. And yet . . . 'I'm enjoying it but I'm not sure it's the life I dreamed for,' he concludes thoughtfully.

In contrast to Waché, Christian Horner has an innate ability to look relaxed even when the pressure mounts, be that the overspend of the 2021 season when the team was fined $7 million, or facing public allegations about his private life. Now, just before testing begins, he laughs and jokes with all members of the team from the pit-wall hierarchy to the mechanics in the garage and staff in the team's hospitality suite. The public messaging is that life and F1 is ever-changing. 'Pierre's day-to-day job hasn't really changed at all. It's just that he is the figure name at the front of the car so inevitably there'll be scrutiny. It's the nature of the beast. I think he's well equipped to deal with that with the team that he has. He's been with the team a long time. Everybody knows their job inside out and it's part of that evolution of Red Bull Racing, you have to keep moving forward.'

Come day one of the three days of testing, it is always like a game of poker, teams reluctant to fully show their hand before the season start in Melbourne. Although, indicators are there, not necessarily in fastest lap times but in each car's race pace on their longer runs. Trying to ascertain the pecking order in winter testing is an inexact science, each team with different programmes to each other or else running different fuel loads which equate to vastly different lap times – a far-from-accurate gauge of how the season will play out.

Each time the car comes in or out of the garage, screens are put in place by team members to avoid prying eyes and signs are up: NO PHOTOGRAPHY. To the uninitiated tuning into the team radio, what Verstappen is saying to his race engineer Gianpiero Lambiase is like a foreign language, expressions like 'torque four', 'b-bal eight' coming over the comms system. There is constant tinkering to the car's settings from within the cockpit, with a nod to Verstappen to make an adjustment on his steering wheel, often done while travelling in excess of 200mph, such is his car control and capacity to multitask at such unimaginable speeds.

Amid it all, the noise of the garage comes and goes. There are moments of peace: staff sitting on discarded tyres or standing still or making delicate preparations for the car's return to the garage. Then there is the roar each time the car is started up or the wheel guns erupt into life to put on fresh rubber, the tinkle of spanners and the turning of screwdrivers. It's a ballet, a technical, technological choreography where everyone knows their role fully. But there are periods of silence, too, bar the dulcet tones of the drivers over the team radio and their engineers during their stints in the car. Each team has only one driver on the track in any given session – be that a morning or afternoon session, or the full day. This season, Red Bull are no longer the first garage in the pit lane but the third, a nod to last year's championships when they ended up in third place behind both McLaren and Ferrari. The aim is to get back to number one.

At the end of the current cycle of regulations, reliability is understandably good for most teams, this year's cars more an evolution than a revolution on the year before. That evolution, anticipates Horner, means a closing up of the grid beyond the top two – McLaren and Red Bull – who battled it out last season. There is a sense this season could equate to a four-team battle for the title. 'It's the last year of these current regulations and, as always, these cars have converged and it's going to be very tight,' he predicts. 'Five drivers' championships in a row is what we're looking to achieve with Max and reclaim the constructors' championship. So, it's going to be a tough fight from start to finish. It's like the first day back at school. Everyone's in their new shoes, clothes, uniform, we've got a new car to work with, a few changes with positions in the team, but it's the same faces and largely the same group of people. It's always exciting to go into a race season because you never know what lies ahead. Have we done enough, is the car quick enough, has somebody else found some kind of magic bullet? There's always a nervous excitement to this time of year.'

It's clear Red Bull have some gremlins – giving testing a stop-start feel – such as water pressure failure on day two. The consensus is they're on the back foot, having driven the fewest laps of any team during the three days of testing – 306 in all. Despite Waché admitting it has not gone as smoothly as hoped, it is not quite alarm bells either. The RB18, for example – the car that dominated the 2022 season, winning all but five races – stalled as it rolled out of the garage for its first pre-season test, and kept on doing so, hardly indicative of what would follow. While testing is never the truest indicator of the hierarchy for the upcoming races, Mercedes driver George Russell estimates that it takes just five laps in an F1 car at the start of a season to know if you have a dud or not. At this stage, there is not the sense that Verstappen has a dud at his disposal nor that he is set to replicate the utter dominance of 2023 when the team won every race bar one.

It is towards the back that gives the greatest reveal of changes to the RB21. Each of the teams – and Red Bull are no exception – employ a 'spy' photographer to capture shots of their rivals to see if they have uncovered other innovations they themselves have not conjured up over the winter and the primary area of interest is often the rear of the car, where changes are more visible to the trained eye. F1 is as much about what your rivals are doing as what you are doing yourselves.

Whatever the case, Verstappen does not look overly concerned with how events play out. He is relaxed to the point that he is able to take a nap at the circuit on the morning of the first testing day. While he has been known to have some fractious encounters over the airwaves with his race engineer, not so this time. His biggest initial gripe is an earpiece digging in uncomfortably from his helmet. His assessment of day one is 'everything felt good', the car responding well to him and no bad surprises thrown up. For Lawson – strapped into the car and with his helmet on – between runs he simply wants to know if there is time to go to the toilet. It's not all glamour in Formula 1, in fact there is a banality to testing, not so for the team but for observers. There are short stints on the track, lengthy spells off it where changes are made to the car to assess different set-ups and then lap after lap garnering as much information as humanly possible to feed back to the team both at the track and back in the operations room in Milton Keynes.

McLaren are the clear standard-bearers after the trio of days but Horner is not about to make predictions . . . good or otherwise. He says: 'I think if anything, last year teaches us we finished first and second in the first two races and McLaren were nowhere. By Miami, they started to come on strong. So, things can change and quickly in this sport. We also have a significant regulation shift in race nine this year, where the regulations with the wings change. So again you just don't know what effect that is going to have, either detrimentally or beneficially, for each of the teams. The drivers' championship is priority number one – to try and retain that trophy. Five would be simply unbelievable. On the constructors', it's going to be difficult for us.'

Waché's own take is that the test has not gone as smoothly as the team would have hoped but his assessment is Red Bull are one of the four in the mix along with McLaren, Ferrari and Mercedes. The car is said to be going in the right direction but will that destination be met in time for a race that is now just days away?

Verstappen briefly courts controversy on the final day of the test when he is caught on camera raising a middle finger from the cockpit of his car. Having previously fallen foul of Draconian new swearing rules, and with nine points on his licence and in danger of a one-race ban, there is briefly a concern over possible censure. It later transpires the middle finger was tongue-in-cheek and aimed at a photographer trying to get a picture of the RB21 outside the Williams garage.

The next time Verstappen will sit in the car will be in Australia.

8

CRUNCH TIME

It is the Monday before race one. After months of work, there is a growing sense of anticipation for the team to finally find out where they stand on the grid. In Formula 1, it is sometimes hard to cut through the bluff and bravado and get a true sense of where individual teams lie before the lights go out for race one. No one will know for sure until Sunday's Grand Prix in Melbourne, and even then probably not until a few races in, such has been the event's propensity to throw up outlier results.

Christian Horner gathers together hundreds of staff inside MK-7. Music with a deep, pumping base is thudding out of giant speakers as he strides in and makes his way to a lectern for his pre-season rallying cry. There has been plenty to shout about in seasons past, and yet in 2024 McLaren whittled away at Red Bull's early advantage to comfortably win the constructors' championship. This season, Max Verstappen's run of drivers' titles is under greater threat than ever before from both Lando Norris and Oscar Piastri. Is this the year the hunted becomes the hunter?

Horner has earmarked Norris, the more experienced of the duo, as the favourite for the title. He addresses staff, confident of his position at the helm and having won a lengthy internal fight to stay in control. The narrative – as is often the case with Red Bull – is one of us versus them, telling his workforce to continue to be 'fearlessly us'. He says: 'Teams look at us and think, *why can't we be like that?* And that provokes a lot of jealousy. Sometimes we can be unpopular with our rivals. But who gives a shit as long as we're happy? We're unashamedly who we are and it's important to enjoy it and celebrate it.'

There has been plenty to celebrate in this recent period of dominance, but this season could finally be the reality check. Horner insists that testing has gone well despite some reliability issues and the team running fewer laps than any of the other nine teams on the grid. Not one to give an inch to rivals, he concedes McLaren have the qualifying pace to beat them and the rest of the grid, and that Red Bull are 0.2 seconds a lap behind them in terms of race pace – not an insurmountable sum with which to close the gap.

Before a steering wheel has been turned in competition, already Horner admits Red Bull are among those pushing the FIA hard on the legalities of the flexing rear wings of the current F1 cars. A clampdown is set to come into place at the Spanish Grand Prix, nine races into the season. Horner and the Red Bull top brass believe McLaren are gaining the greatest advantage from it and the revision will be to their rivals' detriment while boosting Red Bull's own cause. But nine races is a long time to wait to close the gap on their opponents.

Turning his attention to the drivers, he talks of Verstappen being very motivated and upbeat while praising Lawson for having a balanced head on his shoulders. It helps, he says, that he likes the car to be set up in a similar fashion to Verstappen – unlike Pérez – and that the technical feedback from the cockpit of his car has been extremely positive. But the message is also that the Kiwi's job is subordinate to Verstappen's: Lawson is there to earn points in the constructors' championship but not do anything that might harm the Dutchman's chances. Having had all manner of issues with the RB20 – the previous year's car – Horner says there are reasons for optimism over its successor and the way he delivers that pronouncement it's hard for anyone watching not to buy into what he is saying.

Staff have worked for months around the clock to make a competitive car in the RB21 and iron out the glitches its predecessor possessed. Horner is quick to tell his workforce, 'You've got to be slightly mad to work in this organisation in Formula 1 with the hours, sometimes you've got to go above and beyond.' And yet he expects staff to do that again this season and reminds them it is a privilege to be working for a team at the front end of the grid. The overriding message is of a mission to win, doing everything feasible in that quest and to celebrate every win as largely and loudly as everyone can, if and when the time comes.

But there is also what seems like a dig at those who tried to topple him last season. 'When I first came to this team it was common to blame each other for the lack of performance. By working together and supporting each other, what we've managed to achieve are statistics others can only dream of.' While Marko, Jos Verstappen and Oliver Mintzlaff, Horner's boss at Red Bull, are not in the room, the message is clear:

stop the infighting for the good of Red Bull Racing. 'We are one team.'

Sometimes, he might come across as too bullish. He argues that Red Bull Racing are bigger than Manchester United and the Dallas Cowboys and that if it was a country it would be the fifth largest in the world. It's perhaps fanciful, but whatever the actual reality of where they rank, as rallying cries go, for a Monday it is a truly effective one. And then he ends with a reminder of the target: 'It's only ever been achieved once, winning five world titles in a row. We have the driver to do that.'

9

LIGHTS OUT

By the Wednesday of race week, the paddock has decamped to Melbourne. This particular travelling circus takes over the Crowne Plaza, one of the city's premier hotels, and Red Bull have commandeered a platform along the Yarra River that morning just at the foot of the hotel. Fans gather outside in the sunshine, some in Red Bull tops, others in the gear of their rivals, all desperate to get eyes on the defending world champion. It is this season's first public appearance of Max Verstappen alongside Liam Lawson, and already the rapport looks good between the pair. They are being put through their paces by the social media team using a series of jigsaw pieces to recreate the Albert Park circuit and to also rate their favourite tracks. To one side is the shell of the new-for-2025 liveried Red Bull car as music blares loudly and David Coulthard whips up the crowd.

The drivers' appearance is short-lived and both are quickly whisked away by team members and security. Walking in the wake of an F1 driver in the age of social media gives an eye-opening insight into the attention and spotlight they find themselves under. Despite security flanking Lawson and his small entourage of Red Bull staff, repeated requests via flailing arms, shouts and protruding mobile phones come in for signed mini helmets and photographs. Lawson tries to oblige where possible and there is a sense of relief as the entourage squeezes into the lift to head to the top floor with its panoramic view of the city's vista for a series of media interviews. Lawson flits from one with his national television channel in New Zealand to a quirkier challenge with two well-known Australian YouTubers. The attention must surely be exhausting. 'It can be a bit of a shock,' he admits with a shrug. 'But at the same time we're exposed to it for years leading up to it. In F1, it's a different level and it comes with the job.'

If he is nervous about his first competitive foray in the car this weekend it's not showing, and he says it's more a case of excitement than nerves. 'The higher you go, the closer to the front the pressure builds,' he concedes. 'That's something that comes with it.' For his mum Kirsty and dad Jared, the feelings are mixed. For Jared it's the pinnacle, having been alongside his son for each stage of motorsport from go-kart to F1. For Kirsty, the higher he goes, the harder it gets. Come the race, she struggles to watch, so she either takes a walk around the paddock or else puts on her headphones to view a series on Netflix until the chequered flag is waved and she knows her son is safe.

The following day – race day – there is a freshness to the paddock, an added zip around the place. Part of the excitement comes from the built-up nervousness as they await the first official results of months of work, much of it starting early in the 2024 season.

It is the biggest sporting weekend in Melbourne's history, some 900,000 fans are expected to congregate at various venues across the city to watch live sport, with an estimated 450,000 alone over the three days of the Grand Prix weekend and hundreds of thousands more at the various games on the opening weekend of the AFL (Aussie rules football). The city loves its sport and has one of its own to cheer in Piastri, who was born in Melbourne 24 years ago. Albert Park is the perfect venue for the season start, greeted with generally fine weather for much of the weekend, packed stands and genuine enthusiasm for a driver who grew up walking distance from the circuit driving the car of the title favourites.

The walk into Albert Park is different to any other race, almost like a stroll down the red carpet at a film premiere. Drivers and team bosses arrive in their cars ready to walk the gauntlet where fans in various team guises press against the barriers, rows deep, with small helmets and giant cardboard cut-out faces aiming for the selfies and signatures.

Amid the paddock buzz, there is an anxiousness too. The mechanics and engineers have been working to get the car in race trim long before the drivers arrive, checking and double-checking everything even more than usual as this is the first time to ensure the car flown over has been built correctly and is capable of getting their team off to a fast start.

Overseeing that is Gianpiero Lambiase, a constant in Verstappen's ear. The London-born Anglo-Italian's F1 career began at Jordan but he arrived at Red Bull Racing for the 2015 season, first as Daniil Kvyat's race engineer and then Verstappen's when, four races into the season, the Russian was axed and dropped down to Scuderia Toro Rosso. GP, as he's known, has a way of getting the best out of Verstappen and will not hesitate to speak back after choice words from his driver over the team radio. There is a feistiness to him but he clicks with Verstappen better than anyone on the team. In the shake-up of the winter exits he has been promoted to head of racing while remaining Verstappen's race engineer. The pair have enjoyed a remarkable run of success, but GP has no idea if that will continue this season. 'As engineers, we like to think that we have control over our destiny,' he says. 'But the first race every year is very much an unknown. It rests slightly uneasily compared to what you expect in terms of day-to-day. It's exciting and you feel that atmosphere at race one, lots of anticipation. It's not nerves necessarily but a few butterflies and mostly not wanting anything to happen into turn one, lap one, as we've all worked so hard to get to this point, spent three or four months of the winter leading up to it and you just want to see the race play out on merit.'

After the two practice sessions on the Friday, Verstappen is only seventh quickest and 0.6 seconds off the pace of the McLarens. He is behind the Ferraris and Mercedes too. Verstappen describes the performance as 'so-so', lacking outright pace as he falls into conversation in the garage with Horner and Marko the moment he steps out of the car. It is an inauspicious start for the team. While they have a remarkable ability to turn things around, there is a lot to rectify in time for the following day's qualifying. The RB21 is a handful to drive and Marko is already talking about needing the 'Max factor' for a good qualifying result.

In qualifying, itself, the Max factor is evident, where he is quick from the moment of his first flying lap to lay down a marker to his rivals. However, it is not enough to halt a McLaren lockout on the front row of the grid, Verstappen having to make do with third. It is a track where Verstappen has not always gone well and he is struggling with the balance of the car.

The following morning, the sun has been replaced by rain, which is predicted to continue throughout the race. As the front-runners, you rarely want rain; for anyone chasing, Verstappen included, it is the ideal, capable of ripping up the form book and levelling the field.

Hannah Schmitz is the principal strategy engineer with Red Bull and the buck stops with her on when to pit and what tyres to pit for. The goal is simple: 'To score as many points as possible. The weather for strategists makes it more unpredictable, there's a lot more unknowns.' But it also means a greater capacity for risk – good if you're the hunter rather than the hunted. She continues: 'You're trying to manage the risk and make the best call on what you know.'

As Schmitz takes her place on the pit wall, inside the engineering office, a makeshift hub in the paddock that pulls out from one of the team's containers, some dozen members of staff are glued to screens showing in-car telemetry, meteorology reports ahead of the incoming rain, in-car footage of the drivers and more besides. There is an eerie quiet in the room and just a few words exchanged over the team radio pre-race, last directions to both drivers from their engineers about their settings from the start. After the lights go off for the 2025 season, there are all manner of conversations to listen in to, that between driver and engineer, on the pit wall, among the strategists and back at the factory.

Verstappen nearly gets into the lead at the start and again following a late safety car towards the end of the race, but cannot force his way past Norris. The hush of the room of engineers is broken by oohs and aaahs when Verstappen narrowly misses out on an overtake not long before the chequered flag.

Schmitz's roll of the dice is for Verstappen to stay out on slick tyres as Piastri skids off and Norris pits. It briefly gives the Dutchman the lead before he too needs to pit to change rubber. In the end, Norris wins by less than a second, a deserving victory but far closer than it should have been considering the McLaren advantage. For Red Bull, second place is beyond what they had expected for Verstappen during the course of the weekend. It is first blood to McLaren but Australia is never the be-all and end-all, and in any case Red Bull at least look competitive, despite not having a full understanding of the nuances of the RB21.

Horner is relatively happy with the weekend's and the winter's work as he prepares to pack up to fly home. 'We took a bit of a gamble,' he says of the late tyre strategy call. 'We stayed out and obviously that worked out well for us. In the end, the McLaren was a bit too strong. That left Max in second place and it was an eight-lap shoot-out to the end of the race. He came so, so close. I was thinking this might just go our way. It's a track that's notoriously difficult to overtake at and literally he was within a few metres of achieving that overtake. Who knows? Another lap or two he might have done it as it felt like Lando was just tightening up at the end there.'

It's 18 points for second, and 18 points more than Verstappen achieved at the same race a year ago. How does it look for the rest of the season? 'After a sample of one of 24 races and what we saw last year, it's way, way too early to be making any predictions,' Horner tells me. 'It will take two or three races to get a clear idea but it's a battle from the first session until the last in Abu Dhabi in December. We're in the mix. You always want to win but, if you can't win, you want to score as many points as you can. You've got to go with the punches.' The message: it's a marathon, not a sprint. For Lawson, on the other side of the Tasman Sea to where he grew up, the experience is infinitely worse.

10

THE AXE

On the eve of the season start, Liam Lawson is remarkably laid-back as he sits atop the Crowne Plaza hotel with a 180-degree view of the Melbourne skyline and the Yarra River that runs through the heart of the city. Despite the enormity of what awaits him, his focus is on what seems to the 23-year-old the rather more pressing matter of grabbing some caffeine from one of the city's notoriously good coffee spots. With energy to burn, he is toying with changing out of his Red Bull gear, running the gauntlet and trying to go out incognito to do so. In a section of the city awash with eagle-eyed F1 fans, the decision is eventually made to instead bring the hot drink to him.

As the clock ticks down to his first practice session, weeks of conjecture about whether he is the right pick to replace Pérez instead of Tsunoda will get a first reality check. It is a circuit he has never driven before beyond the team's cutting-edge simulator. On the surface, his mood looks relaxed but, underneath, the pressure must feel unsurmountable, a lifetime of having dreamed of this moment since joining the Red Bull driver programme as a teenager. He is acutely aware of his position: 'I know I won't have this forever and I'll miss this feeling as well,' he says. 'So, I think we have to learn to embrace it a little bit, learn to love that feeling and learn to understand that one day I'm going to miss having that. It means you care if you're nervous and you feel that pressure. It means you care about what you're doing. I'm looking forward to it.'

Red Bull have tried not to amp up the pressure on him but it becomes hard not to do so when his immediate barometer is the best driver on the grid. But Horner is abundantly confident the Kiwi is the right man for the job as Red Bull Racing's number two. Speaking before the opening session, he says: 'Liam we picked because we just feel he's got the right fortitude to be Max's teammate. He's got great mental strength, he's a very talented racing driver, he's very adaptable, he drives a car in a similar fashion to Max. He's not afraid of the front of the car being particularly sharp on the entry to corners. And I think he could be a surprise this year, I really do. But you have to remember he only has 11 Grands Prix experience and it's a big ask for him to step up, so he's going to need a bit of time, but I think he's got that Kiwi grittiness about him and the mental strength to take this role on. I'm excited to see what he can achieve. The feedback coming back to the engineering and design team is consistent across the two cars. Liam has been very strong in that aspect with the testing he's done and the work behind the scenes. While he's new to us as a race driver, he's very well known to us, having performed two years as a test and reserve driver.'

The racer in Lawson can't help but want to try to beat

Verstappen – at least in his head – but it is an approach Horner and the rest of Red Bull's top brass have tried to steer him away from. The team principal adds: 'Every driver on the grid is trying to beat Max. To beat him in the same equipment obviously will be tough. He's going up against the best in the world. He recognises that his job, particularly this year, is to learn from Max, to support Max, to support he team. Max is the reigning four-time world champion, he's the best driver currently in Formula 1. And I think that it would be foolish of Liam to think that 11 Grands Prix in he can go out and beat him, but he's going to of course be given all the same equipment. He needs to build up and support the team, and Liam will feel his way into that seat. For us, I think it's just a matter of trying to protect him a little bit and just allow him to grow and develop, and everything he does will get picked apart, scrutinised and analysed, such is the interest in the sport. I think we just need to give him a bit of breathing space to allow him to flourish. I think he will.'

As the clock ticks to FP1 (free practice one, the first of three on-track practice sessions at a Grand Prix weekend), then qualifying and then his first race in the full Red Bull colours, the question inevitably arises about the expectations on his shoulders this weekend. Lawson himself has no idea quite what to predict. He says: 'Honestly, it's quite hard to know. We've done testing and I know where we think we are but I don't truly know until the cars roll out for qualifying and everyone's engines are turned up and there's low fuel loads pushing the car to the limit. Then we'll find out where exactly we sit pace-wise. So, I think a successful weekend for me will be being close to Max. That's the target coming in. And I think that's the goal.'

The lead-up to qualifying is far from ideal at a time when he needs more lap time than most as a novice at Albert Park. A turbo issue prevents him from running in FP3 and he's back in the garage before even completing a lap. 'Is it anything major?' he asks over the race radio, 'Come in' is the curt reply, the team not wanting to give anything away to rivals potentially listening in. It is a problem that can be rectified in time for qualifying but it has cost him valuable time in a car in which he is unfamiliar, and without having tried a flying lap on the Saturday morning before qualifying. Set-up changes are made on his car in the hope it will give him the ideal pace for a quick lap but, on his last outing in Q1 – the first part of the qualifying three-parter – he makes a mistake in the last sector, damaging his tyres and scuppering his chances of getting through. He has struggled to get the soft C5 Pirelli tyres up to speed, unable to make the rear tyres stick to the track like his teammate, and the car repeatedly snaps out of his control, costing him the fluidity of a smooth quick run. In simple numbers terms, it is damning compared to his teammate, who's more than a second ahead of him. He is quick to put his hands up and take the blame rather than make any excuses: 'Obviously a silly mistake, so probably one that didn't need to happen. I think we were in a decent position building up from the lap we were on anyway, so it's pretty frustrating.' The fact that his rival for the Red Bull seat in Tsunoda qualifies in fifth is not lost on him. The questions are: would the Japanese driver have done any better in the Red Bull? And are Red Bull themselves thinking it?

Things don't get much better as the weekend progresses and hopes of a turnaround in the race are not realised. Starting from the pit lane enables his mechanics to make further changes to his car pre-race and the team take a gamble when the rain comes down to leave him on the slick medium tyres in the hope of the track drying and him getting the jump on his rivals – a bolder strategy worth taking from the back of the grid. Instead, on lap 47 he ends up in the wall at turn two after spinning. It is an apt finale in some ways for what has been a difficult race, prior to which he has not really shown signs of the raw pace that had earned him the seat in the first place.

With the paddock already being packed up post-race to relocate to Grand Prix weekend number two in China, Horner is not about to admonish his new driver. Helmut Marko publicly lambasts Racing Bull's Isack Hadjar for his tearful exit on the formation lap prior to the Grand Prix but is less damning of Lawson. Although, in perhaps an early warning, he says, 'We have to let him cool down a bit now and observe his development over the first three to five races.' Horner is softer towards both Hadjar and Lawson. On the latter, he says: 'Liam'll reflect on this weekend. He'll be glad to get out of Melbourne, I would have thought. It's been a baptism of fire for him and he'll be looking to bounce back in China next week. It's a completely different circuit, it's more of a normal circuit. It'll be very interesting to see how we go. McLaren at this stage of the season have a very fast race car. We've got a good basis and some areas where we know we can improve, and some stuff in the pipeline.'

Despite the chance for a reset and to work closely with his race engineer Richard Wood at the next event on the calendar, the Chinese Grand Prix isn't much better. Shanghai International Circuit was designed by Hermann Tilke, the mastermind of circuits in Singapore, Bahrain and Austin among others. It cost nearly £300 million to build and 3,000 workers toiled on it for 18 months. It was first added to the F1 calendar in 2004, a race won by Ferrari's Rubens Barrichello, and the track is designed around the symbol 'Shang', the first character in the name Shanghai. It boasts one of the longest straights on the F1 calendar between turns 13 and 14, while the opening straight leads into two narrow turns before the drivers snap back to the left for turns three and four. It had a brief hiatus on the calendar from 2020 to 2023 with no races held courtesy of its suspension during Covid, but returned in 2024 with Verstappen a comfortable winner. However, going into the weekend, Red Bull appear to lack the pace for a repeat.

For Lawson, at another circuit he has never driven, the race weekend throws up more than one scenario in which to impress with both a sprint race and the main Grand Prix. In qualifying for both, he is dead last: no Red Bull driver has ever qualified in last spot in the team's rich history. His times are closer to Verstappen than in Melbourne but, in a season where the field is so bunched up, being eight-tenths of a second slower per lap sees him in 20th and final place. After qualifying for the main race, Horner is accosted by Sky Sports' Ted Kravitz, who asks, 'Do we have a Liam problem here?' Clearly irritated by the question, Horner purses his lips, narrows his eyes and brushes it off as 'a tough day at the office today for him'. When pushed if paying off Pérez to replace him with Lawson has worked, Horner says simply, 'We'll have a good look at it.'

The Kiwi makes no excuses for the shortcomings, putting the responsibility for it firmly on his shoulders. 'I've got to get a handle on it, it's still not good enough,' he admits before ruing the fact, 'I really don't have time to get it right.' Already, the conversations have been held behind closed doors about what the solution is, whispers emanating that he could have the shortest-lived Red Bull career yet and get the chop just two races in. Even by Formula 1 and Red Bull's standards, that would be particularly brutal.

The Grand Prix itself doesn't get much better, perhaps the one saving grace being that he avoids being lapped by race winner Oscar Piastri. On the surface his 12th place on the official results looks reasonable, having started from the pit lane, were it not for the fact that three drivers ahead of him are disqualified for illegalities with their cars – the Ferrari duo of Lewis Hamilton and Charles Leclerc, as well as Alpine's Pierre Gasly. In the aftermath, Lawson talks about another tough weekend, having a lot to learn and getting a handle of a car he is finding frustratingly hard to drive while Verstappen, for the most part, makes crossing the line in fourth place look relatively easy.

As it transpires, Lawson won't be granted the time to get a handle on the RB21. After just two races, he is told by Horner that his services will no longer be needed and he will be demoted to the sister team Racing Bulls in a straight seat swap with Tsunoda.

It's a very public humiliation and comes as a big shock to Lawson, who says conversations had never hinted that such an outcome was likely. After just 133 competitive laps, his brief stint is over. It is not quite as damning as Ernst Loof, who boasts the record for the shortest F1 career in history after driving two metres of the 1953 German Grand Prix before suffering fuel pump failure, or Marco Apicella's 800-metre run at the 1993 Italian Grand Prix that ended up with him crashing at turn one, but it is still brutally succinct. Red Bull make the case that this is not the end of Lawson's time in F1 and he will be given the season to settle and find his feet away from the spotlight. And yet it feels like a damnatory assessment of him as a racing driver.

Horner is gracious enough to admit that the team are partly responsible for how it played out for the young driver. 'Had the car been easier it would have been easier for Liam,' he says, back in his office at Milton Keynes. 'We chose to make this decision early, not to procrastinate. It was obvious he had a very difficult Australia weekend and he seemed in a bit of a spiral in China too. It was becoming an awful lot for him. Everybody noticed that. It's a very difficult decision to make as you're taking away someone's dreams and hopes. But we're saying, "Look, this isn't the end of your Grand Prix career, we're going to switch you between teams." Two teams gives us a unique opportunity so we're saying to Liam that we still believe in you but you need more time to develop. And I think he's responded very maturely.' But it is a long road to build up the belief in a 23-year-old whose confidence has taken an almighty hit. The long dreamed-for drive he had talked so effusively about is over after just two outings.

The cutthroat move is understandably the talk of the paddock. Former driver Giedo van der Garde, who drove a season in F1 with Caterham back in 2013, posts on Instagram that 'this comes closer to bullying or a panic move than actual high athlete achievements. They made a decision – fully aware – gave Liam two races only to crush his spirit. Yes, he underperformed the first two races but, if anyone's aware of that, it's himself.' Tellingly, it is a post liked by Verstappen.

When pressed on that by reporters once the racing resumes

the following weekend in Japan, he says simply: 'Well, I liked the comment, the text, so I guess that speaks for itself; it was not a mistake.'

The star driver is clearly not happy, while all eyes are now on Tsunoda to see if he can fare any better. Can he do what so many others have failed to do alongside his illustrious teammate?

11

RACER TURNED LEADER

It was a single corner of a track in Portugal where Christian Horner's racing career came to a dramatic halt. A driver in his own right, Horner competed for two full seasons in Formula 3000, then the main feeder series for racers into F1. But while following Juan Pablo Montoya into a high-speed turn as he exited the pit lane during a pre-season test in 1998 in Estoril, Montoya took that corner in a manner Horner knew he never could, suddenly abundantly aware he lacked the utter commitment behind the steering wheel to get to the upper echelons of motorsport. The Colombian would win that year's title and then step up to F1, Horner would finish 33rd. Already owner of Arden Motorsport, the team he set up with father Garry in 1997, at that point he decided to move into management full-time. It was there he cut his teeth as a team boss, doing everything from balancing the books – sometimes a precarious occupation in F3000 – to signing the drivers and even washing the team's truck.

As a child, he was obsessed with going fast, whether on

his BMX bike or a go-kart. After much persuasion, his mother Sara finally bought one after spotting an advert for a second-hand go-kart in the local newspaper. The plan had been for the young Horner simply to have a toy to drive around the garden but, unbeknown to his parents, what they'd purchased was a low-to-the-ground racing kart that could only be deployed at a track. Fortuitously, Shenington go-kart track was just down the road, so they took their speed-hungry son there and, from that moment, he was hooked. He relished the idea of man and machine going as fast as humanly possibly around a racetrack lap after lap.

When years later the Montoya revelation meant those racing ambitions were no more, he pursued them in a different manner, encouraged by his parents, who nudged him to chase his dreams. It was his work at Arden that brought him into contact with Helmut Marko, at the time a team owner of RSM Marko before he sold it to launch Red Bull's driver programme. Horner's team brokered a deal with one of Red Bull's early stars, Vitantonio Liuzzi, to drive for Horner's team in F3000, which equated to Red Bull paying £50,000 per win. Liuzzi won seven of 10 races, the resulting jackpot enriching the team's coffers. In the process, it marked a third consecutive team championship and Marko saw enough in Horner's entrepreneurial make-up to think he was worth the risk and so, in time, he turned up on the F1 grid – a masterstroke, as it would turn out.

When Horner arrived at Red Bull as its new team principal, fresh-faced and younger than a large proportion of his new workforce, he fully admits he was just a kid. He recalls arriving at his desk to find a half-drunk cup of coffee by his predecessor Tony Purnell and his secretary in tears at his sudden sacking. When he addressed staff for the first time he saw shell-shocked faces truly unconvinced by their new team principal. Only two of the workforce knew Horner from the junior formulae, although he enjoyed a relationship with driver David Coulthard, who became a vital crux in those early days. Horner simply got his head down and spent the next six months talking to everyone in the factory and slowly beginning to get his head around the complexities of the business, understanding its people and what the organisation was lacking. He had an innate sense of understanding how a business operated and how to make it better.

He wasn't afraid to lean on others, too, not just Coulthard. F1 boss Bernie Ecclestone became a close confidant and saw something of his younger self in Horner. The pair, neither afraid to ruffle a few feathers, hit it off, a friendship that endures to this day. Other friends on the grid include the likes of Flavio Briatore – a fellow disruptor – and the pair are thick as thieves, but only when, Horner likes to joke, he can understand what the Italian's saying.

For a long time, Horner was the youngest team principal in the paddock, although he now has more junior rivals: the likes of James Vowles, who he calls 'The Reverend', at Williams; Haas' Ayao Komatsu; and Laurent Mekies, who he brought in from Ferrari to head up Red Bull's sister team. His recruitment has always been impressive, Mekies the latest example, the Frenchman's reputation having risen due to the manner he has steadied the ship at Racing Bulls and turned them into a regular points-scoring outfit. Red Bull Austria's hierarchy have been impressed. At Red Bull Racing, much of how the team functions is down to Horner, not just in terms of his decision-making as CEO and team principal but his relentless work ethic. Today, it is reflected in the manner in which each and every member of Red Bull Racing goes above and beyond.

Horner lured Mark Webber from Williams to partner Coulthard for 2007, the team's third season on the grid. Webber, who now manages one of Red Bull's main rivals in McLaren's Oscar Piastri, was partly persuaded to join by Horner as a motorsport purist first and foremost. 'He's a racer who cut his teeth in junior categories,' he said, 'and having been one, he had a good understanding of drivers. That was one of his strengths, for sure. And he had big stamina levels too. Christian can be polarising for some people, too, but the Christian you saw when the cars are at the factory, he worked hard, he worked very hard. I think he saw the gaps in the team and deployed people to fill those gaps. His biggest strength was probably accepting what wasn't in his lane and filling that. And politically he was good for the team as well.'

Much like Verstappen, Horner's public persona is not the same one as behind closed doors. In *Drive to Survive* he is often portrayed as the pantomime villain – one that he relishes. He's pugnacious, scrappy, and like Verstappen, willing to do anything for the betterment of the team's on-track chances. Toto Wolff once likened him to a yapping little terrier, and at times the analogy is remarkably on point. Horner is always happy to be the one doing the scrapping on behalf of his team and readily bears the brunt of any subsequent fallout. But he is amiable and engaging company; funny too.

Paul Monaghan, chief engineer, says that despite the growing demands on Horner overseeing a constantly evolving organisation, 'He's never stressed, always approachable. And you just need to walk into reception and look at the trophies to see what he's achieved. Who would have thought an energy drinks company would beat Ferrari and Mercedes in 2010, and we did, didn't we?' Horner appears to be the ultimate plate spinner, juggling 101 things without giving the impression that it could all collapse around him at any minute, even though there has often been the danger of exactly that happening. On camera, there is no shortage of swearing; off camera too. At the family home, there is a swear jar in place to help curtail his language although he likes to point out he isn't the family's biggest culprit. 'My wife is contributing more to the jar than I am,' he laughs. 'The problem for me is sometimes I'm not aware the cameras are there, but it's made me realise I do swear quite a lot.' Despite the realisation, don't expect that to change.

For a man in charge of a staff of nearly 2,000, Horner is remarkably approachable. Despite being a multimillionaire with a private jet, one of his skills is to seem like a man of the people – he's popular back on base. And he has brought an F3000 philosophy to his management style, being nimble to any changing situation in an all-hands-on-the-pump way. He is also optimistic in his approach – he calls himself a 'glass-half-full kind of person' – who perpetually pushes himself and the people around him to be better. He is not afraid to make mistakes and there is allowance for others to falter too. One of his big mantras is simply: if you make a mistake, just make sure you don't make the same one again.

The bigger the organisation has grown, the bigger both the pressure and the expectation. Somehow, he has managed to not let that pressure get the better of him, although he readily admits it can be lonely at the top. His approach is not to let the bigger picture overwhelm him. While he and former McLaren boss Ron Dennis did not always see eye to eye, there is a piece of advice from Dennis that still resonates in the back of his mind: 'To eat an elephant, you've got to eat it piece by piece.'

Horner is one for the rousing speech, regularly addressing the wider workforce at MK-7 in Milton Keynes, and it is hard not to be convinced by him. He has an ability to make staff raise their game even when already pushing themselves to the hilt and would go into battle for them as individuals and as a team. It creates that us-against-them philosophy that has been such a key part to their ongoing success and makes them so competitive and, at times, combative.

Getting people in the business to buy into what he was saying began with the recruitment of Adrian Newey. Once that deal was sealed, it enabled others to follow and made his rivals realise Red Bull were more than just 'a drinks company' as Lewis Hamilton once famously branded them – a comment he later admitted regretting. And the key truth is that Horner has never tired of racing; or winning for that matter. Just like that kid at Shenington, racing for the first time with the second-hand kart bought from the local paper, he still loves the smell of engines, the noise, the energy and, in particular, the adrenaline rush of race day.

Looking over the campus he has played no small part in building up, I ask him, is it strange that he has not sought a new challenge? But he doesn't see it that way. For him, this is his home from home, a wider family for whom he feels immense fondness and loyalty. Despite the combative front he shows at a race weekend, he cares deeply for his employees. He says he has never felt more assured of his future, and there is the not insurmountable project of building an engine in-house for next season. Asked why he is still here after two decades, he says: 'I never once thought about walking away.

Of course, this job is tremendously demanding on family time – you're away a lot and I have a relatively young family. My passion and motivation and determination still burn strongly enough that I'm genuinely excited when I come to work every day. You have a tough weekend, you brush yourself down, pick yourself up and get ready to go again. And I enjoy the competition. I'm still relatively young, only 51 years of age, and I enjoy working with the people, the team spirit, the competition and energy. If I ever lost that then there's easier things to be doing in your life than travelling to 24 races a year. I'm excited by this next chapter, assembling a group of people in Powertrains. That is our biggest challenge in our 21-year history in F1. If we can do it on the engine side, too, that will be hugely rewarding.'

Horner understands better than most that, for much of the time, F1 is a game, particularly when the Netflix cameras are rolling. It's intriguing, as he appears to care deeply how he's perceived and at other times acts like he couldn't care less. Of his public persona on the screen, he says: 'You have to remember that *Drive to Survive* is a TV show, and a heavily edited one. The personalities aren't always reflective of real life. But the viewing numbers are off the charts and it's been phenomenal for the sport. It's brought a whole new younger and more diverse fanbase, which is fantastic. F1 has never had the popularity that it currently enjoys and the Netflix series has played a pivotal role in it.'

It has made him a celebrity in his own right, although he laughs at the suggestion, before admitting that gone are the days he used to be able to pass through airports and the like – particularly in the United States – without anyone noticing him. 'Now the customs guys in the US, for example, know who you are,' he says, smiling. 'Seven or eight years ago they wouldn't have had a clue. Now they're like, "You're the guy from that TV show, you look much shorter in real life!" But it's amazing and you have to be grateful for it because that means interest in the sport. Without it, there wouldn't be all these people here. It's the fans who drive the business and the sport globally. Without them, we don't exist.'

So, has it come to a point where he is more famous than Geri, his Spice Girl wife? He concedes there's still no competition in that regard and yet there are moments when she is the one to play second fiddle. 'It's funny when they ask her to take a picture, but she doesn't mind at all,' he adds with a chuckle. Long before the couple met, Horner's career was interlinked with that of the Spice Girls. One of his sponsors in his racing days made confectionery cakes. Back in 1996, they had two main ones: Dennis the Menace through a deal with the *Beano*, the other with an up-and-coming girl band. It turned out to be a masterstroke as every girl wanted a Spice Girl cake and, as Horner puts it, 'that ultimately funded my career'.

Family life is split between Hampstead in north-west London and the Oxfordshire countryside where he likes to play the role of the country gent. It is in the latter locale where he has often helped get lucrative sponsorship deals over the line for the team. His children are beginning to show an interest in Formula 1 too. His oldest, 19-year-old stepdaughter Bluebell, is a *Drive to Survive* watcher along with her friends. His 12-year-old daughter Olivia, with former wife Beverley Allen, is a big admirer of one particular F1 driver and he isn't in a Red Bull. 'She's an enormous Charles Leclerc fan,' he says with a warm smile, knowing she won't thank him for the public admission. 'She's crushing on him. She even has him as her screensaver on her phone. She loves our two drivers as well but I think if Charles Leclerc could come round for a play date she'd be massively impressed by that!'

When not at a racetrack, Horner and his wife enjoy horsepower of another kind as amateur racing enthusiasts with a growing number of racehorses in their stable. Each is named after a former Geri hit, including Lift Me Up, Look at Me and, aptly, Scream if You Wanna Go Faster. 'We haven't got a Stop Right Now at the moment but that's not a great name for a horse,' Horner quips. When asked for his favourite song by his wife, he diplomatically says: 'I like them all equally.' As for his love of horse racing, it is driven by his insatiable appetite for competition. Comparing flitting from horse racing in Garthorpe to F1 in, say, Suzuka, he says: 'They're two very contrasting paddocks but the competitive buzz is just the same. And I get more nervous watching the horses than I do the cars and drivers. It's a control thing. With horse and rider, you don't know how they're going to wake up on the day and the size of the fences they have to jump. It's a hell of a buzz and very exciting and rewarding when you see a horse that's been trained at home. It's not a hugely serious level but it's still very competitive and rewarding when you see your horse get a result.'

Unlike Horner, Dietrich Mateschitz preferred to eschew the spotlight, rarely giving interviews and only occasionally appearing at a Grand Prix weekend. And yet it was his vision that enabled Red Bull Racing to get off the ground and his trust in the likes of Horner, Newey and Marko that saw it grow rapidly into the relentless winning machine it became. Despite the thousands of people employed by Red Bull as an organisation, Mateschitz was both its visionary and its decision maker, and that equated to the F1 team as well. He was known as quick to settle on a plan of action, going primarily on instinct, and he was effectively left to his own devices to run Red Bull from Austria by his Thai co-founder Chaleo Yoovidhya, who had little complaint as long as the can kept on selling. While Mateschitz relished the world titles and the dominance first of Sebastian Vettel and, in his latter years as he battled pancreatic cancer, Max Verstappen – his message was always the same: the can was the star, the F1 team set up as the ultimate sales platform for his energy drink while also feeding his own personal passion for motorsport.

Horner revelled in the freedom awarded to him by Mateschitz, enabling him and his team to be operationally agile and make key decisions – however costly they might sometimes be – quickly. While Mateschitz was still alive, Horner raised the idea of him being rewarded for his success with shares in the team as part of his pay package but the Austrian billionaire pushed back. Horner tried again in that regard following Mateschitz's death at the age of 78 in October, 2022, and was rebuffed again. The team and the wider brand were to remain in the ownership of the same two Austrian and Thai families as it had been from the outset. They weren't budging. After Mateschitz's passing, Horner said: 'So many of us have to be so grateful to him for the opportunities he provided and the vision that he had, the strength of character and never being afraid to chase your dreams. That's what he did here in Formula 1, proving that you can make a difference. We're just incredibly grateful.' But also, as the overseer of the whole Red Bull operation, his death merely enabled a clash of personalities, which his leadership had kept at bay, to open up a power vacuum that resulted in nearly three years of squabbling.

Mark Webber still boasts close links to his former Red Bull team where he drove from 2007 to 2013 and won 10 Grands Prix, coming close to winning the world title in 2010 only to be denied by teammate Sebastian Vettel in a four-way tussle at the final race in Abu Dhabi that year. He marks the beginning of Red Bull's internal struggles with the death of Mateschitz in 2022. 'There'd be a lot more harmony if Dietrich was still here,' the Australian muses. 'I think the team suffered very quickly with his passing. If Dietrich was still alive today, I think the team would be in a different situation. It just would have been calmer.' With his death came an end to the business's autocratic nature leading to a more managerial structure headed by Oliver Mintzlaff, who had enjoyed great success as CEO of Bundesliga side RB Leipzig and was rewarded for that success by being appointed chief executive officer of corporate projects and investments. That lengthy job title effectively meant him overseeing Red Bull's entire sports portfolio, including Red Bull Racing, football and the professional cycling team. Horner now answered to Mintzlaff.

At the age of 30, Mateschitz's son Mark had become an overnight billionaire by inheriting his father's 49 per cent stake in the business. Previously the head of Red Bull's Organics division, its range of natural soft drinks, he resigned his post on becoming a major shareholder. In a memo to employees, he wrote: 'I do not believe one should be both an employee and a shareholder of the same company. I will concentrate on my role as a shareholder, and I will interpret this and express myself in a way that makes sense to me.' A group of directors, Mintzlaff included, was set up to run the business.

What this means is that Horner and the team have more people to answer to than simply an enthusiastic founder and owner with a love for motorsport. In some quarters, there was an initial push for Mark Mateschitz to be appointed CEO of the overall business but Horner was among those to push back on the idea of a relatively inexperienced thirty-something undertaking such a role. That did little to create warm relations between Horner and the younger Mateschitz. And added to that, Horner and Mintzlaff did not hit it off. The German took umbrage at the power that Horner wielded towards the team and the salary he was paid . . . notably more than Mintzlaff's annual income.

There was a growing sense on the Austrian side of the business that Red Bull had become Team Horner, which rankled. Amid the power struggle, Horner tried to get rid of Marko, which was ironic, bearing in mind the Austrian had been the one who suggested Horner to Mateschitz as team principal in the first place. It wasn't until October, 2024, when Verstappen said he would leave the team if Marko left, that the ageing Austrian's place was cemented. Verstappen, who, like Horner, was lured to Red Bull Racing by Marko, told reporters: 'If such an important pillar falls away, that's not good for my situation as well. My loyalty to him is very big. I've always expressed this to everyone within the team, everyone high up, that he's an important part in my decision-making. He has built this team together with Dietrich from day one and he's always been very loyal to the team, to everyone with the team, to make sure that everyone would keep their positions from back in the day. And I think it's also very important that you give the man a lot of respect for what he has done. And that comes back also to loyalty and integrity.' At the time of Verstappen's comments, Marko had said publicly he was under threat of being suspended by Red Bull without divulging further details. Following the Dutchman's public support and a meeting with Mintzlaff, Marko was told he could see out the rest of his contract.

Another rift at the forefront of the team was between Horner and Jos Verstappen. A clash of personalities from the outset, it reached a head in 2024 when Verstappen Snr accused Horner of being responsible for the warring factions at the team. Central to it were allegations of coercive and controlling behaviour levelled at Horner by a female employee, allegations of which he was later cleared. Horner remained tight-lipped throughout the whole saga, arguing he was contractually restrained from speaking about the matter, and put on a very public front with his wife at the 2024 Bahrain Grand Prix.

Despite the scandal, at the beginning of the 2025 race season he seems to have survived, thanks in no small part to the public backing of Chalerm Yoovidhya, the majority shareholder of Red Bull with a 51 per cent stake. In contrast, the Austrian side of the business – owned by Mateschitz Jnr – had leaned towards parting company with Horner following the whole unedifying saga. Yoovidhya and Horner, in the end, won out, the latter no doubt aided by results on track and the fourth Verstappen world title that would follow.

So, an uneasy peace remains in the early part of the 2025 season when results are going well, the fissures reappearing when the team are taking a beating from the McLarens on track. Despite that, the likes of Horner, Verstappen Snr and Marko are all aligned in the shared ambition of pushing for

Red Bull to remain at the front of the grid. The reality is that trio as well as Verstappen and Red Bull know they do not have the quickest car in what is the final season of regulations. Horner's position has remained strong while results are going well, Verstappen's fourth drivers' title sufficient to keep him in power despite being dethroned as constructors' champions by rivals McLaren. In 2025, for the first time, doubts creep into the head of Yoovidhya about whether Horner is the right man to head up the team. Was Horner's rising profile overshadowing Dietrich Mateschitz's belief that the 'can must be the star'?

12

HIGH-SPEED CHESS

On a raised platform of concrete stands seven high stools with their backs to the Red Bull garage. There is no set formula, each team differing on the number and make-up of their pit wall – Mercedes have just four individuals in place, Toto Wolff preferring to watch from the garage, while Ferrari's line-up is a six-seater. In front at Red Bull's garage are screens showing live data from the race cars of Max Verstappen and Yuki Tsunoda, every twist and turn of a track session, be that practice, qualifying or the race. Each seat has an assignee, each acutely aware of their place on this prestigious bank of chairs. At Red Bull for the start of the 2025 season, there is a new look to the line-up. Central to it is the ever-present Horner, who makes the ultimate call on the key decisions. He has not missed a race since Red Bull Racing came into being. Horner, outwardly calm, is prone to nervously tapping his left foot with his legs crossed beneath him.

To the left of the team principal and CEO sits Pierre Waché, who in contrast to Horner looks constantly pensive. Now that

Jonathan Wheatley has swapped his Red Bull racing outfit for the green and black of Kick Sauber as their team principal, Steve Knowles has taken over part of his role on the sporting regulations side and sits to the right of Horner. Knowles had experience of the pit wall in the latter part of 2024 and was bedded-in to prepare him to take over that mantle. Wheatley also used to oversee the pit crew, during which he made them the best-drilled on the grid. That has now been taken up by Rich Wolverson, the new head of race operations, who takes a seat to the far left of the septet.

For any Grand Prix and qualifying session sit the two race engineers, Gianpiero Lambiase and Richard Wood, on the far right – for practice sessions they sit either side of the garage. Seat five alternates between Will Courtenay and Hannah Schmitz, sharing the 24 Grands Prix between them. Courtenay, the team's head of strategy, has been a mainstay of Red Bull for the entirety of its lifespan: Schmitz will step up in 2026 when Courtenay leaves the team to become McLaren's sporting director. Such are the terms of his contract and his importance to the team, he still has a season's worth of notice to work through before he can be released, despite the move being announced in September 2024. Even though his contract runs a few months into the 2026 season, the aim for both parties is that Courtenay will be allowed to leave the team in time for that season start and thereby not fall under Red Bull's cost-cap spending.

For such different characters among the seven, it is remarkable how smooth and calm an operation it is. It needs to be, in the heat of the competition. Courtenay or Schmitz will decide the team's strategy at the key moments, be that the timing and/or number of pit stops, tyre choices or anything else for that matter. They have to be the coolest person on the wall, their voice calm and collected even in the fraught nature of a race. Courtenay and Schmitz have worked with each other long enough that they're remarkably aligned in their decision-making, so slotting in and out of a race weekend does not destabilise the team. And in any case, the one absent from the pit wall is still deeply entrenched from the operations room back at the team's Milton Keynes base.

Both are very easy-going and laid-back individuals, quick to smile and laugh. Even in the most stressful moments of a race when an entire result can rest on a split-second decision they are remarkably unflappable as the pressure mounts. Is being calm the number-one prerequisite of the job? 'It is important that you are exactly that,' Schmitz says. 'It is high pressure. You have to be calm to make the right decisions and make sure you're trusted and listened to.'

Stripped down to the most basic principles, a team strategist's role is to give each driver the best chance of scoring the most points possible. It is a high-paced game of calculated risk, not for the faint-hearted. There are mathematical models, statistics, data, but, as ever with a merging of person and machine, there is a human element to it. 'In strategy, a lot of things are a grey area, so there's not a definite right and wrong answer,' she says. 'You're trying to manage the risk and make the best call on what you know yourself. We discuss it a lot – it really is a team sport – and come up with the lowest-risk option. It's not just a numbers game but opinion, thoughts, experience and gut feel. At some stage of the season, you'll take more risks than others.'

Schmitz studied mechanical engineering at the University of Cambridge and before she started working at Red Bull in modelling and simulation she had little idea that the job of a Formula 1 strategist existed. Back then, the strategists weren't shown on the TV footage as they are now. It was only by getting to know strategists at Red Bull that she realised it appealed to her. She recalls: 'That combined everything I'm interested in. I've always enjoyed playing games and done that a lot in my free time. So for me that was using the strategic bit of my mind, but also being directly related to the race and travelling and all of that which is what I really wanted to do, and get trackside. It felt like a really good fit. And yeah, luckily an opportunity came up and I was able to start doing it. I do still really really love my job, so I do think it was the right call. It's a pretty unique job.'

What makes a good strategist? In her eyes, a head for numbers and analysis, but it is beyond the necessary technical skills: 'It's about communication, the way you think and take risks. It's more like playing a game, taking a risk and being confident making a decision when it's not clear what's wrong. It's building trust and relationships as well.'

In her early days as a strategist, Schmitz would have a recurring dream on the Saturday night after qualifying. It would typically entail something going awry such as her laptop not turning on just moments before the race. As she has become more established in the role and encountered all manner of racing outcomes, the dreams have gone away. That's not to say the nerves aren't there. 'As soon as the lights go out I feel very calm,' she says. This is when she and Courtenay are in their element.

Strategists are almost masochists too. They welcome the close races, the tough decision-making. To them, there are different facets which appeal. Seasons like 2023 are fun as a team, when Verstappen was streets ahead of the field, but, from a strategy point of view, calls could be conservative. What they seem to relish most are the riskier calls – when they come off, that is. 'Being the underdog is an interesting thing,' she continues. 'People aren't expecting you to win, so then you can actually make calls which are a bit different or unusual. When that pays off, that's when you notice a strategist, because normally people shouldn't notice you.'

For China, Schmitz takes her seat on the pit wall 20 minutes before the race to prepare herself mentally and ensure nothing is missed in the minutes before the lights go out. Essentially if your driver has landed the car on pole in qualifying, as a strategist you want the race to be boring and straightforward with no surprises. But when not the quickest, unpredictability and jeopardy – be that rain, a safety car, a 50–50 choice between the number of pit stops – are highly welcome.

Listening to the strategy calls is like experiencing high-speed chess with a constant array of moving parts. There is a growing understanding of how the new car works, both the mathematical model of how it behaves and then the reality of its behaviour on track. The aim is for those two things to be as aligned as closely as humanly possible, making it easier to change the model and tweak the car straightforwardly. That is a constant evolution, particularly in the early part of the season. Until the final lap, a strategist's role is constant, acutely aware of the unknown element, be that a virtual or full safety car. A safety car is deployed following an accident when the track is no longer deemed safe to race on, while a virtual safety car forces drivers to reduce their speed for more minor incidents without the safety car itself coming out on track. Either has the propensity to turn a race on its head – good or bad. 'It's trickier than it seems,' says Courtenay, and listening in to the team radio from the engineering office it's hard to disagree. Perhaps unsurprisingly, for both Courtenay and Schmitz it is the mistaken calls that still stick in the memory rather than the masterstrokes of strategy. Schmitz remembers a couple in particular she prefers not to name which she is still disappointed by. But even on a good day she admits it's extremely rare to finish a race and say, 'I did everything perfectly.' Perfectionism is the holy grail but rarely attained.

Strategy for a race weekend begins on a Monday. The wider team of strategists will meet and those talks continue once at the track. Strategists, engineers, drivers and team leaders will come together for a pre-weekend briefing to feed in their thoughts on what the strategy might entail. Being on the pit wall rather than the ops room is the more appealing, as it's where the pressure is greater and adrenaline is at its peak. But flitting from the ops room to the pit wall, argues Courtenay, has made him better all-round at his job. In that ops room, the strategist's role is to come up with ideas and suggestions, crunch the numbers and data and be able to feed in from a more removed position in case anything might be missed front and centre in the heat of battle. 'We can take on more information, process that, cut it down and really provide Hannah and the team at track with really specific information they need amid all the noise and data,' he says. Both agree that role is all about looking at the bigger picture. When back at base, it's important to work out how necessary one piece of information is, deciding when something is urgent, whether it might be missed by the pit wall and whether it can help their counterpart in making the right call at the racetrack.

It's pitch black on a cold and early Sunday morning in March. There's barely a car coming along the A4146, and the car park out the front of Red Bull Racing is almost empty. The clock has just turned 5am and there's two hours before the start of the Chinese Grand Prix. While Schmitz and the rest of the 60-strong race team are putting together their final preparations for the race in Shanghai, here an off-shoot of the team will be playing an integral part in how the events of the 56-lap race play out. Welcome to the ops room which acts as another set of additional eyes and ears removed from the race team and the racetrack but integral in tracking the performance of the drivers. It looks like something from NASA command, albeit on a smaller scale, with rows of seating, each one stacked marginally higher than the next. To one side is a viewing platform where sponsors are sometimes invited to watch the racing unfold while tuned into the team radio. Some 20 engineers are plugged into their radio channels with individual screens of information running to varying degrees of complexity.

On a giant screen spanning the entire main wall plays out all manner of information. It has live footage from the cockpits of the two Red Bull drivers and five of their rivals – Lando Norris, Oscar Piastri, Lewis Hamilton, Charles Leclerc and George Russell – indicating where they feel the threats will come from. The rest of the space is made up of shots of and information from Verstappen's and Lawson's cars, including live footage from their respective halves of the garage.

A step removed from the racetrack, in the ops room

Courtenay and his colleagues can look at the data in more detail, do more thorough analysis on tyre performance, pace, strategy or listen in to the various team radios and feed any pertinent information back to the team at the racetrack, adding to Schmitz's decision-making ability come race time. Courtenay explains: 'There's an ongoing communication throughout the race. Ideas, suggestions, data, analysing. But also looking in more detail about opportunities perhaps missed by the team at the track. Is it worth a two- or three-stop? We've got a bit more time and capacity to look at those options.'

With Schmitz attending the opening two races, Courtenay has been on Australian time and is now aligning with the clock in Shanghai. Today, the alarm was set for 3am. 'It's quite gruelling working funny hours and getting up in middle of night,' he admits. 'You don't see your family or friends for two weeks, which is quite tough. I think we're all looking forward to this weekend being finished.' His two kids find it funny that Daddy goes to bed before them while his wife, who also works for Red Bull, has grown accustomed to keeping them quiet during their dad's sleep times.

Courtenay has lost count of the number of races he has overseen, which might explain the lack of pre-race nerves. Not long before the start, he happily tucks into breakfast and talks calmly about the possible perils of Shanghai International Circuit. Like Schmitz, he is an engineering alumni of Cambridge University, where he was a member of his college's boat, pool, squash and automobile club. His F1 career began with Jaguar before moving into Red Bull after its takeover. A strategy engineer and then senior analyst, he has been head of race strategy since midway through the 2010 season.

For the Shanghai race, the team's two drivers are split on their strategy. Verstappen will start on the medium tyre while Lawson, towards the back of the grid after another tough qualifying session, will begin the race on the hard. In part, Lawson is like a guinea pig testing out how the harder tyre fares before Verstappen changes to it himself later in the race. The default position is for two pit stops, as it will be for most of the grid, but a one-stopper is also a possibility, while a three-stop is even a consideration. 'We really do have to be so open-minded going into this race about what to do,' says Courtenay. 'Until we get going it's hard to know for sure.' As a strategist, the race is never run until the chequered flag. It is forecast for a dry, sunny Grand Prix, so the intermediate or extreme wet tyres are not a consideration, while there is the slight unknown of how the tyre degradation will be with the Shanghai circuit having been fully resurfaced for this year's race.

Verstappen starts in fourth but his pace hasn't been a million miles away from the two McLarens and the Mercedes of Russell in front of him. In contrast, Lawson qualifies in last spot and will start from the pit lane, enabling his mechanics to make some late set-up changes to his car. But the Kiwi is expecting potential carnage into turn one. As he says over the team radio: 'Let's hope this isn't fucking chaos.' Wolverson readies his pit crew by warning them to be ready for a first-lap pit stop. No such chaos materialises. But while Lawson quickly makes up two spots, Verstappen drops two, passed by the two Ferraris of Leclerc and Hamilton, leaving the ambition of a podium finish far harder to attain.

The track resurfacing means tyre wear is a lot less brutal in Shanghai than in the past, the pre-race planned two-stopper quickly becoming a one-stopper for most of the grid, thereby reducing the drama, intrigue and possibility for more place swaps. But Verstappen is struggling with the rear of his car and losing speed on the medium tyres. When he exits the pits, having changed to the hard tyre, his pace and his race kick into life, enabling him to pass both the Ferraris and return to P4 where he'd begun on the grid. As GP says to Max mid-race: 'Better late than never.' To improve the balance of his car, in the pit stop his front wing is adjusted by four clicks – effectively four turns of what looks like a glorified screw-driver – although footage played back later shows it hasn't been done sufficiently – it transpires its impact has been limited. There is concern too about Verstappen's fuel consumption. He is asked to lift a little in turns six and 14. Racers have the ability to only hear what they want to hear. And never wanting to be one to be told to slow down, Verstappen pays no attention until a slightly more curt reminder comes from GP – this time he obliges.

The team are reasonably satisfied with P4 for Verstappen, though it's neither cause for celebration nor great commiseration. With upgrades to improve the car looming in a few races' time, Horner tells Verstappen over the radio: 'There's lessons to be learned from this race.' As for Courtenay, it's not the two-stopper he and his rival strategists had planned for but neither is he surprised. Of the result, he says: 'Not great but not bad. It would have been difficult to catch the top three. We're just learning about our pace and performance.' As the teams pack up on track and in the ops room, strategists, engineers and drivers plug in for the post-race debrief to dissect what went wrong and where to improve as the calendar moves to Japan for race three.

13

THE MAX FACTOR

Falling behind his teammate in the drivers' championship during his first full Formula 1 season in 1985, Gerhard Berger was pondering his own F1 future at his home race, the Austrian Grand Prix, when he was approached by a smiling figure unknown to him. The man in question – a fellow Austrian – said he was looking to get into sports sponsorship. For a young driver scrabbling around to raise enough cash, Berger's ears pricked up at the prospect of a possible sponsorship deal before being informed the company had not quite come into being but would do so soon. The early promise of financial support ebbed away, in Berger's mind at least, although there was something that intrigued him about this enthusiastic personality and he agreed to meet for a beer. It was there that Dietrich Mateschitz spelled out his plans for an energy drinks company called Red Bull, later leading to Berger becoming the first athlete to be sponsored by the brand, one of what would prove to be thousands of athlete sponsorships.

Berger would go on to win 10 Grands Prix driving for the

likes of Ferrari, McLaren and Benetton, and twice finish in the top three of the championship. A decade into racing retirement – and a measure of his everlasting relationship with Mateschitz – Berger would initially take a 50–50 split in the ownership of Toro Rosso when Mateschitz decided to buy Minardi and form his second F1 team. It was here, many years later in 2015, that Max Verstappen would go on to make his F1 debut.

Another aspect of Mateschitz's motorsport arm was acting as a backer for Helmut Marko's RSM Marko Formula 3000 team with Marko, then going on to establish Red Bull's junior driver programme in 2001 aimed at discovering and developing talent. The goal was achieved when Austrian Christian Klien was signed by Jaguar in 2004. That deal came into being the year before Mateschitz bought Jaguar and turned it into his own.

Primarily, what Marko is looking for in junior talent is pure speed, after that it's what lies between the ears. When on the lookout to sign a teenage driver, the typical approach is for him to allocate a half-hour slot with them to get a sense of what they're like in conversation as well as seeing their capabilities on the track. Marko's first sit-down meeting with Verstappen lasted an hour and a half. 'The impression was there was a very wise man in the body of a 15-year-old boy,' Marko recalls, 12 years on from that encounter. 'He was far ahead already in his development. Even then, he was special, he was very committed and he knew what he wanted. Already he had a clear vision of what he wanted to achieve and how to achieve it. And at that stage we were just talking about being a member of the junior team. We didn't even talk about F1.'

Formula 1 team bosses had already taken note of

Verstappen's talent, which was drawn into sharp focus by him winning back-to-back race weekend triple headers at Spa-Francorchamps and then Norisring in F3. Toto Wolff was among those who tried to sign him for Mercedes but Red Bull offered the quicker route into F1 with its sister team and Marko got the deal done. Within two years of that 90-minute face to face, Verstappen, when he got in the cockpit of a Toro Rosso, at 17 years and 166 days was the youngest driver in history to start a World Championship race, driving the 300 kilometres in an F1 car to earn his Super Licence and thereby take his place on the grid. Even now, 200-plus races into Verstappen's Grand Prix career, there are moments when Marko is blown away by what the team's lead driver can do behind the wheel.

The results, the four world titles, the race wins, the overtaking manoeuvres and the remarkable race craft are well documented. Ask people in the team and across the F1 paddock for Verstappen's all-time stand-out drive and there is no shortage of contenders. There's the race-long duel with Lewis Hamilton at the 2021 United States Grand Prix, which went a long way to deciding that year's championship in Verstappen's favour. There was making up 13 places at the Belgian Grand Prix the following year to take the chequered flag. Or there was his first ever race for Red Bull as an 18-year-old when he won the 2016 Spanish Grand Prix. Most within the four walls of Red Bull would lean to Interlagos at the São Paulo Grand Prix towards the latter part of last season for their personal on-track Verstappen highlight. A poor qualifying combined with a five-place grid penalty saw him start the race in 17th. His grasp on a fourth drivers' title was potentially slipping away in the wet conditions. Undeterred, by lap 12, he had already made up 11 spots. He took the win by nearly

20 seconds, setting the fastest lap of the Grand Prix on 17 different occasions. It was comfortably one of the all-time great wet weather drives in F1's long and illustrious annals.

Add to that list Japan, 2025.

Suzuka is a driver's circuit, with its figure-of-eight configuration and high-speed corners. It was originally created by Honda, who still own it as a test track. It was here in 1987 where Nigel Mansell conceded the title to Nelson Piquet when a back injury, sustained in a crash in qualifying, denied him the chance to compete in the race. The following year in heavy rain Ayrton Senna sealed the title at the circuit over arch-rival and McLaren teammate Alain Prost after clawing his way back from 14th to take a thrilling win. The pair clashed on track the following year, Prost out of the race and Senna able to make his way back onto the tarmac to take the win, although he was later disqualified. This time, Prost was the world champion. A third head-to-head in 1990 saw the same pair clash in dramatic circumstances.

For Honda's home race – round three of the 2025 Formula 1 World Championship – and to mark the final year of a partnership as Red Bull's engine supplier, which has led to Verstappen's four driver titles, the team unveil a special red and white livery in honour of the RA272, the first Honda-powered car to win an F1 race, back in 1965. In a country where pride is of vital importance, Red Bull putting on a good show is integral to its standing with Honda, but the team are well off the pace in practice and the early stages of qualifying, a good 0.2 seconds behind McLaren. With one flying lap remaining of Q3, Verstappen decides to go all out – to 'send it', as he puts it afterwards, braking late, attacking the kerb and fighting the handling of a car which has been understeering all weekend. He blitzes the exit of turn one, shows great pace in turns two, six, seven and eight before the track's iconic Spoon curve. In his mind, he is saying, *I hope it's going to stick*, having more faith in his handling skills than what is proving to be a tricky car.

Horner is on the pit wall, readying himself for a place on the second row of the grid and likely behind Mercedes' George Russell and the two McLarens. Throughout the one minute and 27 seconds of the lap he is completely transfixed by his driver's times to that of the preceding lap. Later, Horner says: 'He comes down to Spoon and he absolutely nails it and then you can see the comparison. You see he's gained a tenth and a half, two-tenths on his last lap and then you're thinking, "OK, if he can hang on to this then there's a sniff of a front row here." It's going to be close. You're watching that comparing time and he loses a hundredth on the straight and you're thinking, "Oh no," and then he absolutely nails the last chicane and finds another three-quarters of a tenth there, has a good exit, keeps it tight to the line and, by the narrowest of margins gets pole. It is completely against the run of form. That lap was just outstanding. The team did a good job to give him a car he could work with and he had to extract every ounce of performance and be inch-perfect and Max did, and left nothing on the table.'

It is enough by the smallest of margins – just a hundredth of a second over Oscar Piastri – clocking a time more than half a second quicker than Verstappen had been in Q2. It draws comparisons to some of the great qualifying laps in the history of the sport. Verstappen admits it is very special but won't say if it's the best of his 41 pole positions to date. But it is surely one of the more unexpected, coming 17 months after his last pole at Red Bull's home race in Austria. After a stuttering start to the season, the team celebrates as if it is a race win.

The dumbfounded reaction on the pit wall says it all, the faces of Horner, who calls it 'one of the best qualifying laps ever', and of Pierre Waché best summing up the shock of it all. GP says simply over the radio: 'That is insane.' Rival drivers and team bosses share the sentiment, most with a shrug of the shoulders as if to say, 'that's just Max'. It is a lap that perhaps none of his current peers could have produced, that few in the sport's history might have been able to muster. It is a pole that sets up a lights-to-flag victory for Verstappen despite race-long pressure from the McLarens, including a tight side-by-side tussle for the lead as Lando Norris exits the pits having to weave onto the grass when Verstappen, within his rights, refuses to cede his track position. Red Bull's workforce are still talking about the qualifying lap into Sunday night and over the start of the working week, those arriving bleary eyed at the factory from Japan reliving it to those colleagues who could only watch on TV. It is not quite secondary that he goes on to win the race but it is that pole lap that makes it all possible.

In the wake of such a lap, Marko shakes his head, almost incredulous at the concept that Verstappen is still not the finished article after a weekend that has reinvigorated hopes of a successful title defence. 'He definitely is the best driver we ever had and he's still developing,' he says, speaking in his slow, methodical way. 'I don't see the end of his progress yet. He always comes with something extra. He's getting faster with less risk and more calm. He doesn't have to push every lap. I wouldn't say relaxed but he's not pushing or it doesn't look like he's on the limit. When it matters, he delivers. He has an unbelievable talent, he's committed, he's just interested in racing and he has quite a simple life. All that together makes a very strong racing personality.'

But what is it that makes him the driver who it is almost universally agreed to be the best on the grid? The answer is multilayered. One thing that stands Verstappen out from the conveyor belt of driver talent in the Red Bull programme is his ability to be switched on from the second he steps into a car, be it a practice run, qualifying or a race. Other drivers tend to like some warm-up laps or at least a little prior knowledge of what they're undertaking. In the wet, for example, Verstappen can go out and be two or three seconds quicker over just one lap than his rivals, who need maybe three or four laps to get up to the same pace. That wet-weather pace stems from dad Jos, who would teach his son to learn any track in just five laps, the message always to be on the limit straight away.

Horner likens Verstappen behind the wheel to Roger Federer in his tennis pomp, performing with a confident knowledge that he is the best in his sport. 'He does it with such precision and timing,' he says. 'We're seeing a driver – and it's such a joy to watch – be totally at one, totally confident in himself and extracting every ounce of performance, and his timing and accuracy has been outstanding. We've been blessed to have some great drivers in this team, including a four-time world champion in Sebastian Vettel, but Max even takes it a step further than that. His talent and determination and combination that he has are great to see. He never disappoints when he gets in the car. He has to be talked about in the same bracket as some of the greats of all time in this sport.'

For both Horner and dad Jos, one thing they can actually agree on is that Brazil 2024 marks the stand-out too. And that drive brings an element of pride from Verstappen Snr with the time spent doing lap after lap in wet conditions, Jos often putting his son on slick tyres in the wet conditions to challenge him further. But he puts Max's impressive track performances down to more than just pure speed and an ability to master the wet. For him, it goes back to the days of playing driving games on his Sony PlayStation. That, in turn, led to a passion for sim racing, which continues to this day. 'For sure it's the talent,' he says of his son's standing as the best driver currently on the grid, 'But I think it's also the sim racing that he does. In the sim, it's not about feeling, it's about everything you see with your eyes. When you make a corner on sim racing you judge speed, it's only eyes, not feeling. And because he does it that much, that in combination with talent and feeling, that makes him really good.' Verstappen Snr remembers the little legs dangling off the chair, unable to touch the floor, playing on the PlayStation and then the step-up to the sim. It was something he would have to peel him off, having been glued to it for hours at a time. Even now, Max admits to spending on average one to two hours a day on his sim.

A deep thinker, his technical knowledge base is also excellent. Verstappen's race engineers talk effusively about his technical feedback and you only need to be tuned into the team radio to experience it first-hand. He is acutely aware of even the slightest tweak in tyre pressure, a minute modification to a wing flap, a switch in break balance, and can feed back with a calm immediacy. This brilliant technical mind is at odds with the public's impression of him as simply an aggressive racer, which he also has in his armoury. Unlike many of his peers, he does not do a track-walk to get an understanding of its layout. Simply put, he finds it boring and, instead, he uses his first lap of practice as a track-walk of sorts, albeit a high-speed one. And what's remarkable is that he virtually never makes a mistake in the car, be that practice, qualifying or a race.

Ask the Verstappens for their favourite time in motorsport and it is not the Grand Prix victories, the championship titles, the ever-growing bank balance or the super stardom that they turn to. Rather, it is the stripped-down simplicity of the pair's karting days. Obsessed with racing from a young age, Max hopped on a quad bike at two, was just four when placed in a kart for the first time and seven by the time he started racing them against kids four years his senior. The young boy and the dad he idolised would travel around Europe competing against the likes of Charles Leclerc and Esteban Ocon, still his peers on the F1 grid today. School would end on a Friday afternoon and his dad would be waiting in a van to drive 700 miles to Italy where the majority of karting circuits were. They would practise or race all weekend and be back in time for school on Monday morning, Max spending much of the travel time sleeping in the van.

The Verstappens have always been close – Max going to live with his father when his parents split when he was just 11 years old, while his younger sister Victoria settled with their mother, Sophie. Jos is a regular at race weekends when his own driving commitments – now in rallying – don't clash. An F1 driver of some repute in his own right, Verstappen began his F1 career as Michael Schumacher's teammate at Benetton and went on to drive for a series of F1 teams: Arrows, Minardi, Stewart, Tyrrell and Footwork. He scored two podiums and enjoyed a best finish of 10th in the drivers' championship. Perhaps most famously, he became a fireball in his debut season in 1994 during a refuelling incident at the German Grand Prix from which he escaped remarkably unscathed. Fuel accidentally spilled over the body of his Benetton, suddenly ignited and team members quickly directed fire extinguishers onto the car, Verstappen climbing clear and later doused in a bottle of water to cool down his overheating head. Max was only six when his father's F1 career ended following a final season with Minardi. Jos recalls: 'I took him to the circuit and he was running around. He knew everything about it all already at a very young age. He was so sad if I didn't take him to a race, he was crying when I left home. He understood in the end I had to go away a lot from home and he had to stay behind because he had to go to school.'

There is obvious parental pride whenever he talks of his son and he admits that Max's achievements on track have made him reflective about his own career. 'I think in my time I thought I was good,' he says. 'But seeing him, I'm now wondering how good I was. But I'm fine. I'm more than happy the way that he's doing things and how many championships he won, and I have no issues with that. So I'm happy.'

He is well aware of the accusations that he was excessively pushy towards his son's motorsport career, particularly in the early days. There is a story of Jos leaving Max at a garage in the south of Italy over a row following a karting race, although Jos says the reality was quite different. His son was overtaken by a rival on the opening lap but, too eager to win that spot back immediately, he went for an overtaking manoeuvre at a fast corner – the wrong choice as it transpired – and the pair clashed on track. It denied him what should have been a very easy win. Jos, angered by his son's actions following a weekend of hard work – Jos acted as mechanic, pit crew, the lot back then — sparked the race debrief into a loud and lengthy in-car row.

'That time that I didn't speak to him for a week because of him making a mistake. That was really hard but the good thing after that, we talked about it, we understood it,' says Verstappen Snr. 'Since then, he was always really using his head on the racetrack. You could see the difference the next year — he was so good. It's bad to say but he really needed it, so it's fine, and it's also created the guy he is now. People talk sometimes about how badly I treated him, but we had a very good relationship — only sometimes he needed a hard hand to really push him. He's very relaxed sometimes, that was one of my worries — is he not too relaxed to perform? And that's how I challenge him. He needed it and he liked it, and he could handle it. But yeah, in the first place you are a parent, you want to give him the right opportunities and we were doing a sport where we wanted to win. You know your child and you see him. I'm also very motivated and sometimes I saw him driving like he was not interested. And then I was challenging him. At the end of the day, he enjoyed it. When you ask him what really were the nicest years, I think he will come up with go-kart. For sure, it was a good time together.'

The Verstappens remain a tight unit and, even in the high-paced world of F1, still take time to reflect on those early days. Surrounded by close family, both are quick to poke fun at that time of their lives. But Jos points out it goes a long way to explain the sportsperson his son has become today. As well as toughening him up mentally, Jos worked diligently on making him understand the technicalities of a car, the set-up, the engineering and the complexities of racing, including in the wet, resulting in Max being one of the most adept drivers on the grid in such conditions. But there were ways in which Verstappen found his own path. His passion for sim racing – he owns Team Redline – has been well documented, and he is all about getting drivers from sim racing into different genres of motorsport. When not in the cockpit of an F1 car or trying his luck in GT3 racing, he is still racing on the sim. 'The push for sim racing comes from him,' explains his father. 'It started on the PlayStation and then when he was older we got him a sim and he was really into that. He just wanted to drive.' And the Verstappens did just that come rain, shine or freezing weather on track, or else back on the sim in the comfort of their home.

The crowning glory for the pair will forever be the first world title in 2021 in Abu Dhabi, an emotional and controversial finale after a rollercoaster season in which the championship lead ebbed and flowed between Verstappen and Lewis Hamilton. But amid all the titles, race wins, pole positions and audacious passing manoeuvres, there are still points when the younger Verstappen takes the elder by surprise. But he swats back suggestions that his son has exceeded expectations. Jos's curt reply is, 'No, he can do a lot more.'

Jos loved to test his son on the technical side of things to help build up his knowledge during their karting days together. 'I think it's also what he learned in go-kart. I was always asking him specific questions and he was answering them all the time. We had a dyno [a dynamometer to measure the force, torque and power output of an engine] to test the engines at the workshop, and he had to stay in the same room where I was testing the engines to understand what I was doing, the piston and doing this and that. That's where he started to understand. I think it only went better and better during his time in Formula 1. He technically understands what's happening and that's good. Now, he drives the car, comes in and really pinpoints what he needs and what's important to go faster. So he understands very well. Now he knows how to set up a car even in GT3. When he sees people driving in the car, he can see what they need to go quicker.' To highlight the point, he recalls sending a clip of him rallying alongside co-driver Renaud Jamoul from a recent foray in the European Rally Championship. The response came back, 'Daddy, you have understeer in the car,' and Verstappen breaks into a laugh. 'And I was like "you're right", it's unbelievable he can just see that from outside the car.'

The man who gets to see Max Verstappen up close and personal the most is Gianpiero Lambiase. Asked to explain what makes Verstappen so quick, Lambiase says: 'He has an innate feeling for the connection between himself, the car and the road, so being able to feel what the car is doing on what is ultimately four contact patches of tyres to the ground. It's an incredible raw talent to understand what the car is doing but then relay that in a very succinct and concise fashion such that we can improve that for him, not only short-term at a race weekend but longer-term in the development philosophy of the car.'

The team's chief engineer, Paul Monaghan, has worked with a raft of leading drivers over his years in F1, among them Ayrton Senna, Fernando Alonso and Sebastian Vettel. He says the thing that aligns them all is a ruthless aggression when it's required but the other great strength of Verstappen, he points out, is being a team player despite being its clear superstar, another facet not often known outside the four walls of the team. 'Even on a day when we haven't been as successful as we might want to be, he's dusted himself down and contributed,' says Monaghan. 'He's like, "We're in this together and off we go". That's one of his greatest strengths that people don't see.'

There is almost an effortlessness to it all. Watch onboard footage of Verstappen, be it a qualifying lap or within a race, and to the uninitiated it doesn't necessarily look outstanding. But each movement, every decision, every flick of a switch is meticulously thought out. And for a teammate, it can be hard to fully comprehend, particularly when one's handling of the car is often mystifyingly different. For Yuki Tsunoda, it is all down to how readily Verstappen is dialled in, while he prefers a few laps to get up to speed like many of his peers. 'He's just able to nail it every time when it counts,' he says.

And the scary part when watching his Suzuka lap is he's hugely motivated to get better and still doesn't think he's yet reached his peak.

14

IN THE PITS

It is a carefully choreographed dance, months in the planning and just two seconds in its execution, even fractionally less if absolutely everything goes to plan. It is punctuated either end by just two sounds, four wheel guns whirring noisily and rhythmically in unison, the physical movements in between the two sounds a mere blur. Three people stand over each tyre: one to remove the old one, another to add the new rubber and a third with a wheel gun. The target point for the driver is the front-jack man, ready to hoist up the car as it hits the jack at 80kph, ridiculously fast as you face it even with the reduction in pace with a speed limit in the pit lane. At the rear is another jack to additionally lift up the car while a third holds a spare jack should either fail and, at the front, two people are primed to adjust the front flaps as directed by the engineers. Either side of the briefly stationary car a person holds it steady while it's balanced in the air, another checks the coast is clear to return to the pit lane, while a further team member holds a fire extinguisher in case of an emergency. And finally there is someone to restart the car in the unlikely event that it should stall.

It scarcely seems credible that inside a two- to three-second time frame teams are planning to cram in hoisting up a one-tonne car, attaching four wheel guns, removing the old tyres, replacing with new, reattaching with the wheel guns, lowering and releasing. When done well and fluently it is a thing of beauty and crews immediately know as much by the sound as the sense of speed. As the tyres screech and the RB21 disappears into the distance there's a quick round of back-patting in brief celebration before the team return to their regular roles in the garage.

Many years ago at the Australian Grand Prix, a hapless group of us journalists were given the chance to do a pit stop on Jenson Button's BAR Honda. The timer went past 20 seconds, which seemed quick for our inexperienced makeshift crew. How F1 teams can do it in less than a tenth of that time is nothing short of a miracle. For Red Bull, it all begins with a simple request from Rich Wolverson – 'Pit crew get ready' – helmets are slotted on in response, each member of the team knowing their exact place. The best pit stops feel like the driver has barely halted.

Back at the factory, outside the frenzied nature of a race weekend, there are regular pit-stop practices, although it is hard to replicate the speed, noise, heat and pressure of a race weekend pit stop at HQ with what is an electric version of the RB21. The trick is to do a sufficient number so the stops become second nature while also not overdoing it so they become monotonous and repetitive. While speed is of the essence, the team are told not to go chasing records, as that will come organically. The record of a single pit stop is currently held by McLaren, set on Lando Norris's car at the 2023 Qatar Grand Prix. The clock stopped at 1.80 seconds, two-hundredths of a second quicker than Red Bull's previous best mark. But Red Bull have long prided themselves on being the fastest pit crew on the grid. Each season, one of F1's partners, DHL, gives out an award to the fastest crew over the course of the season. For the past seven years that gong has gone to Red Bull, as dominant in the pit lane as Verstappen has been on track. But the crew have undergone big changes for 2025. Gone is Jonathan Wheatley – replaced by Wolverson. It is the first time for almost the entire pit crew that they have a new boss. In addition, for the first time this season Red Bull are rotating their pit crews in response to the marathon nature of the season, 24 races now cemented annually on the calendar, and allowing crew members to have time off mid-season with family and friends. It is also hoped that lessening the load will help with staff retention, the attritional nature of life in the garage meaning it is increasingly becoming a young person's game. With that rotational nature, the understanding is that there will be hiccups as new recruits try to bed-in to the team and their roles in the fast-paced world of the pit stop.

Jon Caller, the number-one mechanic for Yuki Tsunoda, says there are pluses and minuses to such a change of approach. 'It means we've got to have a bigger strength in depth of the pit crew which is a challenge,' he says. 'Before we had a set pit crew and that leads to everyone knowing what they need to do every week pretty consistently. This time we're getting new members in different positions so we're doing a lot more practice with different members to try to get that consistency throughout our range of positions. There's always going to be a bit of a learning curve with that. Other teams have been through that process already, so there's going to be some teething issues and slower pit stops because of it. But I think going forward it's going to mean longevity in the race team is possible because it's such a long season and this means a few races off a year each.'

The teething issues play out as anticipated. A year ago, in races one to three, they were quickest at two Grands Prix and third-fastest at the other. Twelve months on, they record the seventh quickest individual stop in Australia, the sixth best in China, which includes that front-flap adjustment on Verstappen's car, and don't even register in the top 10 in race three in Japan. It is to be expected; any gremlins set to be ironed out as the season and the stops progress.

Pit-stop crews are not employed solely in that role by the team, they all have their own day jobs. Front jack-man Ed Hemsworth is the race-team coordinator; gun-man Callum Adams is the composite events team leader; and the front- and rear-left wheel guns are powered by the Caller twins, Matt and Jon. There are try-outs back at base for who's best where and there are varying attributes required: strength to lift the 12kg tyres as well as a calm, unflappable nature for something like the gun-man role. It's also no longer the preserve of an all-male world, although Michaelagh Tennyson, responsible for front flap adjustment, is currently the only female member of Red Bull's pit crew. Her role with the team is that of race parts and lifing controller. All have to be equally quick, there's no point in, say, one gun-man being faster than the others.

The Callers are one of two sets of twins at Red Bull, the other pair based back at the factory, engineers Craig and

Carl Lawson. Of the on-track twins, Matt is the older by just 30 minutes. He joined the team first in 2015, working initially in car-build and then on the support team. Then word went out at the factory that Red Bull were looking for more mechanics without being able to find suitable candidates. 'I was asked, "Do you know anyone you'd recommend that's half-decent?"' he recalls, 'and I said, "I don't know if he's half-decent but, yeah, I know someone who can swing spanners and he looks a bit like me."' So, he rang his brother to ask if he'd be interested in switching life as the chief mechanic for a team in the British Touring Car Championship for Formula 1. Jon says: 'I was looking for a new challenge at the time and Matt just rang at the right moment.' He went in the next day and was offered a job. That was back in 2016 and the pair have been there ever since, making the step up to working as part of the race team in 2018.

Initially, trying to work out who's who can be a challenge and even now the team's chief engineer Paul Monaghan repeatedly gets the Callers muddled up. But Jon has a slight gap in his front teeth and there's slight differences in the way they walk and work. Until this season where races off have become a prerequisite, they have been ever-present in the garage, directing their team of mechanics, both working with a quiet authority to guide out their drivers when the time arises.

Seven years from their first race together, the pressure hasn't dissipated. Matt says: 'They say pressure's a privilege and to be at a top team in the most competitive championship in the world is amazing. Red Bull have always pushed the boundaries in every respect. And so we're trying to always be the fastest in everything, whether that's pit stops or human performance or car floors – everything. Even the music level is always pushed to the highest degree, and it's always nice to be a part of it.'

In spite of all that pressure, watching them at work is almost a calming experience. On the floor to one side of the garage is marked No.1 – Verstappen and Matt Caller's domain – the other half of the garage bears a 22, the number of Tsunoda. In his karting days, Tsunoda raced under the number 11 but, with that taken on the F1 grid by Sergio Pérez when he arrived in F1, he instead doubled it and came up with 22. The mechanics may often be working at top speed to fix a problem before qualifying or a race, or else changing a major component on the car that hasn't worked mid-practice session with the clock ticking in often unpleasantly hot working conditions. There is little chatter, everyone fully focused on their individual task.

On Verstappen's side of the garage, Helmut Marko sits on a high stool with Verstappen's engineers either side of him. Centrally, Monaghan is seated, inspecting a screen with various information, sometimes tyres, sometimes numbers, sometimes footage of a rival's cars. Some of the pit crew working on the tyres have knee pads as they need to get low to the ground. Amid it all, scrutineers loiter around the garage ensuring everything the team is doing is above board; so too is someone from Pirelli, there to help in case of any issues with the tyres. That they miraculously all avoid each other in such a cramped environment is no small wonder.

'A lot of people who come into the garage are amazed we don't bump into each other,' says Jon. 'Especially in tight garages like Monaco with a lot going on. It's kind of like organised chaos. Everyone knows their place and it's fairly regimented. When you do 24 races a year you get pretty used to where you need to be and when. It's when things go wrong that you earn your money.'

A good number-one mechanic, aside from the obvious technical skills, primarily needs to be a good communicator, as they are the bridge between the engineers and those on the garage floor, funnelling all the information from both sides and sharing that to the right people at the right time. They also need to step back as much as possible to take an overview – not easy when a mechanic's natural instinct is to be completely hands-on. Both Matt and Jon are perpetually looking at what the next obstacle might be, what might slow them down, and thereby enabling their respective crews to be as quick as possible.

Now pit stops are very much second nature, muscle memory instilled in them by repeated practice. At the factory they'll do two sessions a day, 10 stops at a time. Then at race weekends there are stops throughout Thursday, Friday, Saturday and the Sunday morning before the race. They've got so good at it they even did a project where they did a pit stop in the pitch black, all of them fully blindfolded, unable to see a single sliver of light. The first few attempts were as you might expect – shambolic. By the end, they'd got the pit stop down to a rapid 2.8 seconds. 'That was a cool human experiment,' says Jon, 'to take away one of your senses. But it showed that muscle memory plays a massive part in what we do, and that's down to all the practice.'

The Callers have done a variety of different jobs in the pit crew over the years, from flap adjustments to taking wheels on and off, before landing what Matt calls the Hollywood job as gun-men. The irony is that such a short operation takes months to get right: practice makes perfect. Essentially, the more they do it, the more it becomes muscle memory and they can blank out the fact that there's millions of people watching on TV. 'It almost happens on autopilot now, you don't remember you've done it,' says Jon of the experience. But human error creeps in, often to catastrophic consequences. It's rare to win a race in a pit stop but it's perfectly possible to lose one when pitting.

The Callers travel to Japan for race three but fly home on the Friday morning when their father is taken ill. In their absence, Verstappen goes on to win the race as they watch it from their dad's bedside. With the three of them seeing events play out on the television screen from the hospital, his dad quips after the race: 'I think you're out of a job now!' Following the Japan win, expectations from outside the team are high of a repeat in Bahrain. But the team knows that with its rough track surface and far higher temperatures, it will highlight the issues with the RB21. While Suzuka – resurfaced in sector one and hence less abrasive and with cooler temperatures than expected – proved the perfect window in which the car could operate in, Bahrain is its antithesis. As Verstappen lists the issues afterwards it is lengthy: no pace, overheating tyres, poor balance and even poor pit stops – not a criticism usually levelled at Red Bull. Summing up, he says, 'Everything went wrong.'

He has a point. At a time when the target is a two-second pit stop, his two stops in Bahrain are 4.7 and 6.2 seconds apiece. The reason for the first, which also afflicts Tsunoda, is simple and frustrating, a wiring loom having worn away in the pit gantry. It could have happened at any point, but it decided to strike then. The red light held by chief mechanic Phil Turner, who oversees the two mechanic crews, never goes out as a result and hence both Verstappen and Tsunoda remain temporarily rooted to the spot. As Jon Caller says: 'It is frustrating, as that could have happened at any point during the weekend and Sod's Law says it's the first pit stop of the race. That's just the way racing goes and we had to adapt from that point. We have a very bullet-proof system and that was an absolutely freak fault that never happened before. We reacted well to it, did the best we could, salvaged some places, put in processes in the hope that never happens again.' As for the second, there was an issue with changing the front-right tyre.

The pit stop errors mirror a hit-and-miss start to the season but, as the new members of the pit crew gel into the line-up, the mistakes will steadily dissolve and Red Bull's motley crew in the pits will rapidly climb its way back up to being one of F1's stand-outs. And in any case, the Callers have both experienced worse than the events in Bahrain. Like the rest of their teammates, there is an element of pride in the quick pit stops, although they do not stick in the memory bank as much as the howlers. Both have encountered moments they'd rather forget.

For Jon, that goes back to Mexico in 2022 on Sergio Pérez's car. He under-gunned the left rear on his car and a two-second stop built to a four-, five-second one. Such time loss might not appear gargantuan but, in an era where the field is bunched up more than in recent memory, it can be costly. 'We were chasing down a podium and probably the reason we didn't get one was because of that. It was Checo's home race too.' The error circulated around his head time and time again in the aftermath but his fellow pit crew took him out for a few drinks that night and it was quickly forgotten. It is often with humour that the crew move on from errors. For 24 hours, people can have a laugh about it, the comedy almost acting as a way to trigger a pressure valve. And it is that humour that bonds the team tighter. But they all know that mistakes are permissible as long as they're not repeated.

Matt grimaces as he begins to recall his own pit-stop nadir five years ago at the United States Grand Prix in Texas when the team were on the precipice of the constructors' championship. His under-gunning of Verstappen's car proved even more costly, equating to a 10-second stop, which to Matt felt like an absolute lifetime. 'From memory, Max was pretty vocal on the radio about that one! But he still won the race and dug me out of a pretty big hole. Had he not won that weekend, and us the constructors', that would have been firmly on my shoulders. I felt devastated but, as we always say, you win as a team and lose as a team.'

The target is to now get back to winning.

15

THE DIVA

A year on from 2024's season opener in Bahrain where Horner found himself in the very public eye of the storm, the public-facing message is that peace reigns; but the reality is the fractures have not been fully mended and the future is uncertain. Helmut Marko tells Sky Germany in the aftermath of the race that there is a very real possibility that Verstappen could leave, which co-owner Mark Mateschitz warns internally is the worst thing that could ever happen to Red Bull. 'The concern is great,' says Marko. 'Improvements have to come in the near future so that he has a car with which he can win again. We have to create a basis with the car so that he can fight for the world championship.'

The team have gone from the glory of Suzuka to the despair of Bahrain the following Grand Prix weekend: a four-time world champion should not be battling with Pierre Gasly for sixth place on the last lap in Sakhir. At one point in the race, he was briefly running dead last. The contrast from one weekend to the next is stark, but the RB21 appears to be somewhere in between the performance in Suzuka, where Verstappen was a pole sitter and race winner, and the desert of Bahrain. The balance problems of the previous year are fundamentally the same as they were with the RB20, which proved something of a riddle for the engineers to solve even as the season progressed. The team estimates only a quarter of the issues with it have been remedied with its successor, the RB21.

The RB21 currently has a narrow operating window, essentially meaning the set-up and track conditions have to be just right for it to be in its sweet spot. In Suzuka, the stars aligned with its high-speed corners and much cooler temperatures than in past seasons in Japan, meaning tyre management – something the McLarens are the current masters of – was less of an issue. Far hotter temperatures in Bahrain – in contrast to the cool February test there – and its abrasive surface prove a nightmare for Red Bull's car, more suited to a fast-flowing circuit than the medium-speed corners of Sakhir. Combined, it causes issues with the Brembo brakes, the tyres and the balance of the car, which means that as the race goes on it skids and slides all over the place.

Red Bull is confident it knows what's wrong with the car but finding the answers is a harder one to solve. Horner talks of it being 'engineering problems requiring engineering solutions'. Reflecting on the early part of the season, he says: 'I think for the engineering team it has been a head-scratcher. The car's been a little bit of a diva so far this season. We're starting to get a much better understanding of the RB21 and where we need to improve. We're working very hard on that and the whole team are very focused. But hopefully as we're getting to know each other better and updates start to subtly appear on the car over coming races we'll be able to have a more predictable car and better balance.'

Horner is all too aware the buck stops with him but his head has been on the chopping block too many times for him to worry about this issue. But digging him and the team out of the hole is not straightforward. One of the big issues is that the team has not seen a direct correlation from the wind tunnel to the circuits and the team's simulation tools are not properly replicating what then takes place on track. The team currently use a wind tunnel in Bedford. While a new one is being built on the Milton Keynes campus, that won't be finished until 2026. So, the inference is that there might be yet more engineering gremlins to come, and things could get worse before they get better.

The nimbleness of Red Bull means they are one of the best at finding solutions mid-season, capable of putting an in-house development race into place with speed. The question is whether they can pull it off with their first truly Newey-free season. Horner is bullish about the chances. 'The thing that marks this team out is that we'll always pull a result out of the bag,' he muses. 'We're a team of racers and that DNA runs throughout the entire company. It's frustrating we're not consistently in a winning position yet. But there's drive and determination in this business and team, and competitiveness in that people don't like losing. That is the biggest motivation to get back into a winning position.'

And yet he knows full well the pressure is on him to spark a turnaround, with Marko's fears over Verstappen's future and the hierarchy in Austria so used to success that it demands it imminently. The pressure is on Pierre Waché too. At the moment, the message has been that if the car wins, as was the case in Suzuka, it is down to the brilliance of the driver; if Verstappen is sixth, as he was in Bahrain, then that rests with the car and the engineers – the group Waché oversees as technical director. While not admitting defeat, the Frenchman makes the confession that fortunes could indeed go further downhill before any upswing. 'It's difficult to expect anything at the moment,' he concedes. 'I think the window of the car to find performance is very narrow and it's very easy to be out of it. That's one aspect. The second aspect is the difference between the teams is very low. A small mistake or better job from others changes our position massively. Everything we are doing currently after the first races, we learn a lot about the car. It will be a very difficult season and tight, but very interesting.' The engineer in him is fascinated by the problems, the competitor in him clearly irritated and itching to get back to winning ways more regularly than just the Suzuka one-off.

While he does not quite see the car as a diva, he concedes it is a vehicle that needs a lot of attention to get it in the right window and that too much time is being spent searching for performance. And it's not as simple as widening the operating window of the car to find that fix. 'What we have to try to do is optimise and understand the window of the car to suit the driver, and development-wise try to widen that window. The problem is that widening the window can also reduce the performance of the car. We try not to reduce it when making it wider but, in parallel, understand how with the set-up that we can play around with this car to make it easier to use.'

Explaining where the issue lies, he says: 'I think the main problem is the link between the through-corner balance, which means how the car behaves during the braking phase until the apex.'

On its day and at the right track, the car is quick, but the other side of that there are race weekends where it never features at the front end of the pack. While not quite as confident as Horner, Waché says he and his team have a better understanding of the car and are already moving it in the right direction with their in-season development. But he laughs when conceding, 'It doesn't mean it's easy to fix.' He is feeling the pressure of finding solutions and, while he admits the wind tunnel and simulation tools are an issue, it is not something he insists that he and the team can use as an excuse. 'We had some issues from that, for sure, but I will not hide myself only from that aspect,' he insists. 'Our toolware was maybe a little bit out of date and at the end of a set of regulations. When you have to find some small detail it's more difficult when you have a tool that with a repeatability is not as good as some others.'

Another difficulty is, counter-intuitively, the brilliance of Verstappen. Such is his ability he can cover up some of the issues and limitations of the car, driving it beyond its capabilities. 'This guy is able to use the car better than everyone else. We have to listen to him and try to adapt the car based on what he can do with it. We are following what he tells us and what he can choose. His capacity to drive already gives us a lot more opportunity to make the quickest car because he has a different limit than others. However, he's also hiding some problems that you struggle to fix.' Does that mean he's simply too good for everyone else around him? 'This is the problem you have with these talented people,' Waché says. 'You know exactly what he wants but, because he's pushing the limits, for sure on some occasions it's creating some big problems. As you may know the development of the car is a massive operation, it's not like in a day you can change it. And for the second driver, it's more difficult to follow the same direction.'

The grid is bunched so tight that a simple mistake can have huge consequences from one race to the next. While hard to believe, Waché argues he doesn't mind the low points of 'being bad', as he puts it, as long as they can understand and learn from it, but he is impatient to improve the car. Change is coming with a new floor and Waché and his technical team are hopeful it will provide a big step forwards. Internally, it is seen as the key to unlocking the potential of the RB21, which is lurking underneath the chassis but so far evading Red Bull's greatest minds.

Verstappen Snr rails against those who suggest the car has been 'built for Max'. Instead, he argues the team have built the quickest car possible, it's simply that 'Max has a very special feeling and can drive anything'. As for solving the issues, he says: 'Obviously they don't understand otherwise they would have built the car differently. That's the difficulty of wind tunnels, you have the sim and everything has to correlate together. At the moment, they're a little bit lost on that otherwise they would have fixed it. Sometimes it's a very difficult car to find a sweet spot.'

His son would dearly love change too. Despite the poor showing by the team, he leaves Bahrain just eight points behind championship leader Lando Norris, which doesn't quite seem to reflect the advantage of the McLarens. A race later in Saudi Arabia, he is 12 points off the top spot, this time Oscar Piastri replacing his teammate as championship leader. In Jeddah, a week after Bahrain, the performance effectively flips again, Red Bull with genuine pace to match the McLarens but Verstappen having to make do with second place after a five-second penalty for gaining an advantage over Piastri at the start of the race. Then in Miami two weeks later, Verstappen finishes 40 seconds behind Piastri, never once able to get close to the Australian. Is this simply a period of damage limitation for Red Bull before the flexing wing change in Spain, a title fight that's slowly ebbing away or is drivers' crown number five still possible? Horner is unfazed: 'Quite a bit's happened in the first few races. Statistics [before Miami] were second, fourth, sixth and another second and two pole positions. We know there are areas of the car we really need to improve. Max has extracted every ounce of performance and we've optimised race weekends so far. There's a lot of positives to take out of the first few races.'

But Verstappen and Red Bull have grown accustomed to being a winning machine in recent years. Finishes in and around the podium are not sufficient to battle for the title. Clearly off the pace of the McLaren – sometimes alarmingly so, as in Miami – quick solutions are needed. It begs the question: is the car good enough for a title charge? Horner shrugs his shoulders and says: 'Only the points table will tell us at the end of the year. There's a lot of the year to go. We're not even a quarter of the way through the season. With what we've had, it's not too bad. The key is getting performance on the car and dealing with some of its vices.' And again his mind moves on to Spain and the in-season rule change. 'Whether that benefits some or is to the detriment only time will tell,' he adds. 'It's very hard to predict, but for sure it'll have an impact.'

16

IN THE BARRIERS

Getting up to speed on his first fast lap in qualifying for the Emilia-Romagna Grand Prix, Yuki Tsunoda hits the Variante Villeneuve Chicane aggressively, far too aggressively. In practice earlier in the day his best lap time is a second behind that of his teammate. All-out attack is his only response as he tries to claw back even a fraction of the time deficit. Taking too much kerb on entry to Villeneuve, he spins violently out of control, flips upside down and clatters into the Armco barriers at 150mph, leaving all four corners of his Red Bull badly damaged. As he sears towards the barrier at breakneck speed, he removes his hands from the steering wheel – thereby diminishing the threat of breaking his hands or wrists – and prepares his body and mind for impact. He thinks to himself, *Oh, this is going to hurt*, but back to front, and therefore unsighted, he is unclear of when to brace for the exact moment of impact. 'And then for a few seconds I'm upside down and I'm like, *What's going on? I shouldn't be like this*, and each time thinking, *Oh my God, this is going to be a massive crash*.

I just made sure I didn't get too hurt. But in the back of my mind I knew the barrier was kind of like a sponge, an FIA-protective barrier, so I knew it maybe wouldn't hurt as much.' On impact, the barrier's metal outer coating rips apart just like it's a sheet of cardboard, doing its best to wrap itself around the top of Tsunoda's car. He flips back down to the ground, the shell of his car coming to rest on four badly damaged wheels with him still strapped into the cockpit.

There are heads in hands and complete hush in the Red Bull garage in the immediate moments afterwards. Waiting to hear from the driver over the team radio can feel like a lifetime. Following a pause in which he catches his breath and dusts himself off, he delivers the reassuring words 'I'm OK' over the team radio, which is met with collective sighs of relief all round. And from there, Tsunoda gets up, removes his safety belts and steps out of the car remarkably unaided despite the vehemence of the shunt. That he is unscathed is nothing short of astonishing and he is given a clear bill of health to compete in the following day's race, albeit from the back of the grid. As he walks away from the car with the session red-flagged he keeps on looking back at it, partly to see the level of damage, partly in amazement that he is completely in one piece and walking, the halo encasing him still fully intact.

Imola back in 1994 remains one of Formula 1's darkest and deadliest Grand Prix weekends. First, Roland Ratzenberger lost his life at the same corner where Tsunoda flew into the barriers 31 years later, and then Ayrton Senna at Tamburello. Three decades on, massive strides have been made in driver safety, pushed by the likes of former F1 medical director Sid Watkins. In the intervening years, there has been just one driver death: Jules Bianchi, following his crash at the Japanese Grand Prix in 2014.

The halo is one such innovation, introduced in 2018 and originally designed by Mercedes, a titanium protective barrier for drivers inside the cockpit. At its introduction, it received a mixed response from cynical drivers but has undoubtedly gone on to save lives. Romain Grosjean's halo deflected the barrier when he crashed at the 2020 Bahrain Grand Prix, and it acted as a vital protective layer for Zhou Guanyu when he was flipped upside down in dramatic fashion at the British Grand Prix in 2022. Tsunoda is another of those clearly in debt to the halo for what will be the biggest crash of the entire season from any driver.

He admonishes himself, calling the accident a stupid mistake on his part and, while drivers are quick to move on from such incidents – you have to – he is still bothered by aspects of it. Reflecting on the crash, he says: 'It was more of a shunt than I expected. I was a bit unlucky that I had a bit of a jump before the barrier, which I think made it slightly worse. The speed I went into the barrier was quite fast.' And there is a realisation just three races into life at his new team that his group of mechanics will not be thanking him for having to work relentlessly and late into Saturday night to rebuild the car in time for the following afternoon's race. That his car was fitted with the new floor is a particularly big setback, having to revert back to an older, less efficient floor for the next race and subsequent weekends. 'It wasn't my finest moment,' he says. 'I made a huge impact and it was such a big backward step for the mechanics to have to rebuild the car overnight. I felt really really bad as it was one of the worst turns of my career, so I really wanted to bounce back strong.' Such is his strength of feelings that he struggles to sleep that night, reliving the crash, analysing where he went wrong before resolving that he will finish in the points as a way to thank his mechanics for their toil. 'I'm happy I did that,' he says, when he finishes in 10th place.

Hiroshi Fushida was the first Japanese driver in Formula 1 after qualifying for the Dutch Grand Prix at Zandvoort in 1975, only for a blown engine to prevent him from taking the start. He tried his luck again at the British Grand Prix but failed to qualify for the race. Fushida included, there have been 21 Japanese drivers to make it to F1, with varying degrees of success. The first full-time Japanese F1 driver, Satoru Nakajima, signed as the teammate of Ayrton Senna at Lotus in 1987 and scored points in two of his opening three races. Nakajima, who would go on to become a motorsport executive after his racing days, got his fascination for cars from his older brothers, driving in his family's garden unbeknown to their father. His son Kazuki would later drive for Williams, for whom his father was nearly signed back in 1986, losing out instead to Nigel Mansell. Nakajima Snr lasted five seasons on the grid, his son just two. Other notable Japanese drivers in F1 include Aguri Suzuki, responsible for a first podium among his countrymen at his home race in 1990 before in later life bringing his own eponymous F1 team to the grid, Super Aguri, for a brief stint with another Japanese driver, Takuma Sato. Then there was Ukyo Katayama, until Tsunoda the most capped Japanese F1 driver of all time even though he had the unwanted statistic of failing to finish 63 of the 95 races he started. In 2009, he had to be rescued from Mount Fuji when the tents in which he and his fellow climbers were staying were blown away. Two people died in the incident but Katayama survived.

Tsunoda will later surpass Katayama's national record for Grand Prix starts at the Spanish Grand Prix, race nine of the 2025 season, his fifth on the F1 grid after a meteoric rise through the junior ranks. His passion for motorsport was sparked by his father, Nobuaki, who took his four-year-old son to Nakai Inter Circuit in Kanazawa to try his hand at karting. The Tsunoda family still recall him being a natural, and that led to him attending his first F1 race three years later in 2007, which was won by Lewis Hamilton in his rookie season – he was hooked. From then on, motorsport was the only path he wanted to pursue and he decided he wanted to join the likes of Hamilton on the grid. But his motorsport dreams reached a crossroads at the age of 16 at the final trials for the Honda Formula Dream Project, Honda's junior driver programme. If successful, he would be snapped up for the coming season of Japanese F4; if not, his plan was to walk away from motorsport and focus on his education instead.

Overtaken by a crippling bout of nerves, he froze at the wheel of the car and made a false start, the worst possible beginning. He ended up third and missed out on a spot on the driver programme, bawling his eyes out on the train ride home. As fate would have it, Nakajima Snr had already spotted his racing talent, standing on the final corner of the trials as Tsunoda pushed desperately but ultimately unsuccessfully to close the gap on the leaders. So, instead, on the recommendation of Nakajima, he was snapped up by the Suzuka Racing School (another Honda project) and made his way into the national F4 championship courtesy of that secondary route. He would do two full seasons in that formula, capped by winning the title at his second attempt. From there, thanks to Honda's ties to the F1 team, he joined the Red Bull junior team for the following season where he drove for Jenzer Motorsport in F3. On his arrival in Europe in 2019, his English was limited, learning predominantly from the team mechanics, which would explain the occasionally choice language used by the Japanese driver over the team radio, particularly in his early days in F1. Despite the burgeoning vocabulary, his season never quite ignited, except for Monza in the latter stages where he won the sprint and finished on the podium in the feature race, enough to see him move up to the much-heralded Carlin team in F2. In the feeder series for F1 he finished third in the championship standings, earning him rookie of the year, just 15 points behind champion Mick Schumacher, with wins on the F1 tracks of Silverstone, Spa and Bahrain.

From there, AlphaTauri (Racing Bulls under another of its former names) came calling, snapping up the 20-year-old for the 2021 season. Announcing his arrival, then team principal Franz Tost said: 'In F2 this year, Yuki has demonstrated the right mix of racing aggression and good technical understanding. I am sure he will be a great asset to our team.' For his part, Tsunoda spoke of realising a lifelong ambition but also carrying the hopes of a lot of Japanese F1 fans.

He immediately started strongly, with a top-10 points finish at the season-opening Bahrain Grand Prix. And yet he earned himself a reputation for being rash, his four-letter rants over the team radio aimed at his race engineer Mattia Spini becoming a feature of race weekends. To the ever-watchful wider leadership team, such outbursts didn't go unnoticed. Reflecting, Tsunoda believes both the low point and the turning point came in Bahrain at the start of his 2024 campaign. Ordered to let Daniel Ricciardo past during the race, after the chequered flag Tsunoda scythed past his teammate on the slowdown lap before braking heavily and then returning to the track to pass the Australian close-up and at pace. Afterwards, he sarcastically said over the radio: 'Yeah, thanks guys, I appreciate it.' Ricciardo didn't take his words too kindly, replying: 'What the fuck is wrong? Fucking helmet', and neither did Red Bull's top brass, it not helping the perception held by some that he lacked the maturity to make the step-up to the A team. Looking back on that moment, Tsunoda admits he used to take his stress out on the track and found it liberating, before clicking into a more affable mode off it. It was a moment that made him see the error of his ways and seek a shift.

Including cleaning up his in-cockpit behaviour, Tsunoda felt he'd done enough to warrant the Red Bull seat for the start of the 2025 campaign, instead it has come two races later and without a winter of testing embedded in the team. Of being initially overlooked just a few races into his new role, he says: 'I think I was proving enough to show that I can be in this team. For me, it didn't make sense at all. I was kind of frustrated but, at the same time, this is Formula 1. It's not just about performance. I still saw opportunity and I knew I had to be the lead driver [at Racing Bulls], and unlock a new level in myself. In the end, they chose Liam and I wasn't happy about that but, at the same time, I was prepared and that made me a little bit calmer, so I didn't feel really frustrated.'

He's now on a fast track to getting to grips with a second new car in a single season and, under the glare of his Red Bull debut in front of his home crowd in Suzuka, he struggled to

12th as teammate Verstappen won. The opening few week-ends, his form ebbed and flowed through practice, qualifying and the races. 'It's quite a rollercoaster in a way with my sessions,' he says. 'But the team have made it as easy as possible for me to feel at home and feel comfortable. The up-and-down performance is natural. That's part of the journey, and learning about the time – there's such limited time and pressure going on. I think I'm on the right path and just need to keep doing what I'm doing.'

He believes his stint over the winter and early this season has changed him. Having felt like a junior driver at the team for three seasons he has instead felt like a leader, impressing Racing Bulls principal Laurent Mekies and the rest of the team with his approach. As such, the switch up is not so daunting. 'This year people were really relying on my comments and the team was trusting in my performance, and trying to get feedback from myself to develop the car for the future,' he says. 'So, I was already feeling quite a lot of pressure. Here, it's a different kind of pressure. Red Bull have had a lot of success. They'd just won the drivers' championships so they have a strong winning mindset and expectation from each race is higher. From that, you have more pressure but I'm quite enjoying it.'

The task set for him by the team is to consistently score points. In the early days, he has had varying degrees of success. He picks up his first points for the team in only his second race, coming ninth in Bahrain just three spots behind Verstappen, but then crashes out on lap one with Pierre Gasly in the next race in Saudi Arabia. In Miami, he is back in the team's hospitality area to watch the remainder of sprint qualifying after going out in Q1. Sat with his manager Diego

Menchaca, he does not speak for the remainder of the session, left to ponder a chance gone begging. Come Imola, he recovers from his crash to sneak into the points, an impressive recovery drive after his 150mph smash-up.

The man tasked with getting Tsunoda up to speed is his race engineer Richard Wood. Having spent a winter and two races with Lawson, he now has to form a new bond with Tsunoda. Wood says: 'You don't have to have common interests or be best buddies but you need to have a mutual understanding so you kind of know how their minds are working and what they're thinking. But he's fun, he's up for a laugh, too, quite a joker. We talk nonsense – it's important to chat – and play a bit of padel. You spend so much time with drivers, almost more than you do with your families, so it's good to have that understanding and that relationship.'

It is up to Tsunoda and Wood to work out how to get consistent points finishes and catch Verstappen. Rather than feel daunted by Verstappen and what he can do in the likes of Suzuka and Imola, where Verstappen picks up a second race win of the season, pulling off what is later chosen as the overtake of the season around the outside at turn one on Oscar Piastri, Tsunoda feels inspired. 'He is one of the best drivers in history, and I clearly see why,' he says. 'In a good way it makes me realise I'm not far away. I know if I bring myself to the level that I want, I think I can perform very closely. I would like to be scoring points as consistently as possible. Currently, I'm slightly behind compared to Max. It's not easy to build up confidence and learnings in a race week but, at the same time, you can't keep saying there's not much time. I think I'm on the right path. Once I learn things from Max then hopefully I can be at the level that Max is right now.'

Paul Monaghan is among his backers, arguing, 'He's done enough rodeos that he's not intimidated by the calibre of driver he is trying to match. He's not worried by the fact he's sitting opposite a four-time world champion and says what he wants.'

And yet Imola is a massive setback in that quest to close the gap, financially damaging in the cost-cap era where every penny counts, but also denting the Tsunoda confidence. And the clock is ticking in his bid to catch up.

17

WELCOME TO MONACO

If Formula 1 is a circus, then Monaco is the ultimate attraction, an abundance of ostentation, unapologetically brash in the wealth it oozes from every pore. Long before the race, every mooring is filled by superyachts. It is the must-see, must-be-seen-at event on the calendar for everyone from billionaires to celebrities and influencers.

Formula 1 has an obsession with its celebrity attendees, from the screen time they are allocated to the document listing the expected VIPs at each race weekend, as well as their number of Instagram followers, crucial in the social media age. At this year's Monaco Grand Prix, there's famous figures from music: Dua Lipa and Future; from the silver screen: Jude Law, James McAvoy and Woody Harrelson; and sporting icons from the past, such as Zinedine Zidane and present like Real Madrid's Kylian Mbappé, French rugby star Antoine Dupont and the world's best cyclist, Tadej Pogačar.

Fans flock in from neighbouring France and Italy as well as from further around the globe, most staying in the far more affordable Nice – a picturesque train ride away, taking in such stunning locales as Villefranche-sur-Mer, Beaulieu-sur-Mer and Èze. The plethora of international accents on the short rail journey into Monaco at the beginning and end of each day sums up its universal appeal. Unsurprisingly, it is one of the richest stretches of property on the planet. Few baulk at the price of Monaco – the high spending is just part of the allure. At La Rascasse bar and nightclub, which gives its name to one of the circuit's iconic corners, the barman will happily deprive you of €25 for a single drink.

Monaco is the sport's supposed jewel in the crown but, in truth, for all its beauty, it is ultimately an incredibly dull race, a procession from start to finish, albeit an eye-catching one. The size of these current F1 cars – both in terms of their width and length – is too enormous for pursuing drivers to overtake at any point through this iconic street circuit. A quirk of the place is that its famous track is made up of public roads, opened up between sessions, those on foot able to pass over a tyre mark left moments before by a late-braking Formula 1 car. It makes the up-close-and-personal nature of it feel even more real and, for the majority of the drivers, it is the place they call home. Some say it is the ultimate training ground, the surrounding mountains the perfect place to cycle, as many of them do. The more cynical, perhaps even accurate, view is that the tax haven is an ideal location for these fast-paced millionaires and their sizeable bank balances.

Ordinarily, Max Verstappen can walk around the streets of Monaco – where he too lives – unbothered, the mixture of celebrities and multimillionaires unfazed to be brushing shoulders with a four-time world champion. But despite living a relatively short stroll away from the street circuit on the other side of the Rock of Monaco, walking around on a race weekend is an impossibility. Everywhere he goes, he is mobbed by fans wanting selfies and autographs, admittedly not helped by him being easy to spot dressed in his Red Bull-branded gear. Even outside the confines of the F1 paddock standing on La Rascasse, the corner where Michael Schumacher infamously parked his car nearly two decades earlier to halt the advances of rival Fernando Alonso, an elderly gentleman accosts Verstappen, telling him his granddaughter and Verstappen's stepdaughter Penelope are friends and like going cartwheeling together. 'Oh really?' comes the response, Verstappen genuinely engaged by the interaction. Be it Monaco or Montreal, it's impressive to see how gracious and generous he is with his time.

So then, who is the real Max Verstappen? He is often portrayed as a villain of the track, but in fact, outside of the car, he is a gentle giant and a hugely likeable character. Unlike many of his peers he has never had the desire to play to the cameras, which may be a part of him being misunderstood. In the Netherlands, he is adored – there is no current sporting figure held in higher esteem, not even the likes of footballers Virgil van Dijk and Frenkie de Jong. In the country's all-time sporting annals, he arguably sits behind only Johan Cruyff, who guided the Netherlands to the 1974 World Cup final and was a multiple European Cup winner as both a player and manager, in the public's affections. But globally, perceptions vary. Elsewhere, he can be perceived as spiky and overly aggressive, while in the UK, he has often been earmarked as the enemy of Lewis Hamilton, after those dramatic and controversial circumstances in Abu Dhabi in 2021. Since then, the Anglo–Dutch rivalry has been more with Lando Norris, who challenged Verstappen for the title in 2024, and George Russell, with whom Verstappen has endured a fractious relationship.

But off the track, it's a different story. 'It's the way he is as a person, that's what I'm most proud of,' says his father Jos. 'He is such a gentle, sweet, nice guy. I think mainly the English press put him in a bad light, let's say, but at the end of the day it doesn't matter. We know and the people around him know how he is and that's our main thing. That's fine and really it doesn't bother him at all. He really is just a normal guy who is a special person in the car. And he stays happy in life and I think that's a good thing.'

He has definitely inherited a double dose of drive and aggression from both parents, his mother Sophie herself an impressive go-karter in her youth, driving against the likes of 2009 Formula 1 world champion Jenson Button and Verstappen's current boss, Christian Horner. But from the outside looking in, the softer personality appears to come from his mum. Despite the demands of a Grand Prix weekend, he dotes on her and his two grandmothers when they are occasionally at track side.

Family has always been important to him, even more so since becoming a father himself just a few weeks earlier ahead of the Miami Grand Prix. He's happy to know he can go back to daughter Lily and his partner Kelly and stepdaughter Penelope at the end of a working day in Monaco. I ask if his nappy-changing speed is up to his F1 standards. 'I've done it before with Penelope,' he says. 'But honestly, it's probably more complicated when they're very little as they don't work with you. Luckily as a dad in the beginning it's not too hectic, and anyway they're so attached to the mum that as a dad you're more like a passenger. Just make sure that everyone is doing well and there's not too much chaos.' Ex-F1 world champion Button had said he never wanted to become a parent during his career as he felt it might slow him down. Put that to Verstappen and he is in full disagreement: 'I don't think you should change as a driver. Once I get to the track, I know what I have to do and I know what needs to be done. It's nice when you come home and there's this little girl there. But when I sit in the car I think about the performance. It definitely doesn't make you slower. Then again if it's a good or bad weekend, when you come home it doesn't matter. I like to just switch off and not think about Formula 1 and racing.'

That softer side is also seen in the way in which he treats the younger drivers on the grid. At the start of the season he was warmly mocked on social media for his patient treatment of rookies like Gabriel Bortoleto and Kimi Antonelli. All talk hugely favourably about how much time he has for them – teammates or rivals – and how willing he is to help. Lawson recalls that when he was snapped up by Racing Bulls mid-season Verstappen reached out to ask how he might be able to help him. While a cold-blooded racer, the truer Verstappen repeatedly emerges in his dealings with the team. In seasons past, I'd observed him from a distance and it was hard to get a true picture of him, the man behind the visor. But witnessing him within the team has been enlightening. The 27-year-old could not be more humble and down-to-earth. He poses with a smile for selfies and autographs and his interactions with teammates have nothing to do with status, treating every member of staff equally, from the mechanics surrounding his car to the team's ultimate hierarchy, be it Christian Horner, Oliver Mintzlaff or even the wider company's co-owners. To me, he is immediately courteous, quick to say hello and ready for a smile, which is far more in abundance than his racing persona would suggest.

The race team spend more time with each other than they do their loved ones. For some, they're away for more than half of the year, such is the nature of the F1 calendar. There are varying degrees of sacrifice to do what they love and, for the mechanics, as Matt Caller puts it, that means, 'We're lucky enough to work with a guy called Max Verstappen who's phenomenal at his job, and it's our job to give everything to that to make it [the car] as reliable and quick as we can.' There is a mystified feeling within the team for the skewed public perception. 'A lot of people say it in the team, but he's so misinterpreted across social media and the F1 audience,' says Caller. 'There's this perception of him as demanding and angry. Sure, there's times when he's unhappy with the car but it's not anger and it's not aimed at anyone in particular. It's just a frustration, as he wants more grip, feeling, aero balance or whatever. When it's not going the right way there is a frustration born out of competitiveness and we're all the same. He couldn't be further from that perception of demanding and angry. He's the most laid-back, friendly, funny, personable guy. He knows what he wants to do, he wants to win, so do we, so we're going to work really bloody hard to give him a race car he wants and he's going to get us race wins so we can have champagne on a Sunday. Outside of that, you can chat to him about anything. He's incredibly funny – with a hell of a sense of humour – smart, switched on, he's a nice guy to work with. And in the car he's just amazing to watch. He's so naturally talented, so, so quick, so that's easy for us. If we give him the car, he'll deliver. And for any of the guys that go up against him in the team it must be quite hard. You can do as much as you can and you still come second best while it looks like Max is doing it fairly effortlessly. He's very easy to work with.'

Each season – this year planned for the Hungarian Grand Prix – Verstappen takes his engineers and mechanics out for pizza and beers, a rare moment for the team around him to come together as one and a small token of his appreciation for their efforts. There, all talk of Formula 1 and racing is put on hold, instead the conversation as a group can veer in every which way aside from the subject they spend so much time discussing at the racetrack and back at the factory. There is also a full team get-together come Brazil of the entire racing workforce for which he again foots the bill. In those moments and the post-race celebrations, he relishes being one of the boys.

In conversation, it's sometimes easy to forget he's this superstar racer, although that's different when you're sitting with him in the passenger seat of a Ford Mustang Dark Horse for some laps of F1's most iconic circuit. Photographers talk about a different look on his face when he puts on his racing helmet and goes into driver mode. At a track with a top speed of 177mph this is slow for the Dutchman, despite the speedometer getting up to three figures, but such is his passion for racing he is still in his element for his first ever laps at the venue in a road car. 'I think you chose the right one,' he says of me being alongside him at this one-of-24 circuits on the calendar.

He raises his eyebrows at the fact the car, complete with a UK number plate, is right-hand drive, he adjusts the seat and the position of the steering wheel to his liking, checks the controls and powers up the car. And then he's off, but not before ominously saying, 'I've had a few shunts around here.' On his debut in the race as a 17-year-old in 2015 he clipped Romain Grosjean's Lotus when trying to overtake him and hit the barriers full-on at 30G with his front-left wheel already dangling off. Three years later in FP3 he again found himself in the barriers at Rascasse, leaving debris scattered all over the track. Those barriers come at you fast in Monaco, even at speeds well below that of an F1 car. The confines of the track seem smaller than on television, the ferocity of the braking a notable jolt for the uninitiated. Verstappen stays firmly rooted to his seat; I am bobbing around at every bump, turn and change of speed, almost like jelly in a helmet. Away from the circus of the race weekend, he is in his element. 'I don't normally get to drive here that fast in a road car,' he says, still capable of being impressed by Monaco despite countless laps around the course. And all the while he is seeing what nuggets of learning he can take on this Thursday of a race weekend. New tarmac has been laid down at different places, he is quick to point out, and he muses at the possibility of having better grip than in past years.

He turns onto the home straight as we near 100mph, some way slower than the speeds he will hit in first practice the following morning. His brakes properly kick into action for the first time at Sainte Dévote before he returns his foot to the accelerator through Beau Rivage, observing more new tarmac that has been laid. Here the climb is much steeper than it looks on television. Into Massenet, he observes the fast corner, Mirabeau, which brings with it the first screech of tyres. Moments later, an alarming beep sounds from the controls. Verstappen is unperturbed; I pretend not to be. We enter the Tunnel, the quickest part of the circuit, where drivers can approach a speed of nearly 180mph in a Formula 1 car. Verstappen points out this can normally be taken flat-out. Not this time in a Ford, with whom Red Bull are partnering for their in-house engine creation for next season. It brings us to the Nouvelle Chicane, where you feel the force of the braking again, and then by the Swimming Pool Verstappen has been told not to go more than 50kph for safety reasons. It is a briefing shared with the other drivers on track but not everyone has paid close attention, as another car scythes past. Not used to being overtaken all that often, Verstappen appears both a little irritated and amused by the fact. 'They told me to only go 50 here,' and off he sets on a second lap that's quicker still, particularly through to the Tunnel and that speed-limited final section.

Winning Monaco is one of the must-have wins on a driver's CV and he has done so twice, first in 2021 and again in his ultimate season of dominance, 2023, leading both races from start to finish. He would dearly love to do so again but, even before a wheel has turned in anger, he knows his chances rest almost solely on having a quick car in qualifying. With the RB21 blowing hot and cold from one race weekend to the next, it is unclear where he stands in the pecking order. McLaren very much remain the benchmark, the only question appears to be which of the drivers in papaya take the chequered flag.

Looking ahead to qualifying, he says: 'I think Monaco is one of these races that's very challenging, tough to win. It can also be very hectic. It's one of the races that you do want to win and, when you do it, it's very special. Luckily I got to do it twice. It's a good day but also a good night! Qualifying is by far the most difficult part here. In the race, it is more keeping your concentration up. You know that qualifying is super important. Hopefully the car works here. I honestly always do the best I can. Let's see.'

F1's rule-makers are acutely aware of the processional nature of the race, while the grid – from top to bottom – knows that Monaco is here to stay despite any gripes some might have about it as a race spectacle. Later in the season, it's announced that it will continue to host an annual F1 race until 2035. This year, there is intended to be manufactured jeopardy, a rule – agreed by all the teams – for an additional pit stop in a bid to shake up the order. Will it have the desired effect? At this stage, no one really knows. 'It can be very straightforward or very chaotic,' Verstappen muses. 'It all depends on the safety car.' The previous year, there were just four overtakes over 78 laps of the 3.338-kilometre circuit and the top 10 all finished in the order they started the race, which concluded with Verstappen, in sixth place, who called it boring and said he wished he'd brought his pillow along. Having beaten the McLarens to pole at three of the last five Grand Prix weekends despite being in a slower car, it begs the question: has he got in the heads of their two drivers? With a shrug of the shoulders, he says: 'I don't know. I just do the best I can.' It makes the hour-long qualifying on the Saturday even more vital, and thereby thrilling, as Lando Norris parks his car on pole, leaving it late to deny Charles Leclerc, born and raised in Monaco, by just a tenth of a second. Verstappen will start in fifth more than half-a-second a lap slower than Norris and struggling in the RB21 with the low-speed corners.

Monaco is the reserve of the ridiculous experience even by F1 standards. In the past, I've found myself on a superyacht, watching Bernie Ecclestone and then Force India owner Vijay Mallya smoke cigars, drink and laugh at the media assembled on the surrounding deck. And there's been over-the-top team and sponsor nights at the Amber Lounge nightclub along Avenue Princess Grace in the principality. On the day of qualifying, I'm on a speedboat bobbing up and down outside the back of the Monte Carlo Bay Hotel, waiting for Yuki Tsunoda, who is running late after breakfast, as well as his parents, Nobuaki and Minako, both immaculately dressed for the Formula 1 paddock. Monaco is the first race since the Japanese driver's high-speed crash in the Emilia-Romagna Grand Prix at Imola. If it's had any impact, it's not showing, his obsession for thrill-seeking undiminished. Above is a clear blue sky and the water is completely calm, much to Tsunoda's chagrin. 'Yesterday was much choppier and I had so much fun,' he explains, revelling in the bumps be they on land or sea.

A fan of the sport, wakeboarder Dominik Gührs, a fellow Red Bull athlete, is hiding in the front of the boat in order to surprise Tsunoda. Midway through our conversation, we are interrupted by Gührs, who explains he is set to put on an impromptu show in the water for the driver. He jokes the Japanese driver needs to get his board shorts on to join him and, whether it's lost in translation or not, Tsunoda doesn't get the joke and is fully prepared to join in. 'Am I doing wakeboarding? Fuck yeah,' he says with delight before a slight look of concern comes across his face. 'I hope there's no sharks inside, hopefully I don't get eaten by a shark.' But his concerns – unwarranted in any case – fall on deaf ears over the roar of the motorboat. Conditions are not ideal for wakeboarding but Gührs proceeds to enthrall his star audience Tsunoda, a keen wakeboarder himself, learning at a cable park near his home in Milan and having mastered a front flip but yet to get to grips with the intricacies of a backward iteration. Once back in the boat, the German world champion is passing on his best tips as the vessel weaves into Monaco harbour and slots straight into the F1 paddock, meaning the usual accosting by hordes of fans is short-lived. His well-dressed parents, meanwhile, are a little sodden by a splashier ride at the front of the boat. 'I love this,' says Tsunoda. 'You can't complain with this life. Travelling by boat every morning, literally parked by hospitality and straight into the team.'

Luck is a big element of Japanese culture and Tsunoda is undecided if his parents bring it. He was eighth a year ago in Monaco with them in attendance and he is hoping for a similar points finish, perhaps better, come the race. Asked if they give him good luck, he says: 'I had a good race last year and they were here but I'm not sure if they're a lucky charm or not. I'm still investigating.' Imola is still raw for Mum and Dad, it's hard to see your son hurtle upside down into solid metal barriers. Tsunoda is non-plussed by it all but he readily admits his mother is less so. 'My mum, I think, is still not fully comfortable and probably is never going to be,' he admits. 'The Imola thing didn't help but still she trusts me.'

In Monaco, everything is compact, and not just the tight and twisty street circuit. There is barely room to swing a proverbial cat in the garages where the teams of mechanics are more tightly packed than usual. On the floor above sits a room of spare parts and team members again cramped in, while on the top floor is a small, understated hospitality area. There, a guitarist from the band Muse rubs shoulders with the actor

Patrick Dempsey. Separated by the door sits the engineering office where those engineers not on the pit wall or in the garage are tuned in to the race and its data. As a race, Monaco may play out like a procession but for the team's strategists it is one of the most intense. From the moment the lights go out, everyone is primed for the fact a car may hit the barriers at any point – as Bortoleto's Kick Sauber does early on – to bring out a safety car or, if the crash is bigger, a red flag. Red Bull are as interested in the cars ahead as their own.

While at some races, the dialogue over the radio can be limited, in Monaco it is constant. Paul Monaghan is looking at a potential flat spot on one of Norris's tyres after he locks up at the start in the hope it can be a crack in his armour. Verstappen, meanwhile, is accusing Oscar Piastri of brake-testing him. It is reported to race control but it falls on deaf ears – no noting of the incident let alone an investigation. With each driver stuck in their position, the biggest question as ever in Monaco is when to pit at a place where a timely undercut can pick up a crucial place or two. With different opinions, it puts team members at loggerheads. Gianpiero Lambiase, in particular, is getting twitchy about the need to stop from lap 24 onwards, warning, 'we're going to start to lose time now', but head of strategy Will Courtenay tells the team the numbers say otherwise and to hold firm, suggesting now would not be the time to get the jump on Piastri. Getting past Piastri through pitting nearly becomes a reality but the Australian's tyres come back to life to deny that. A deflated GP is on the radio again saying, 'that's sad' about what he sees as a missed opportunity. But in the aftermath there is acceptance the moment was never quite a reality. Horner later calls the incident 'neck and neck' and that, on reflection pitting to attempt the move 'was a massive risk . . . like going to the casino and putting all your money on black'.

There comes another hope of passing Piastri by timing the second round of pit stops differently but, after the Australian takes time for his tyres to come in, he is then clear. And in a final throw of the dice, the decision is made not to pit for a second time until the very last moments of the race, the calculation being that the only way to gain a place is if a red flag is shown. None is forthcoming. At points, there are frustrations within the team. Complaining of his gears, Verstappen moans, 'My shifts feel like Monaco Grand Prix 1972,' while Pierre Waché is cutting about Tsunoda when discussing his pit-stop plans. 'Well, he's fucking slow anyway,' he says succinctly. In Tsunoda's defence, he basically does the entire race on one set of tyres after the team opted to pit him on lap one. The consensus in the team debrief afterwards is that Verstappen's fourth is the best the team could have hoped for.

The result leaves Verstappen third in the championship but 25 points – an entire race win – behind leader Piastri, who is just three points ahead of his teammate. The compulsory two stops has not created the racing that was hoped for, the front of the race still largely processional, with Norris winning from local driver Leclerc, and Verstappen some 20 seconds behind the race winner. Reflecting before flying off in his private jet, Horner backs the sport for having tried something new and yet the racer in him would love more jeopardy still. His solution is for track changes, not easy where virtually every corner of the harbour is taken up with high-rise apartments. It's no wonder one team member calls it the poshest council estate on the planet. 'Is there a way we can make an overtake space work here?' he asks. 'The exit of the Tunnel or turn one, maybe. Is there anywhere on the track where we can nick a little bit more ground or change the trajectory of one of the corners to create a bigger braking zone to essentially create an overtake because that's what it's desperately calling out for?' Monaco's ruler Prince Albert has no immediate plans to send in the diggers to bulldoze the harbour and give it a facelift.

Horner's argument isn't new. As long as Monaco has existed, there has been talk of its lack of overtaking. But with smaller, more nimble cars of past years, overtaking was an option. Liam Lawson has shown the impossibility of it in the manner in which he backs up the rest of the field to aid Racing Bulls teammate Isack Hadjar and give him the space further up the field to make a second pit stop and not lose track position, a masterstroke, as it transpires, by team boss Laurent Mekies, whose stock is rising rapidly. Hadjar and Lawson finish sixth and eighth respectively for the sister team, only piling the pressure on Tsunoda, who has a torrid race to finish in 17th. Of the finishers, only Kimi Antonelli is behind him.

And yet there is still hope looming in the shape of Spain. Could the new rules over the revised front wings by the FIA close the gap on the front-running McLarens? No one knows for sure, including Horner. Before leaving Red Bull's floating palace in Monaco, he says: 'It is a decent change. It's a significant change to the front wing characteristics that will affect all cars. It may very well be neutral up and down but for sure there is an effect. It will probably take two or three races to play out. Barcelona is a very aero-sensitive track and degradation can be quite high there so it will be interesting to see how things play out.'

Is this said in hope rather than expectation?

18

PAIN IN SPAIN

Max Verstappen changes gear from first to second to third, all the way to eighth, each time a rapid whir sounds between every sudden shift. Lacking the same volume and intensity of the V8 or V10 engines of past Formula 1 cars, the shifts in the V6s are more muted, easier to listen to in close proximity. For 66 laps, Verstappen shifts up and down around the 5.5km Circuit de Barcelona-Catalunya. But the driver is absent, all that remains at the team's UK headquarters is his gearbox. It sits proudly in a spotless room, accessed by a single door and viewed through a solitary window. It is powered up by a Dynomater, which proudly boasts the name 'Busty Bertha' on its side, a nod to when former Red Bull driver Sebastian Vettel would name his cars. The German won his maiden world title in Randy Mandy and subsequent championship wins followed with Kinky Kylie, Abbey and Hungry Heidi. It seems some old habits die hard back at Milton Keynes. Verstappen has only ever named one of his F1 cars, the 2023 car, which delivered the knock-out blow to the rest of the grid, appropriately branded Rocky by the Dutchman.

Like other F1 teams, Red Bull have rigs set up back at the factory to test every part of a car. And for 20 years, Barcelona has tended to be a useful repeat test track – albeit remotely – because of it boasting a good mixture of high-speed and low-speed corners. This is effectively a stress-test on the gearbox. A technician uploads Verstappen's Spanish Grand Prix race details into a computer and the gearbox kicks into life, every shift mirroring that carried out by its driver in the reality of the race. It passes muster, evidence in the factory that the gearbox should hold firm to the rigours of this particular F1 track. In Spain, however, it's not the gearbox that will prove to be the problem.

In the on-track world, a half-hour car's ride away from Barcelona – although considerably longer on a Grand Prix weekend where gridlock is commonplace – sits the Circuit de Barcelona-Catalunya, home to the Spanish Grand Prix since 1991. The 1990 Spanish Grand Prix in Jerez saw Martin Donnelly miraculously survive a horrific high-speed crash in practice. Following suspension failure, he hit a wall at 160mph, obliterating his car and seeing him catapulted out. He was treated immediately at the scene by Sid Watkins, F1's former chief medic who did so much to make the sport as safe as it is today. His peers watched aghast as the battle commenced to save the Northern Irishman's life. With brain and lung contusions as well as leg fractures so severe doctors nearly amputated his right leg, he had swallowed his tongue and was placed in a medically induced coma. A local priest even came to read him his last rites.

Donnelly's story is straight out of Hollywood. A month before the crash, *Autosport* had asked on its front page of the young man from Belfast: 'Is Donnelly the next Mansell?'

On the morning of his Jerez run in January, 1990, he signed a $5-million deal to drive for Lotus the following season. By the end of it, he was fighting for his life and yet lived to tell the tale. Years later, the crash is the inspiration behind Brad Pitt's character Sonny Hayes' accident in the *F1* movie, which will premiere in New York in just two weeks' time. Pitt said in interviews around the release that Donnelly's story was as beautiful as any world championship tale.

This newer circuit in Montmeló, a small municipality with a population of just 10,000 people, was opened for a first race the year before Barcelona hosted the Olympics, acting as the start and finish for the team time-trial cycling on the road for those Games. It has been one of F1's most-used circuits and the home for pre-season testing before Bahrain took over that role from 2021. Michael Schumacher and Lewis Hamilton boast the most race wins here with six apiece, while it was also here where Verstappen won on his debut for Red Bull, back in 2016. Aided by a crash between title rivals Hamilton and Nico Rosberg, which put both drivers out of the race, Verstappen became the youngest race winner and podium finisher in F1 history at the age of 18 years and 228 days. For 20 laps, he faultlessly fended off the faster Ferrari of Kimi Räikkönen, who would make an attempt to pass every other lap, using the alternate lap to recharge his car's battery. He was immediately branded the sport's next superstar.

This year's race is the last Spanish Grand Prix to be housed here before relocating to a street circuit in Madrid, although a Barcelona-Catalunya Grand Prix will be held in in alternate years from 2026. Nine races in, this Grand Prix has long been seen as a marker in the sand, a potential turning point for the rest of the 2025 season. It marks a clamp-down by the FIA

Max Verstappen celebrates victory in front of Foro Sol in Mexico 2023.
Verstappen won the Drivers' Championships four years in a row with Red Bull
between 2021 and 2024. Would he make it five in 2025?

© Mark Thompson/Getty Images Sport

Left: A fresh-faced Christian Horner arrives as team principal for the new team Red Bull Racing in 2005. The young upstarts were dismissed as 'just a drinks company' by Lewis Hamilton and other critics.

© Mark Thompson/Getty Images Sport

Right: Verstappen over-taking Lewis Hamilton in Abu Dhabi in 2021 on his way to his maiden title in the most dramatic ending to an F1 season.

© Joe Portlock/Formula 1

Left: Sebastian Vettel celebrates winning his 4th consecutive world title in 2013. It would be an eight year drought until the team won again.

© Vladimir Rys Photography/Getty Images Sport

Right: Dietrich Mateschitz, the entrepreneurial founder of Red Bull and its Formula 1 team. His death in 2022 left a power vacuum at the top of the company.

© Vladimir Rys/Bongarts

Red Bull Headquarters at Milton Keynes. Two thousand workers support the Formula 1 team from this building. *© Marc Atkins/Getty Images News*

Watching Verstappen in pre-season testing in Bahrain. At this stage, no one knows how the other teams are going to perform. *© Clive Mason/Getty Images Sport*

Left: Verstappen celebrates winning at Suzuka in front of the team. Victory in Japan was a rare highlight in the first half of the season.

© Clive Rose/Getty Images Sport

Right: Frustrations boil over when Verstappen collides with the Mercedes of George Russell in Spain, leaving Verstappen under threat of a one-race ban.

© Bradley Collyer/PA Images

Yuki Tsunoda's spectacular high-speed crash at Imola underscored a tough start for the driver. *© Lubomir Asenov/LAP*

Above: Young driver Liam Lawson was ruthlessly axed after just two races.

© Francesca Anna Tantone

Above: Verstappen in discussion with his father, Jos, who has an influential voice in the team. © Peter Fox/Getty Images Sport

Below: Under pressure and facing a power struggle within the team, Christian Horner, team principal for two decades, ultimately loses his job following a string of poor results. © NurPhoto

Below: Helmut Marko – the man who discovered Verstappen – was another hugely influential figure behind the scenes.

© NurPhoto

Left: The Red Bull team is a sum of its parts, including top talent like Gianpiero Lambiase, Verstappen's race engineer, and Hannah Schmitz, team strategist. *© Mark Thompson/Getty Images Sport*

Below: Laurent Mekies replaced Christian Horner halfway through the season. He would bring an engineer's approach. *© Kym Illman/Getty Images Sport*

Verstappen leads at Monza in a dominant weekend for the team, reigniting his championship challenge. *© NurPhoto*

Verstappen makes a pit stop at Mexico. The team can change the tyres in under two seconds. *© Mark Thompson/Getty Images Sport*

Verstappen celebrates in Las Vegas. By winning here and in Qatar he takes the championship to the final race. *© Jeff Speer/Icon Sportswire*

Verstappen seen before the final climactic race of the Formula 1 season.

© SOPA Images/LightRocket

Verstappen leads the two McLarens of Norris and Piastri at Abu Dhabi. Victory for Verstappen and a 4th place for Norris would make Verstappen champion. © NurPhoto

on flexing front wings. The general consensus has been that front-runners McLaren have benefitted most from the way in which they have been able to exploit flexing bodywork. Despite McLaren insisting it is not the silver bullet that has catapulted them towards being the benchmark for the sport, the likes of Red Bull and Ferrari have been pushing behind the scenes for the sport's lawmakers to investigate the legality of McLaren's set-up and thereby make a change. It has echoes of last season when Red Bull suggested McLaren were using some sort of tyre water to cool its tyres. At the Miami Grand Prix – just three races previously – McLaren CEO Zak Brown had taken his place on the pit wall with a reusable bottle with the words 'Tire [sic] Water' emblazoned across it in a light-hearted dig at his rivals.

What this type of front wing does with this iteration of F1 cars is flex to create more downforce in the slow corners but then flexes in the other direction in the high-speed corners and on the fast straights. The front wing is one of the most sensitive components on the car because it's the first time that the air meets the car and dictates the flow and how it interacts with all the other elements. Any change to the behaviour of the front wing will affect everything downstream of that on the car, such as how the wing interacts with the front suspension or when the air hits the floor and bodywork. All 20 cars on the grid currently have to undergo a test on flexing. Previously, an upwards deflection of 15mm was allowed when a load of 1000N (Newtons) was applied on top of two different places on the wing and 20mm if just on one side of the wing. The allowance from Spain onwards is now 10mm and 15mm. In a sport that deals with fractions, such a minuscule shift can turn the grid on its head. Some of

McLaren's rivals have been banking on it having a negative impact on the front-runners of 2025. Ferrari boss Frédéric Vasseur calls it a potential 'game-changer'.

Publicly, at least, Horner has opted for a wait-and-see approach. Talking to me at the onset of the season, he had said: 'We have a significant regulation shift in race nine this year, where the regulations with the wings change. So again you just don't know what effect that is going to have either detrimentally or beneficially for each of the teams. Of the impact, I think the reality is that nobody knows. It's all conjecture at this moment in time. We'll just see and have to adapt to the regulations.' But Horner's lobbying of the sport's authorities behind the scenes and the optimistic way in which he has been viewing it behind closed doors gives him and the team the belief that this could indeed be the game-changer and the start of clawing back the deficit to McLaren. Waché, the man responsible for ensuring Red Bull don't fall foul of the new front-wing tests themselves, calls him and the team 'a passenger trying to fulfil the rules'. But he is hopeful, at least initially. He says: 'We can have some optimism it will affect them more than us but there's no magic. If you want to benefit for yourself, you have to work for it.'

All the while, both Brown and McLaren team principal Andrea Stella have effectively said it is a red herring in explaining their car's superior pace. In an untrusting world like F1, where it is unclear who is bluffing and when, his rivals are unconvinced before steadily coming round to that way of thinking. By the time the teams converge in Barcelona, the general consensus is that the seismic shift some had hoped for will not materialise. And so it proves. By the chequered flag, Piastri is just ahead of teammate Norris while Charles Leclerc is the next best placed driver 10 seconds back. Verstappen is even further down the pecking order.

With a new front wing costing something in the region of £100,000, in the era of the cost cap, Lewis Hamilton is particularly cutting about the new flexing test, calling it 'a waste of money'. Angrily rebuking the sport's rule-makers, after finishing the race in sixth place, he says: 'Just wasted everyone's money. It's literally changed nothing. Everyone's wings still bend, it's just half the bending, and everyone's had to make new wings and spend more money to make these. It just doesn't make sense.'

Is the danger now that McLaren will disappear into the distance, the championship slipping away from Verstappen? Red Bull are among those who will have to renew their focus on improving their own car rather than hoping a change of rules can curtail that of their rival.

19

BAN LOOMING

The red mist. It often bubbles just below the surface of some of Formula 1's greatest of all time. The desire to win can burn so brightly it occasionally has the propensity to overspill into self-destruction. Think Ayrton Senna, think Michael Schumacher, think Max Verstappen: all victims of their own competitiveness at stages in their careers. For many, it simply adds to their appeal while for others, it can take the gloss off the greatness. For Verstappen, this kill switch goes all the way back to his karting days, which dad Jos, himself no shrinking violet, tried to harness to make him a better racer. Verstappen would earn himself a reputation for on-track aggressiveness early in his F1 career, which Red Bull argue sometimes still blights his copybook in the eyes of race stewards and rivals alike. Even with an increasingly mature Verstappen, there has still been those moments in seasons past where he feels like the world is against him, out to get him, and the fallout is his emotion overspilling on the track. And yet prior to Spain in 2025 he has enjoyed an unblemished record in contrast to previous campaigns, not once earning a penalty from the stewards at the opening eight Grand Prix weekends, one of the longer stints without a mark on his licence.

Spain is a perfect example of Red Bull Racing employing a riskier strategy in a bid to make up for the pace deficit to the McLarens and, for a time there, it seems the risk might pay off despite the dominance of Norris and Piastri in practice and qualifying. Quite suddenly, it seems that a win for Red Bull might not be entirely off the cards, that the race in Imola wasn't a one-off. Verstappen qualifies in third, just a tenth of a second off the second McLaren of Norris. A shout of 'yeah, boy' rings out over the Red Bull Racing team radio – unclear whether from someone trackside or back in Milton Keynes – as Verstappen gets the slipstream on Norris to get past at turn one. Just a few laps into the race, Tsunoda is already complaining of understeer. Hannah Schmitz, at track for the race, suggests opting for a three-stopper and bringing him in after just eight laps. Often, the Red Bull number two is used as a guinea pig to try something out for Verstappen. Schmitz is confident this is the best strategy and Horner backs her: 'Fuck it, if we're going for three stops, let's go for it.' The pit stop from the newly revised pit crew, now well back to their slick best, earns congratulations over the airwaves from Rich Wolverson. A few laps later, Verstappen complains of a lack of grip and losing his rears, and so it proves, a sitting duck down the home straight to Norris on lap 13. Schmitz again hints at an early stop for their lead driver, a clear delineation from the pre-race plan of two stops to three. 'We'll still beat Ferrari and Mercedes. I'm not sure we'll beat McLaren on it but it's at least something different,' she insists. The rest of the pit wall concur.

But by lap 27 Verstappen is once again struggling on the Pirelli tyres. 'It's so hard to drive, I can't brake and there's no turn-in in low speed.' Two laps later, Schmitz suggests bringing Verstappen in for mediums, which eventually comes on lap 30 with him pulling out of the pits just ahead of Hamilton, from whom he immediately begins to pull clear of. It's obvious that despite Red Bull's change of plan, McLaren have no intention of shifting from their pre-ordained two-stop strategy.

In Monaco, Verstappen had said his gear shifts were so arcane he likened them to 1972. When GP suggests a repeat of that year in a light-hearted moment at this race's halfway point, Verstappen quips: 'Maybe 1974 now.' A moment later, an apology comes from GP for having hiccups. It's not all cutting-edge over the airwaves. Meanwhile, Norris is overheard by someone at Red Bull saying he is racing Verstappen, while McLaren warn the Briton he has an issue with his tyres. Footage is quickly checked by Paul Monaghan and dismissed, clearly a bluff by McLaren over the radio waves. And then Horner despairs that, 'Piastri's pace is insane' at the front of the pack.

Opinions are divided on when to pit Verstappen for the third and final time. On lap 46, Schmitz suggests an undercut on Hamilton to which GP disagrees. Schmitz argues back: 'I'd personally like to do that this lap.' GP isn't happy but begrudgingly agrees. 'That getaway was shit,' he decries as Verstappen then comes back out behind Tsunoda. 'Let him go quickly, please,' is the instruction from Horner to driver number two, who obliges immediately. On lap 49, Norris comes in for his second stop. He's 1.8 seconds clear initially, which drops down to six-tenths of a second as he struggles to get his tyres to come in. Someone in the engineering office shouts out, 'Come on, Max' but Norris is aided by having DRS,[1] lapping Carlos Sainz, and the chance of an audacious pass for second goes begging. 'Fuck, without DRS we would have had a chance,' concludes Horner.

A few laps later, Verstappen is caught in traffic behind Bearman and Lawson as he tries to lap them. 'Fucking hell, fucking idiots,' he remarks after coming past. On lap 54 disaster strikes when the safety car is deployed when Kimi Antonelli comes off the road. It is a lose–lose situation for Verstappen. Bunching up the field, it effectively gives drivers a free pit stop, a stop that Verstappen doesn't need or want, having already stopped thrice. The decision, which needs to be made in a matter of seconds, is either to pit for the hard tyres – his only fresh set of rubber but a tyre no one, Verstappen included, has used at the Circuit de Barcelona-Catalunya all weekend – switch to a set of scrubbed soft tyres from qualifying or keep Verstappen as he was on his current set of used tyres. None of the choices appeal, but Schmitz argues the hard-tyre option is the lesser of three evils. There are 10 laps left and Verstappen questions the call over the team radio on returning to the track: 'Why the fuck have we? What is this tyre?' GP tells him it is the only option, his driver asks if 'someone has run it in the race'. 'Negative' comes the reply, leaving his driver to try them somewhat blindly and hope for the best.

Verstappen's frustration is spilling over in his dialogue with his race engineer. Things can quickly go from bad to worse. On the hard tyres, Verstappen is a sitting duck. Leclerc hits into the side of him when attempting a pass. 'Oh mate, he

---

1 DRS: drag reduction system; a button whereby a driver following a rival within a second can momentarily reduce aerodynamic drag for a speed boost when overtaking.

rammed into me,' he complains. 'Charles just rammed into me on the straight.' GP asks if the matter is being reported to race control but, no sooner has it happened, there is concern over a subsequent coming together with Russell and potentially gaining an advantage after coming off track. The advice over the airwaves is to give the place back to the Briton, much to Verstappen's chagrin. When the order comes, Verstappen takes umbrage: 'I was ahead. What the fuck?' 'That's the rules,' comes the reply from GP. As he appears to slow down to let Russell past, he then turns into and hits the Mercedes in a moment of madness for which he is handed a 10-second penalty to drop him to ninth as well as earn him three points on his licence, the highest penalty sanction available. What had begun as a strategy masterclass by Schmitz has, through no fault of hers or the team, ended in unmitigated disaster.

Even outside the car, Verstappen's red mist doesn't lift. The irony amid it all is stewards later say there was no case to answer and Verstappen wouldn't have been ordered to give the spot back to Russell. In a championship fight in which Red Bull is struggling to hang on to the coat tails of the McLarens it is a body blow. But when asked in the TV pen by Sky Sports of the dent to his title hopes, he says: 'If there are any. We're way too slow to fight for the title. Maybe it would have been better to stay out but that's easy to say now.'

As the head of sporting, Steve Knowles is the team's representative to race control and the stewards. In the heat of battle, he and the Red Bull pit wall made the decision to give the place back to Russell. Reflecting, Knowles says: 'The question is, has he left the track and gained an advantage or has George? We felt it was quite a marginal call because everyone is so close together after the safety car. If you get a penalty of 10 seconds then that puts you out of the points completely. We felt it might have been George's fault but we weren't totally confident of it going that way.' To make this decision, Knowles has just a single lap – in Barcelona, less than 80 seconds – in which to pore through footage before the officials decide to step in. Knowles continues: 'We decided to give the position back on the basis that, if it ruled against us, it was lower risk. As it turned out, they ruled in our favour and we didn't need to give the position back.'

Red Bull – Horner in particular – are always quick to jump to the defence of Verstappen even when he's in the wrong, but tellingly, no such public backing is forthcoming this time. Verstappen is advised to apologise, which he duly does in the post-race engineering debrief and again on social media the following day. He writes: 'We had an exciting strategy and good race in Barcelona, till the safety car came out. Our tyre choice to the end and some moves after the safety car restart fuelled my frustration, leading to a move that was not right and shouldn't have happened. I always give everything out there for the team and emotions can run high. You win some together, you lose some together. See you in Montreal.'

Post-race inside the Energy Station, there is a confab among the team's head honchos, Horner and the Verstappen camp in quiet conversation. The sentiment is universal. Sitting on the decking to one side of the Energy Station, Waché is vaping post-race. As we reflect on the Grand Prix, Verstappen's actions and the use of hindsight, Verstappen walks past, heading upstairs to his private driver's room. Waché asks the driver about hindsight. He quips back: 'Hindsight is a wonderful thing. If we had hindsight, we'd all be billionaires.'

Later in the season, in an interview with Dutch driver

Giedo van der Garde for the broadcaster Viaplay, Verstappen will admit regret over the incident. 'I'm happy with my season,' he'll say. 'The only point of criticism is the situation in Barcelona. What happened there, of course, wasn't great but it also came from the fact that I really care. I could also have said, "my car isn't fast, I'll let it go". It's in part the fact that I cannot accept from myself when I get out of the car that I haven't done everything and given everything. That makes me mad at myself. I cannot put in 80 per cent effort. I have to get out of the car with the feeling I've tried everything. I was mad about what happened on the straight during the restart, then corner one and then I got the radio message that I have to give back the position. At that moment, all the signs went red. That was not good and you learn from that. And moments like these probably won't happen again. You can be in a similar situation with the car but it's something that you learn from.' It is a rare and unusual admission of fault from him.

'It's a great example with the fullness of hindsight and plenty of time to watch the slow-mos over and over again, you make a different call,' Knowles says. 'When you have a lap to make a decision and look at the overall situation I could imagine that we'd make the same call again should circumstances conspire. Max has gone off the track and maintained position to George. We had a lap to decide.'

The rap sheet for Verstappen reads 11 points. One more and it will take him to 12, warranting a one-race ban. With him just about clinging on to being in contention in the drivers' championship, missing a race entirely would be catastrophic. There is also the added factor of a release clause in the Red Bull star driver's contract allowing him to leave at the end of the season if he's outside the top three in the champion-ship at the summer break. Any racing suspension could be potentially seismic, both for this championship and beyond.

The points date as far back as 30th June, 2024, when he caused a collision with Norris at the Austrian Grand Prix, earning him a two-point penalty. That will be erased from his licence in two races' time, meaning he needs to get through the races in Canada and Austria with an unblemished record. Much like with a regular driver's licence, penalties stay for 12 months, his other points, accrued in a six-week spell last season, have some time to run. He earned two points after being judged to have forced Norris off the track at last year's Mexico Grand Prix. One-point penalties followed for driving too fast under the virtual safety car in the sprint race in São Paulo, and driving unnecessarily slowly and impeding Russell in qualifying for the Qatar Grand Prix. There were also two points for causing a collision with Piastri at the season-ending race in Abu Dhabi just before Christmas.

There was a feeling even before the season started within Red Bull that some were looking to catch out Verstappen both on track and with regards to the new FIA directives around swearing. Speaking in Australia, GP told me: 'The other drivers are looking to destabilise Max and there are certain rules coming in this year so we're working very hard with Max on which he could fall foul of. And there will be some teams looking to gain on that, no doubt, and we just need to make sure that we are scrupulously clean in what we're doing.' That partly explains the decision to give Russell back the spot after their initial on-track difference of opinion in Barcelona.

How costly this misjudgement could be is unclear at this

stage. Following Spain, Verstappen is walking a high-speed tightrope. Horner warns him simply to keep his nose clean. In the dying moments of Montreal the two McLarens come together, bringing out the safety car. Behind it, Verstappen momentarily overtakes Russell after heavy braking from the latter. Knowing the danger of any penalty point infringement, Verstappen is quick to say over the race radio: 'George suddenly just aggressively braked.' Russell meanwhile says to his team: 'Verstappen just overtook me under the safety car.' Two hours after Russell's win, Red Bull lodge a complaint with the stewards for driving erratically and committing unsportsmanlike behaviour for, in their view, trying to get Verstappen penalised. Almost six hours after the chequered flag, leading to some key figures missing their flights home, the stewards decide there is no case to answer. In their ruling, they say: 'We accept the driver of car 63's explanation of the incident and we are satisfied that the driver of car 63 did not drive erratically by braking where he did or to the extent he did. We are not satisfied that by simply reporting to his team that car 1 had overtaken that he engaged in unsportsmanlike conduct. Even though the protest did not allege it, we are also satisfied that by braking where and when he did and to the extent he did the driver of car 63 did not engage in unsportsmanlike conduct.'

Despite getting heat from critics, particularly Toto Wolff, who calls it 'petty' and 'embarrassing', Knowles insists there are no regrets over Red Bull's post-race decision, a view shared by the rest of the team management. 'It depends how you view the protest mechanism and whether or not it was a fair question we asked. We believed it was. The stewards saying it was not deserving of a penalty is totally fair enough but we still think having that hearing was a worthwhile exercise. There are various rules that, if you read them in black and white and take strict interpretation, we'd say we break them every weekend. Drivers break that rule behind the safety car as they have to keep brakes warm and tyres warm. It falls into the grey where George had to do that when Max was right behind him. Max did not anticipate that, flew past him, had to slam on his own brakes to avoid overtaking him and going past the safety car, and then had to give the place back. Then George got on the radio as many drivers do and pointed out that there was an infringement by another driver. Now whether or not you put the two things together and say that's an offence worth a penalty, that's a question for the stewards. We felt it was because of how close all the cars were and how close Max was behind George and we felt the timing of the application of brakes was not particularly safe, and could potentially have caused an incident. We thought it was arguably an attempt to get Max a penalty. The protest system exists for teams to raise questions with the FIA and ultimately have a hearing, and they ruled George was not doing anything unduly erratic and unsportsmanlike. We fully respect that ruling.'

Having escaped censure at one race, there is still a nervousness at the next in Austria, the last major threat to Verstappen getting a one-race ban. Looking ahead to the weekend, Knowles almost pleads: 'A quiet weekend would be great. Max has been doing this a long time. He's very much aware of the various penalties that could add that final penalty point. I'm sure he will weigh that up in his decision-making and take a little bit less risk. We've spoken about it. We're also keeping an eye out for potential attempts from other drivers to get him penalties.

Considering how much is at risk here, we'll try to protect Max as best we can from it.'

Protect him from a penalty, perhaps, but not from a collision caused by Kimi Antonelli. On the opening lap, Verstappen ends the race pointless but penalty-less, although unlucky to be the one car picked up by the out-of-control Italian teenager.

20

WILL HE STAY OR WILL HE GO?

Formula 1 is not known for driver loyalty and longevity. Teams and drivers alike are unapologetically selfish in the quest for ultimate glory. Take Ferrari, who this season unceremoniously dumped Carlos Sainz for Lewis Hamilton after the Spaniard had equipped himself admirably against Charles Leclerc. Such a costly financial move has proved a questionable one, such has been the disappointing nature of Hamilton's debut season for the Prancing Horse. In Red Bull, there was the axing of Liam Lawson, deemed surplus to requirements after just two races. His replacement, Yuki Tsunoda, has hardly been the solution that Red Bull hoped for. But teams are not the only ones guilty of such cross-grid transgressions – drivers, too, give furtive glances across the grid, a case of the grass being greener elsewhere. Sometimes these moves work out, but more often than not the driver regrets their choice.

Since Verstappen made his debut for Scuderia Toro

Rosso in 2015, his F1 career has been entirely in the bosom of the Red Bull family. It has echoes of Hamilton, who was essentially a one-brand man with Mercedes before his shock move to Maranello. Amid the chaos and controversy within Red Bull last season, Verstappen's head was turned and his camp began to hold talks at rival teams. Mercedes' Toto Wolff made no secret of his desire to snap up the star driver, much to Horner's irritation. In the end, such talks came to nothing but the whispers linking Verstappen to Mercedes have never entirely gone away. In Austria at Red Bull's home race and eponymous track, the rumours spark back into life yet again, surprisingly from Mercedes driver George Russell.

Frustrated at his team's inability to agree terms over a new deal, despite being one of the form drivers early in 2025, in a revealing interview with Sky Sports he lays bare the reality of his and Verstappen's situation. 'As Mercedes, they want to be back on top and, if you're going to be back on top you need to make sure you've got the best drivers, the best engineers, the best pit crew, and that's what Mercedes are chasing. So, it's only normal that conversations with the likes of Verstappen are ongoing. I feel with the performance I'm showing at the moment I've got zero reasons to be worried.' And yet by speaking, he is showing genuine concern over a threat to his future. If Mercedes sign Verstappen, what does that mean for Russell? It's no secret there's no love lost between the pair and Wolff knows that it is either Verstappen or Russell, not both. Already this season there have been on-track incidents between the two – notably in Spain and Canada – and there has been plenty prior to that.

This fractious relationship began back in 2022 when Verstappen accused Russell of being overly aggressive in overtaking at the Emilia-Romagna Grand Prix, but it then erupted in Azerbaijan the following year when they collided on lap one of the race. A tetchy exchange followed in the pit lane afterwards, Verstappen calling Russell a 'princess' and the Briton countering his rival had completely lost his head. Then there was Qatar that same season when Verstappen said he had 'lost all respect' for Russell after being penalised for impeding him in qualifying.

Opening talks with Wolff and Mercedes also makes total sense from the perspective of Verstappen and his team. The new regulations for 2026 have the potential to shake up the grid and its quickest driver understandably wants to know where the best option might be. If the F1 rumour mill can be believed – it can't always be trusted – then Mercedes currently have the best engine for next season. The thinking is that the German manufacturer has often shone the brightest at a time of engine regulation change but that doesn't necessarily equate that 2026 will follow suit or that the Mercedes will have the best car, with the Mercedes-powered McLaren having the edge over the works team this season.

There is also the back story of last season, the infighting between Horner, Jos Verstappen and Marko, and Verstappen Jnr's very clear dislike of all that, wishing for greater harmony between those around him. With Red Bull's form on track wobbling for parts of last season too despite Verstappen winning the drivers' title, it makes sense that he would look at where his best options are. As his manager Raymond Vermeulen puts it: 'Max is very respectful of the people. Red Bull was there from day one, they put him in the car, they made the effort. They treated him very well to enter Formula 1, so yes, we are loyal. But on the other hand,

I also told management we have the quickest driver in the paddock and I want to have the quickest material for that, so it seems to be that we're still in the front but it is a very competitive world.'

Then there is the matter of Verstappen's contract, which contains the clause stating that if Verstappen is outside the top three in the drivers' championship going into the summer break after the Hungarian Grand Prix, he can head elsewhere. At the start of the Austrian Grand Prix weekend, Russell is only 19 points away from usurping Verstappen's place in the top three. By the end of the weekend, that will be down to nine when Verstappen is speared into unknowingly by Mercedes' Kimi Antonelli on the opening lap.

The Verstappen camp potentially has a decision to make. So seismic are the regulation changes, no one really knows who will begin next season on top, let alone win the championship. Verstappen's team have to weigh up whether to take the plunge or decide if it is more sensible to see how the new regulations pan out. In so doing he can revisit his options for 2027, be that staying at Red Bull, if their first ever in-house power unit can be successful, switching to rivals Mercedes or else another team on the grid.

Speaking to a huddle of reporters crammed inside the Energy Station at the Austrian Grand Prix, he says: 'I think I've said this before. Naturally, of course, people are talking but it's most important that we have a very competitive car for the future. At the moment, it is very tight but we are working very well as a team to try and improve. For sure, I said this already with the team, we are working and focusing also on next year to try and be competitive again. I've got a long contract with the team, I'm very happy where I'm at and, like I said before, we are focusing already on next year with the things that we can implement on the car. So, I guess that should say enough of where I'm driving next year.' When asked for a direct yes or no on whether he would be at Red Bull in 2026, he says: 'You couldn't get that out of my answer before? I mean, OK, yes. But that's what I said, we are already also working on next year's car. I think when you are very focused on that, that means you are also driving for the team.'

Wolff is also cagey. He says: 'We are going into territory that I don't want to discuss out here, but people talk, people explore. And most important is that in our organisation we are transparent, but it doesn't change a millimetre of my opinion of George, his abilities or anything else.'

At the following race a week later in Silverstone, the rumours of a big-money cross-grid switch haven't gone away. Clearly bristling, Verstappen refuses to answer any questions about 2026. It does little to dampen the whispers. After Silverstone there is still a mathematical chance that Verstappen could leave Red Bull, with his lead in third over Russell at 18 points – one DNF from him and a strong race from Russell in Belgium could see Verstappen bumped down to fourth in the title race, as the crunch point at the Hungarian Grand Prix approaches. The rumour mill goes further into overdrive when he is spotted with Wolff on their yachts in Sardinia, parked up side by side. It leads to the suggestion that further talks over a big-money deal have taken place on the Mediterranean island between the pair. By the time the next race in Belgium comes around, Verstappen laughs it off: 'I don't really care about those things because I went on holiday with my friends, my family. And when other people also are there at the same time, that can happen. I mean there are more people on the island than just me and Toto and the family. If you go to the same island, that can happen.'

The uncertainty also piles the pressure on Horner as team principal. If he can't hold on to his star driver, is he the right man to steady the ship? His public messaging is he is confident Verstappen will stay put and yet, in turn, he opens his own talks with Russell about the potential for a mouth-watering crossover.

21

END OF AN ERA

There's an edginess inside the Energy Station at the Red Bull Ring, a nervousness verging on paranoia, amid whispers and occasionally worried glances. There has long been an unease within the team's top brass ever since the schism left by owner Dietrich Mateschitz's death in October, 2022. On one side, there is Christian Horner as the omnipotent boss of the team – every faction of Red Bull Racing reporting to him from the race team to the marketing operation, a model that, it has to be said, has been hugely successful. But, in some quarters, there is a growing unease at his rising power, the sense that it has become more Team Horner than Team Red Bull. A few are unified in their disquiet about his level of control. While alive, Mateschitz trusted his F1 team boss to get on with the job at hand and largely avoided interfering. Mateschitz's eyes and ears to the F1 team was Helmut Marko, friends since they first met in the 1960s and someone whose perspective he trusted.

Since the Austrian's death, however, the structure of Red

Bull's parent company has been working entirely differently. Oliver Mintzlaff, CEO of corporate projects, now overlooks its portfolio of sports teams, including Red Bull Racing. So the question now was whether a role existed for Marko, now he was into his eighties. He was employed – as he always has been – by Red Bull rather than Red Bull Racing despite being a director in the team. With Mateschitz's passing, Horner may have assumed that he would be able to sidle Marko into retirement.

Crucially throughout all the ups and downs, Marko perpetually has maintained the backing of Max Verstappen and his father Jos. Verstappen Snr, Marko and Mintzlaff have been united in a growing acrimony towards Horner. This has led to fraught relations between Marko and Horner, and Horner and Mintzlaff. Red Bull gives you wings, so the advertising slogan goes, and Horner was in danger of having his clipped.

When reports emerged of a complaint by a female employee ahead of the 2024 season accusing Horner of controlling and coercive behaviour, it paved the way for Horner to be toppled. But he dug in, even when a tranche of WhatsApp messages alleged to be between Horner and his complainant were emailed to most of the team members and media in the paddock. Jos argued that if Horner stayed put the team was in danger of being torn apart. Even Max, who was more a peacekeeper, entered the debate, making it very clear in a press conference that if Marko went, he would too. And yet, Horner survived. He was cleared via an internal investigation by a London KC brought in to look into the case, and again following an appeal by his complainant. Mintzlaff met with both Marko and Horner the previous Saudi Arabian Grand Prix weekend, where both were told they would be staying on in their respective positions. But despite a public front saying otherwise, the distrust has never gone away, never more apparent at the Red Bull Ring than perhaps anywhere on the calendar to date.

Back in Austria, the unease is more notable than usual from the outside looking in. Built in 1969, the Österreichring, as it was then known, hosted the Austrian Grand Prix up until 1987 when it was scrapped and eventually rebuilt following safety concerns. Its esteemed list of winners includes the likes of Niki Lauda, Alain Prost and Jacky Ickx. It is a circuit not without controversy. American driver Mark Donohue lost his life here at the Vost-Hugel Curve in 1975 during a practice session when a tyre failure sent him into the fencing. Twelve years later, Stefan Johansson avoided serious injury when he hit a deer at 150mph at the Jochen Rindt Curve. The deer was not so lucky. Following a reconfiguration, Jochen Rindt again hosted an F1 race from 1996 to 2003 until its contract was terminated, at which point Red Bull owner Mateschitz stepped in to buy it. It wasn't until 2008 that work began on construction. By 2013, it was back on the F1 calendar. It is a circuit where Verstappen has won four times, though Red Bull have struggled here in more recent times, Verstappen's dominant 2023 season aside where the car was quick everywhere. Today, it is a picture-postcard of a track.

Red Bull's top brass are in attendance: Dietrich's son Mark and company co-owner is there, as well as Chalerm Yoovidhya coming over from his native Thailand. The race could barely go worse from a perspective of trying to impress the Red Bull hierarchy. As we've seen, Verstappen is driven into and out of the race on the opening lap; Tsunoda, meanwhile, makes it to the chequered flag but dead last. There is almost a gallows humour on the radio. 'It's exciting this, isn't it?' observes one team member, while another, on lap 24, ponders what flavoured ice pops might be coming post-race, and finally the ultimate observation: 'It's a fucking procession now.' It's a one–two for the McLarens – Norris ahead of Piastri – and they're 20 seconds clear of the next best, Charles Leclerc. Even if Verstappen had not been speared into, he never would have had the pace to match them. A shot at title number five is fast slipping away, the points disadvantage to Piastri now up to 65.

Horner fronts up to a group of huddled media, nervously playing with his signet ring as he bounces back and forth from one question to another. As I wait my turn to speak to him, he is whisked away to the top floor of the Energy Station to talk to the owners. Horner believes he has survived worse. Just a few weeks earlier in Dubai he had met with Yoovidhya. When asked how long a turnaround would take, Horner suggested five years but the Thai co-owner said he had three. Even with that assurance over his future, Red Bull HQ is looking to at least remove an element of Horner's control with the marketing department being overseen by Austria. Horner pushes back, his argument being his way has worked up until now, the hierarchy need to have faith in him or else find someone else.

With barely time to catch breath, a few days later the team relocate to a second home race at Silverstone, and the sense of unease hasn't dissipated. No longer are Red Bull's owners in attendance but Mintzlaff is. The Friday of a race weekend feels like Groundhog Day. From the outset of FP1 both drivers complain of understeer and oversteer. As has now become customary, as Verstappen gets out of the RB21 at the end of the second of two practice sessions, he describes it 'as quite a bad day'. The balance is off, he's struggling from one corner to the next, his biggest gripe 'understeering to the moon', which has been an ever-present problem on the first day of a Grand Prix weekend. Tenth in FP1 hardly suggests he will threaten the front-running McLarens or have aspirations for a race win as at Imola. And all the while the rumours won't go away that Verstappen could switch to Mercedes next season despite Christian Horner's denials.

Horner is in the team bosses' press conference in between Friday's two practice sessions. Despite the internal divisions at Red Bull, the Verstappen rumours and the issues with the car, he looks relaxed as he leans back on the sofa to face the usual barrage of questions. 'We've got some understeer in the car that we just need to tidy up, so it's a bit of a balancing act,' he says. 'We're giving away 90 per cent of our lap time in turns six and seven, but the rest of the lap's looking pretty decent, and actually the long run, if you look at the times, looks pretty sensible. So, I think we've got something we can work with. We've just got to make sure we tune it overnight the right way.'

Forthright views are exchanged in the engineering briefing from drivers, engineers and Horner himself, all acutely aware of the turnaround required in time for practice the following afternoon. And then there is the battle of the elements. The forecast looks dry for the race but Silverstone has a microclimate that baffles even meteorologists, blue skies and sunshine quickly turning to heavy rain in the blink of an eye.

Silverstone is the birthplace of Formula 1, home to the first world championship Grand Prix 75 years ago and host of the British Grand Prix since 1987 despite a battle at times to keep it afloat. Under the circuit's managing director Stuart Pringle, the Northamptonshire track has flourished and remains one of the circuits likely to be on the F1 calendar in perpetuity. It is also the locale for the majority of F1 teams. Aston Martin's headquarters are opposite one entrance while Red Bull are just 20 miles down the road. It is the one race where many of the wider Red Bull workforce can attend, and many do. Like Austria, it's important to do well here. The team can't afford another dire weekend.

A bomber station in the Second World War, Silverstone's three runways lie within the confines of the modern-day track. Lewis Hamilton, with a record nine victories at the circuit, has described a lap as being like flying a fighter jet. It remains one of the fastest tracks on the calendar and a firm favourite with drivers – British or otherwise. Red Bull have won here four times, including Verstappen in 2023, but such an outcome looks unlikely this season and yet Verstappen has already shown in Suzuka and Imola that anything is possible. Despite Friday's gremlins, Marko is quietly predicting a front-row grid slot but it's hard to know if he's being serious, so deadpan is his delivery.

From the off, Verstappen is quick, his Q1 lap the best of the field but not necessarily an indication of where he will start in the following day's race. In Q2, he is eclipsed by Lando Norris. Both McLarens start their final flying lap in Q3 ahead of him, Verstappen well aware of the benchmark he needs to beat. He is purple in sector one – the quickest driver taking in the likes of the Hamilton Straight, Abbey, Aintree and the Wellington Straight. But better is yet to come despite entering Luffield wider than the two McLarens on account of lower downforce on his car. He is flying through

Copse, Becketts and Chapel and, by the time of the DRS line, he is fractionally ahead of Piastri, the pole pacesetter. Wrestling the car in the lower-downforce final sector, he may not pull off his quickest time in the third sector and yet it is enough to edge Piastri to pole by a tenth of a second. In all, just two-tenths of a second separate the top five. GP is the first over the radio, 'You went motor racing, Max. That's pole position. Great lap.' Horner adds, 'What a lap,' to which Verstappen responds with this trademark catchphrase, 'That is simply lovely.' Marko once again talks of the 'Max factor – an incredible lap, flawless once more.' Friday's woes and the infighting suddenly seem a long time ago.

Once the dust has settled, Paul Monaghan has had time to look back at replays and the relevant data, and is in awe. 'He's absolutely incredible,' he says. 'He's a stunning talent, isn't he? Look at Brazil last year, we were not in the top half in qualifying and had an engine penalty. Look at the drive he produced – absolutely incredible. Look at Imola this year around the outside of Oscar; Suzuka was remarkable too. You listen to his radio and he's so calm in the car. You'd think he was sitting next to you driving a road car. He might be pulling 4 or 5G and he seems so placid. I'm not sure the images convey just how good that last lap was. Max just drove the perfect lap. He makes it look easy, it looks just like a video game. The speed they're going is just phenomenal and the car control is so . . . not minor exactly, but you barely see it. For me, it's stunning to watch. He's wrestling it but the resolution of control is so fine it's actually hard to see. The more you dig into it, the more you look and think *wow*.'

That night, Horner hosts his drivers and their entourages at his Cotswolds home. For all the turmoil, it is an evening of smiles. Talk understandably turns to the possibility of a race win the following day. Verstappen still needs a car with which to deliver and Silverstone has been part of the floor upgrade that began back in Imola.

The current era of F1 cars is referred to as the 'ground-effect' era. In the most basic terms, aerodynamic designs are created to generate low pressure on the underside of the car to effectively suck it to the track, thereby creating downforce. Monaghan explains: 'The closer you take them to the ground in a non-linear way, they pick up load. So you want to run them as low as you possibly can. That doesn't work in all circumstances because we have low- and high-speed corners and it goes up and down with speed as much as tyre as anything else. So you try to design a floor that works in a low-speed condition and high-speed condition where it can be very close or occasionally touching the ground. Those demands are quite different. Everyone is trying to extract more lap time from the floor and the methods of doing it are subtly different and the aim is common, which is lap time.'

The other big change for Silverstone is a skinny rear wing. It is gambling on that innovation that enabled Verstappen to get pole. It gives him much greater pace on the high-speed straights – one only needs to look back at his in-car footage of Hamilton and Wellington Straight compared to Norris and Piastri – but to the detriment of downforce in the few lower-speed corners. The argument is Verstappen's car-handling skills are such that he can manage it.

Explaining the wing change, Monaghan says: 'If you look from the front at the depth of the rear wing in terms of its height, the deeper it goes from the bottom of the first element to the top of the second element you're making more load. If you make more load, you make more drag for a given speed. So ultimately we balance the rear wing drag against the engine power, which is why the speed rolls over. If we put a smaller rear wing on, we still balance engine power. So, you ultimately make the same load and same drag just at a higher speed. In other corners you have less load on the car but also less drag. When we put a smaller rear wing on the car we are effectively lowering the drag in the speed ranges of corners but also reducing the downforce. Ultimately, we balance the engine power in higher speed. You're making a trade for a fixed speed. If I go around a corner at X speed, can I do it with less download on the car and do my lap time more on the straights than the corners, which is effectively what a rear wing does for you? Are you competitive against those around you or will they breeze past you on the straight? This is where your trades come in. It's never an easy choice.'

On Saturday, it has led to a good result. There is confidence on Sunday that Verstappen can comfortably win the race if he has a good start and pulls away from the McLarens into clean air, and it doesn't rain. As Monaghan puts it, 'We have made our bed and we will lie in it today. We will find out. Predictions are imperfect. I think Max will have quite a fight on his hands. We're as confident as we can be. We're on pole with the four-time world champion.' As the heavens open before and during the race, defying meteorological reports from earlier in the week, Verstappen knows he is a sitting duck: the heavier the rain gets, the more like Bambi on ice he will be in the lower-speed corners. He is easily picked off by Piastri early on and then disaster strikes following a restart after a safety car on lap 21. He spins and drops from second to ninth. From there, it is a race of damage limitation and he claws his way back to fifth. After Austria, it is another poor result, with the knives that are already out for Horner being further sharpened.

After two consecutive chastening weekends for the team, Horner is called to a meeting in London on the Tuesday morning after the British Grand Prix with Mintzlaff and Marko. His fear is that the pair will inform him that the large marketing arm of Red Bull Racing will be removed from his watch to be overseen by Austria. As he walks in, he sees that also in attendance is Red Bull's global head of human resources and the mood of the meeting doesn't look particularly friendly. The fear that control of marketing is to be removed from him is replaced by a reality which is infinitely worse.

In the meeting Horner is told that his time at Red Bull is up after two decades, eight drivers' titles and six constructors' championships. He will be 'removed of operational duties' with immediate effect and placed on gardening leave while the terms of his exit are thrashed out by the lawyers. For Red Bull it will be costly and cutthroat: Horner is on a salary of £12 million a year and has six years left on his contract. He is given no explanation for his sacking, none. When he presses, he is told the team was beginning to feel more like his than Red Bull's and news of his removal will be announced in 20 minutes' time. He argues that announcing his departure in this way does little to value the people still at Red Bull and asks if, after two decades at the helm, he can address his staff before the press release goes out. Mintzlaff and Marko agree to his final wish.

The following morning, Horner gathers his senior team to tell them the news before giving a tearful address to wider staff. It takes place inside MK-7, scene of so many rabble-rousing speeches, team debriefs, championship celebrations – both drivers and constructors – and ultimately the final act in his remarkable tenure at Red Bull.

Taking to the lectern, he says, 'Yesterday, I was informed by Red Bull that operationally I will no longer be involved with the business for the team moving forward from after this gathering. I'll still remain employed by the company but operationally the baton will be handed over. And that obviously has come as a shock to myself. Obviously I've had a chance to reflect over the last 12 hours or so and I wanted to stand in front of all of you to break this news and just express my gratitude to each and every single member of the team that has given so much during the last 20 and a half years that I've been here. When I arrived 20 years ago, with a few less grey hairs, I walked into a team and didn't know what to expect, but I was immediately welcomed and showed to run-down buildings. We started to build what became a powerhouse in Formula 1. Watching and being a part of this team has been the biggest privilege in my life.'

As he speaks, his voice cracks, a rare show of emotion. There are tears shed by staff, too, a look of loss and bewilderment on many faces as the meeting breaks up. Mintzlaff and Marko wait on the grass outside the main building before addressing staff themselves. Marko's insistence that staff simply have to work harder goes down like a lead balloon. And there are others to follow Horner out the door. Also removed from their roles are two of his closest confidants – chief marketing officer Olly Hughes and Paul Smith, the communications chief – deemed necessary exits by Austria.

In a subsequent Instagram post, what will be his last

of the season, Horner writes to his 2.5 million followers: 'After an incredible journey of twenty years together, it is with a heavy heart that today I say goodbye to the Team I have absolutely loved. Every one of you, the amazing people at the factory, have been the heart and soul of everything that we have achieved. Win and lose, every step of the way, we have stood by each other as one and I will never forget that. It's been a privilege being part of and leading this epic Team and I am so proud of our collective accomplishments and you all. Thanks to the amazing partners and fans who enabled us to go racing. Your support has helped grow the team from its humble beginnings to an F1 powerhouse that laid claim to 6 Constructors' Championships and 8 Drivers' Championships. Equally, thank you to our rivals, with[out] whom there would be no racing at all. You've pushed us, challenged us and enabled us to achieve accolades we never dreamed possible. The competition has made every victory sweeter and every setback an opportunity to develop and grow. Formula 1 is a sport built on relentless ambition, passion and respect. The rivalries have been fierce, but the mutual drive to innovate and raise the bar is what has made this journey so special. It's been an honour to be part of this incredible era of motorsport. I leave with immense pride in what we've achieved and also with what's in the pipeline for 2026 – and huge respect for everyone who's made F1 the pinnacle it is today. Thank You.'

The timing is particularly brutal coming just 10 days after the death from eye cancer of his first wife, Beverley Allen, mother to Horner's daughter Olivia and with whom he had a harmonious relationship despite their split 11 years ago. Her funeral will take place the week after Horner's sacking.

Beyond his primary concern for his daughter and his own position and future, his overriding worry is for the staff members he has left behind, with whom he has a sense of loyalty built up from years at the tiller. It is not the ending he expected after two decades and one only needs to look at the trophy cabinet at Red Bull Racing reception to see what he's achieved.

Moments after his final speech to staff, the press release drops to the entire shock of the F1 paddock and the wider F1 fanbase announcing Horner's exit and his replacement: Laurent Mekies. Many were aware of the warring factions and unease but this has dropped like an unexpected bomb. The Frenchman readily admits 'it came out of the blue' to him, too, broken to him in a joint phone call from Mintzlaff and Marko telling him Horner was on the way out and they wanted him to step into the role. He asks for some time to think over the request. Partly, there is a sense of loyalty to Horner, who brought him into Racing Bulls, but also the enormity of what he is undertaking, a step up from team principal of a far smaller team to CEO and team principal of an F1 winning machine.

There is a sense of irony at Horner being replaced by the man he brought in to head up Racing Bulls. One wonders what would have happened had it stayed dry in Silverstone and Verstappen had won. It's unlikely he would have been sacked the following week but in all likelihood, it would merely have given him a reprieve before results once again fell by the wayside. But for the first time in Red Bull Racing's history, Horner is no longer in charge.

7th December, 2025, Abu Dhabi Grand Prix

Amid all the pre-race talk of potentially backing up the field in Abu Dhabi to aid his championship chances, Max Verstappen has instead attempted to disappear into the distance, pulling clear of a chasing Lando Norris and Oscar Piastri to break any McLaren slipstream.

By the time DRS is enabled on lap two, he is already 1.4 seconds clear of the papaya chasers thereby reducing their chances of getting past him for the race lead.

In contrast to much of the season that has preceded this moment, Verstappen is the quickest man in the quickest car in Yas Marina and looks every bit a race winner in the Grand Prix's early stages.

A championship winner? That is an altogether tougher route to navigate. Even if he wins, he still needs a dose of luck, the requirement being for Norris to finish outside the top three. In an unlikely stepping stone in that quest, he is helped from an unlikely source as Piastri passes Norris around the outside with one of the overtaking manoeuvres of the season.

As Piastri pulls off the pass, there are sharp intakes of breath at McLaren, so too along the grid and the wider F1 paddock. It has echoes of Verstappen on Piastri at Imola so many months earlier. So much has happened in the ensuing races.

Were the race to finish now, Norris would be champion by a mere two points after 24 races, one of the closest championship battles in history.

Verstappen, controlling the Grand Prix at the front of the field, is hardly the focal point. Such is his race craft and control, his team on the pit wall, in the garage and back at Milton Keynes are relatively at ease with his on-track position.

But there are still fingernails being gnawed at the uncertainty that lies behind in what is still a three-way title fight. There are the occasional jitters: the pit crew briefly being unable to hear communications over the race radio before that particular technical gremlin is rectified, or McLaren observing early graining on the tyres of Verstappen's RB21.

There are other potential players aside from the leading triumvirate in how the championship battle might play out. Charles Leclerc had begun the season hoping that Ferrari would force their way into this title fight. With new teammate Lewis Hamilton, it has been a year of despondency and disappointment for the most part and yet Leclerc could still help decide which driver ends up on top come the season's end.

Leclerc is breathing down the neck of Norris but, try as he might, cannot force a way past before Norris pits on lap 17. McLaren know their pit crew need to be rapid as Leclerc comes in for a tyre change just fractionally behind. The clock stops at the McLaren garage at 2.1 seconds for the pit stop and another sigh of relief is expelled from Zak Brown and Andrea Stella.

From lap 18 onwards, Norris now has to cut his way through the field. With Verstappen in first but still needing to pit, the Briton is some way back in ninth. He picks off the Mercedes of Kimi Antonelli and the Williams of former McLaren teammate Carlos Sainz without a fight. In the chain of cars ahead, it next brings him to the back of Lance Stroll, himself in a battle with Liam Lawson.

Can the former Red Bull man do anything to hamper Norris and aid Verstappen's cause? With one audacious move, Norris clears both the Aston Martin and Racing Bulls drivers to scythe past into fifth place. Lawson tries to come back at him with the use of DRS and is briefly alongside the Briton only for the McLaren to abruptly close the door.

It is every bit the drive of a champion but other dangers still lie ahead, notably that of Tsunoda in his last race for Red Bull Racing before a season on the sidelines as reserve driver in 2026. His employers had hoped he could consistently aid Verstappen in the championship battle. Now comes his chance. Over the radio, he is reminded to hold up Norris in what is potentially his last move of note for his employers. 'I know what to do so leave me,' comes the irritated response.

On lap 23 Norris pulls to the outside of Tsunoda to try to slip past, and in turn he goes wide to force him off the track. Red Bull Racing have already been warned by the sport's lawmakers that all manner of sanctions are available to them should they be deemed guilty of any illegalities.

Norris shuns the danger despite a high-speed stint off track while, moments later, Tsunoda is handed a five-second penalty for his crime, reacting in perhaps faux horror when he is informed of that by Richard Wood over the team radio. The reality is he is bang to rights.

More crucially in the championship tussle, in comes word from race control that Norris is under investigation for gaining an advantage by going off the track and, from there, getting past Red Bull's number two. Could there yet be a further twist in the drivers' championship?

PART TWO

THE RESURGENCE

22

THE NEW REGIME

Early Thursday morning of race week it is eerily quiet in the paddock at Spa, home to the Belgian Grand Prix, the relative absence of people accentuated by the fact the paddock is split in two. One half is a level up backing on to the garages, which in turn open up to the racetrack, housing the team's cars and engineering offices. The other paddock is accessed via a set of steps and a small tunnel complete with Formula 1 memorabilia, including one of ex-F1 world champion Jochen Rindt's former race cars.

Thursday is traditionally media day for a Grand Prix weekend, where the drivers are offered up for interviews, and the paddock gradually builds up through the morning with the arrival of team members, journalists and broadcasters. Photographers are poised to grab fleeting images of drivers on their arrival, WhatsApp messages exchanged to warn when and where they will pop up. For once, the greatest anticipation is on the emergence not of a driver but of Red Bull's new boss, Laurent Mekies. The spotlight is very much on this team above all others with its new leader at his first race in charge. Messages arrive from his chauffeur, formerly Horner's driver, to say he has boarded a helicopter with Yuki Tsunoda and will be landing at the circuit. Is this a show of support for the Japanese driver under pressure in the second seat alongside Verstappen or merely a coincidence of their travel arrangements? And then the slim bespectacled Mekies emerges in a pale-coloured zip-up polo shirt under a blue suit with his black bag in his left hand and a broad grin on his face. With him, there's always a grin.

His role as Red Bull Racing CEO and team principal has already begun in earnest with a filming day at Silverstone just a few days previously. His pearly white teeth are also on show there as he presses the flesh and shakes hands with the staff as if to signal that the boss may have changed but it is business as usual. In Spa, the sensation is it is anything but. He is all too aware he has inherited a team that has been struggling but has also lost the only leader it has ever known – one who was popular with staff.

For the first time in 405 races, Horner is watching a Grand Prix from home, having not missed a single one during his tenure, which is testament to his commitment. No other team boss on the grid has been so present. Only two people – Helmut Marko and Ole Schack, one of Verstappen's mechanics – have been in attendance for 400-plus races. He and Horner celebrated their quadruple century with a cake in Imola just a few races ago; Horner had joked of 400 more but would only manage another five. Many of the team are worrying about their futures. For a team so assured of itself and its way of operating, there is now nervousness and uncertainty. Not only Horner has gone but also the head of marketing and the director of communications, that trio an integral part of the operation. But it is Horner's absence that is on the lips of the entire paddock – a big presence leaving a big void by his departure.

Monaghan, for whom a dry sense of humour is the answer to most situations, says: 'It's a bit of a shock, isn't it?' He is clearly fond of Horner and dented by his sudden exit. 'He committed 20 plus years to the team, and the team evolved and grew and changed and succeeded under his tutelage. So, it's an awful shock and full credit to Christian. He had the courage to come and tell a small group of us and then everybody what happened. He could have just gone home and put his head under a pillow but he stood up and said to everyone what had happened. What a courageous thing to be able to do, and he composed himself and held himself – 10 out of 10. I'm not sure I could have done that. Who would have thought the energy drinks company would beat Ferrari and Mercedes in 2010? And we did, didn't we? I wish him every success in whatever he does. If he comes back to the paddock, I hope he'll come here for a coffee.'

But there is warmth for Mekies, too, and an understanding he is in a difficult position, having been jettisoned into the team at the expense of its lifelong leader. Monaghan says he's looking forward to working with him, having known him for years, his concern less about what he brings to the team and more what his football allegiance is. The lifelong Liverpool fan says: 'If it's not Liverpool, he's out!' the delivery typically deadpan. For Mekies, who admits he and Horner have exchanged messages, the job at hand is multifaceted: to get to know his team, how it works and what it needs to turn itself back into race winners . . . and rapidly. Can he get the team back to winning ways as in Suzuka and Imola or are they anomalies in McLaren's charge to the title? The approaches of Mekies and Horner are unsurprisingly different. Horner was the go-to figure for anyone of note during a race weekend, the centre point of everything that played out. There was a certain swagger as he arrived on a Friday as though surveying the empire he had built up, and yet he was still approachable to all his race team. Mekies, in contrast, opts to arrive 24 hours earlier in his quest to get up to speed with the trackside team. The quirk of the Energy Station is that Red Bull staff sit to the right when in attendance for meals or coffee breaks, the Racing Bulls workforce going to the left. Old habits die hard as Mekies arrives and promptly goes left. For the rest of the weekend, he is omnipresent, walking between the Energy Station and the garage to be as hands-on as possible. Monaghan jokes he can't keep up with the former engineer, both physically and mentally.

The next day and the rest of the race weekend, in fact, Mekies gets in the habit of arriving early – around 8am – earlier than most, be that staff, the press or VIP guests. This time he turns to the right and takes a table with a coffee to talk through events with Helmut Marko. Marko relishes having a fellow morning person to chew the fat with. 'I'm an early bird,' he says, 'so, it's the first time I have someone that comes in in the morning with me. The last one was Niki Lauda, who was always up that early. But it's amazing. I haven't seen someone who is not a fan of Laurent. He knows nearly everybody, shakes hands with everybody and it takes a while to get from the gate to our hospitality place.' But where does the power now lie and how much independence does Mekies have to run the team as he sees fit? His overseers from Red Bull head office in the form of Mintzlaff and Ahmet Mercan, Red Bull's global head of motorsports, arrive and there is a mood of anticipation, almost nervousness at their arrival. They meet with the Verstappens, Max and Jos, as well as Marko and there is already a far more relaxed, smiling nature to proceedings, none of the paranoia and infighting of the past months. It is telling that Verstappen Snr is far more present.

But what of Mintzlaff? The German has a strong handshake and a deep stare that can make you feel like he's looking into your soul. He and Marko have achieved their desire of removing Horner but Mintzlaff and Red Bull Austria are not about to publicly delve into the details of Horner's exit – the approach from Austria HQ is not to front up to the press. Despite that, there are initial indications Mintzlaff may give a series of interviews in the build-up to the weekend but he turns down such overtures. The belief is the press release announcing Horner's exit is sufficient and, while the terms of the exit are being worked out through expensive lawyers on both sides, the decision is made that it is better to say nothing at all. Mintzlaff does at least talk to Michel Milewski from German newspaper *Bild*, who he has known from his days in the Bundesliga. Horner is not mentioned but Mintzlaff talks of flipping a switch, looking forwards and standing in unison as a team. He speaks of the greatness achieved in Red Bull's history and predicts more to come in the future. He also declares the world championship has not been lost yet.

Max Verstappen's mother Sophie is also in attendance for this new era, as well as his grandmother Marianne, with whom he enjoys a close relationship. It is touching to see a four-time champion dote so readily on two of the key women in his life. Mum and grandma take their places proudly in the back of the garage for the weekend's sole practice session as Red Bull Racing's bold new era begins.

Verstappen starts the session with a new front wing and also a revised sidepod the team hope can help close the gap on McLaren, as well as the skinny rear wing which gave them pole in Silverstone but saw their race fall apart in the rain. Will the gamble pay off? They have to balance when to stop focusing on the car for the 2025 season and move their attention solely to the 2026 iteration with the biggest regulation overhaul in a generation. The message is to keep the focus on this season for the time being. There is a boost for Tsunoda, too, who profits from a new floor he and his team have been pushing for. It is Mekies who gives the official all-clear, giving him a chance to properly see what Tsunoda can do in similar equipment to his teammate. Would Horner have been so generous?

For Red Bull's brave new world, it is the perfect start in the sprint race. Verstappen gets a slipstream up to Les Combes to pass polesitter Piastri on the opening lap for a lead he won't concede for the duration of the 15-lap race. 'No Horner, no problem' appears to be the message as Verstappen produces a masterclass to win the sprint race, much to the delight of the Orange Army who have swamped over the border from the neighbouring Netherlands to support their sporting hero. Red Bull's parent company breathes a sigh of relief but it is telling that the celebrations are a little muted in the garage. Is that because it is only a sprint win, an indication that the team is still reeling from the seismic change at the top of the organisation or even a bit of both?

With wet weather more clearly forecast than at Silverstone, the skinny wing is gone for qualifying and the race to avoid a repeat of the British Grand Prix issues. And yet the FIA is cautious over driver safety in the wake of Kimi Antonelli going into the back of Isack Hadjar at Silverstone after being unsighted by the heavy rain. But the clock ticks on and the frustration builds as Red Bull, with a car designed for the deluge and the driver to master the conditions, are unable to race. It finally starts an hour and 20 minutes late, a rolling start behind a safety car on a drying track. Verstappen, who has qualified in fourth, ends in exactly the same spot come the race finish with the two McLarens both 20-odd seconds ahead of him up the road. It is a more realistic assessment of where Red Bull currently stand for new boss Mekies. At this point, most pundits and even members within the team are beginning to give up on the possibility of a fifth straight drivers' title. But Mekies' message is clear. Pierre Waché recalls the immediate directive from his fellow countryman as Mekies walked into the factory: 'It's not finished now. We are fighting for the fifth.'

23

MEET THE BOSS

Tucked away on the first floor of the Energy Station sits a corner room sealed behind closed, double glass doors. The walls consist of thin wooden panels with large plant pots dotted around the room and a white-cushioned L-shape sofa. The Budapest sun shines through the windows and onto Laurent Mekies, who has arrived at haste but, despite the obvious length of his to-do list in only his second race as team principal and CEO, sits down and gives the impression that time isn't of the essence even with the clock ticking on another race weekend. Having been a deputy at Ferrari, worked at the FIA and then been team boss at one of the lower-ranked teams, he is well-known up and down the paddock but does not possess the global renown of fellow team bosses like Toto Wolff, Frédéric Vasseur, Zak Brown and the man he replaced at the helm of Red Bull Racing, Christian Horner. Nor does he give the impression he is particularly bothered to attain that. There seems little time for, or interest in, ego.

The sport likes to talk about racers and engineers: Horner

is the former; his successor very much the latter. Mekies studied mechanical engineering in his native France before a specialism in automative engineering brought him to Loughborough University in the UK. He began his F1 journey at Asiatech prior to joining Minardi, which boasted a workforce of just 80 people when he started and where he was the race engineer for the likes of Mark Webber.

He'd been bitten by the F1 bug long before that. As he likes to put it, 'One kid out of two is a car fan and I was on the right side of it.' Growing up, he was shaped by Alain Prost versus Ayrton Senna, a rivalry as acrimonious as it was exhilarating on track. There was the passionate, occasionally hot-headed Senna and the cooler, thoughtful and almost robotic Prost, who earned the moniker 'the Professor'. As a young French lad he was a Prost fan first and foremost, and relished his first encounter with Prost in adulthood and the many the two countrymen have had since. He regrets he never got to meet Senna, tragically gone just as Mekies was beginning his engineering studies. For all his Prost love, he was also able to 'recognise the out-of-this-world talent of Ayrton'. Ask him which driver he'd most like to work with from another era and tellingly, he answers Senna despite the Prost-ian love.

It is a similar sort of talent he recognises in the lead driver he has inherited, already well-versed previously in Verstappen's skill. When he told Racing Bulls rookie Isack Hadjar he was going to become the new CEO and team principal of Red Bull Racing, the younger of the two Frenchmen said, wide-eyed, 'You're going to be working with Max,' almost incredulous at the news. Even at this midway point in the season, there is a suggestion Hadjar could yet be a Verstappen teammate next season. And like his fellow Frenchman, Mekies is similarly in awe. In the first few days of direct working with Verstappen, he has been surprised both by the driver's brilliance first-hand but also in an altogether different, unexpected way.

'His numbers are unbelievable and we've all been witnessing these numbers as competitors,' he says in excellent English with a heavy French accent. 'And suddenly you get to know him a little bit better and then you discover everything that is behind what you see on the track. You understand, *oh yes, that's how you get to such an unbelievable level.* We know the on-track level and how unique that is and then you discover Max off track and discover a completely off-the-chart level of commitment, lover of the sport with a direct approach to the good moment and the bad moment. And suddenly it's becoming very clear that the combination of the two makes him untouchable and unique. It's an unbelievable combination to have that raw talent combined with the absolute love and commitment for the sport and with all the understanding he has. I've been surprised by him well beyond what I was expecting.'

Mekies has a passion for racing but says Verstappen's is on an entirely different plain. He will find to his surprise that, if he contacts him on the Monday after a race, he is typically sim racing rather than taking a break. Publicly, Verstappen has still to commit himself to Red Bull and the new regime, though it seems that he is leaning towards staying put. As well as his surprise in Verstappen, there is also an element of shock that Mekies finds himself in this position, too, although his affiliation with Red Bull goes back a long way. When Mateschitz bought Minardi and turned it into Toro Rosso, as it was then, Mekies was promoted to the role of chief engineer. From there he turned from poacher to gamekeeper at the FIA, first as safety director and then deputy race director. His first job at the FIA was to change the rules of Super Licences for drivers under the supervision of his boss Jean Todt, ironically in response to a certain young Dutchman getting his at the age of 17. From there, Ferrari came calling and he was appointed sporting director before being promoted to deputy team principal. By 2024, he was a team principal when Horner lured him to head up Racing Bulls, and just a year and a half later here he is, sitting at Horner's desk. The fact he has replaced him is not lost on him. He was originally called on the day of Horner's dismissal by Mintzlaff and Marko but had to get them to call back as he couldn't hear them, the line was so bad. Moments later, the phone rang again and he was offered the job. His first reaction was not to immediately grab the opportunity, the engineer in him wanting to methodically think it through. He rang his wife to gauge her opinion before quickly calling back to say he would take one of the biggest jobs on the grid. He's been on a fast-track learning curve in the weeks since.

There appears to be a growing trend of engineers morphing into team principals in F1 – more than half of the current crop come from an engineering background. As an engineer, Mekies hails from an entirely different background to Horner. As such, an alternative approach is to be expected. So what does a Mekies Red Bull look like, I ask him? 'It's not about identity or the way we look at it,' he explains, quick to deflect attention away from him towards the team. 'The first couple of weeks is just about meeting great people, understanding the people, trying to see where the strengths and the weaknesses are, trying to see how we can support them better, try to understand where the limitations will slow us down for more competitive advantage. More competitive advantage will turn us into a faster car in the next years. So, that is what we're trying to do, it's not about identity.' The message is he wants his Red Bull to be the sum of its parts, a point that will go down well with Austria.

The opening days have been a whirlwind of management, getting up to speed with a monster of a team, understanding the whims of Red Bull Austria and reassuring the staff undoubtedly dented by Horner being toppled. There has barely been a moment to breathe. Has he been able to enjoy it? 'I don't think you get an enjoyable feeling,' he is honest enough to admit, 'because A: it came out of the blue, and B: you very quickly realise only full immersion gives you the chance for it to work. It's been full immersion ever since, so there's no space for enjoyment. It's an honour and privilege, of course that's the feeling you get. Does it transfer to enjoyable? I'm sure it will soon.'

But enjoyment has come sooner than anticipated, at least on track, with another Verstappen masterclass for the sprint race win in Spa, a much-needed boost after the past few days and two particularly difficult races in Spielberg and then Silverstone. It is in Spa that Mekies kicks off his racing ritual of speaking to staff in the garage before the start of the race weekend. Each time, he oozes with positivity.

'You may recall there are 24 races,' he says, again smiling and laughing. 'There's been a high number of races for a high number of years and I'm a lucky boy because fundamentally I only worked in the sport. So, after university and a couple of years in junior Formula 1, I ended up in this pit lane and have stayed here ever since. It's a privilege. You get paid for doing your hobby. On the flip side, it takes quite a lot of time, so to answer you more seriously, the best free time is with the family. Any time we are not here in the pit lane or in the office is with the family.'

Despite being based in the UK, home for Mekies is in France, where his wife and three children, aged 11, five and two, live. The older two, he says, are his harshest critics. Take the Spa weekend, what was their reaction? 'It was a mix but they start by looking at the less good, so they keep your feet on the ground,' he says fondly. 'The oldest two are following Formula 1. They are not the most complacent fans, they tell you the truth. You come back, you try to make a good story out of the weekend you had and they are going to give you the harsh reality of what it was.' The youngest of the trio, aged two, is making Mekies aware of the English expression 'the terrible twos' but he says warmly: 'It goes from love to a bit less love but mainly it's a lot of love!' A family man, he wants to bring back the family feel to Red Bull after recent internal battles. He knows the enormity of the job at hand. Is he the right man for it? Only time will tell. Horner himself had talked about how Red Bull Racing needed a rebuild that would take years to pull off. Mekies has 11 races – less than half of the 2025 campaign – to make his mark before the season's end.

The sprint win in Spa is one positive and although Verstappen doesn't spell out his future that weekend there is a growing acceptance that he is staying put. Even Wolff suggests talks are dwindling: 'The direction of travel is definitely that we want to continue with George and Kimi. That is the absolute priority. But you can't look past someone like Max and the plans he has for the future. We did that but I don't think there will be any big surprises.' In any case, Verstappen announcing he is staying put in Belgium is perhaps not the best look, given how closely it would have followed Horner's departure. Finally, in Budapest comes the announcement at his Thursday media huddle, the announcement pre-planned in the days leading up to it.

For Mekies, Verstappen's public declaration he is staying put is a major goal achieved. In front of journalists gathered from around the globe, Verstappen, a microphone in hand so the packed half of the first floor of the Energy Station can hear, tells the crowd: 'The thing is, people are waffling so much throughout the whole season when the only one that actually can or should speak is not speaking. That's me, and I do that on purpose because it makes no sense to start throwing things around, and actually that should be the same for everyone. Some people just like to stir the pot, some people just like to create drama, but for me it's always been quite clear and also for next year. I'm discussing with the team already the plans, the things we want to change next year so that means I'm also staying with the team for next year. I think it's time to basically stop all the rumours, and for me it's always been quite clear that I was staying anyway.'

Mekies readily admits the boost is massive. 'Of course it is,' he says. 'Having that sort of renewed commitment is the right sign to get everyone to give even more.'

Verstappen Snr, protective to the hilt, takes umbrage about some of the stories that have been written about his son in the weeks leading up to his announcement. 'It's a bit too much what the people are writing – 80 per cent is bullshit, it's really bad, people making stories up. And the thing is then he gets the questions, all of them, in the press conference. That pissed him off a little bit, people making up stories and he has to defend himself. The team knew that he would stay. It's more difficult now than it was in my time.'

For now, Verstappen's future with Red Bull is secured at least until the 2026 season when stories about whether he stays or goes will inevitably emerge once again. As for his son's long-term future, Verstappen Snr says: 'Of course, we have a contract until '28. For sure he will do that. It also depends on the regulations and if he still has fun to drive the car. It's important how next year's car will feel like for him – that depends on how long he will drive.' For now, the conversation has gone away but the reality is everyone knows – the Verstappen camp and the wider Red Bull Racing team – that talk of his future will reignite next season if Red Bull struggle in their first season as a power-unit manufacturer. It is at least temporarily no longer an immediate cause for concern for Mekies.

It is the one positive of a difficult weekend in Budapest. From the outset, Red Bull know the Hungaroring will be a tough Grand Prix for them. No longer able to run the skinny front wing, which has worked to such good effect at points during the last two races, Verstappen can only qualify in eighth place. It is quintessentially the sort of track that does not suit the RB21. Complaining of a lack of grip all weekend long, he is overtaken by Liam Lawson for the sister team at the start, struggles throughout and finishes ninth. The only positive is that race stewards opt to take no action against him following a battle for 11th place in which Lewis Hamilton goes off track. Verstappen and Steve Knowles are called to the stewards post-race, argue their case and they evade any sort of reprimand.

In post-race interviews, Marko muses a one-stop strategy

may have been the better approach, such was the difficulty in overtaking, but that fifth or sixth would have been the very best result attainable. Verstappen, meanwhile, gets ready to pack up for a much-needed summer break for him and the team, both in need of a major rethink. As he leaves the paddock, he tells reporters he doesn't expect to win another race in 2025 with 10 left to go and that he needs to switch off from racing for a few weeks.

For Mekies, the summer break is in some ways unwanted with so much to do. With his star driver having slipped down to ninth and Yuki Tsunoda having been lapped in 18th, is there a situation where both drivers will start finishing outside of the points? The new era is in danger of unravelling in its infancy.

24

WHO'S IN THE HOT SEAT?

'Embarrassing.' In one word, Helmut Marko had damningly summed up Isack Hadjar's debut for Racing Bulls. Before the formation lap of the first race of the 2025 season had even been completed, before even having a chance to get off to a first Grand Prix start, he had crashed out of the race. With much excitement over a new breed of highly rated rookies on the grid, the Frenchman had endured the worst possible start and the fallout was hugely public. Afterwards, he sobbed uncontrollably into his helmet, having to eventually be consoled by Anthony Hamilton, Lewis's father, who knows exactly what sort of pressure and expectation is placed on a rookie driver. While Christian Horner was quick to defend Hadjar's youth at the time – just 20 at the start of the season – Marko called him 'embarrassing', more regarding the tears than the spin-off and, when pushed on it, refused to back down. It was hardly a ringing endorsement for longevity in the unforgiving world of Formula 1 where promising drivers are discarded before they've even got their feet in the door. In F1, you can go from hero to zero in a heartbeat.

Marko can be blunt to the point of utter brutality but, despite the harsh delivery, there was truth behind the words: Hadjar needed to toughen up for the upper echelons of motorsport. Before his mishap put him briefly into the spotlight, it was an entirely different debutant, Kimi Antonelli of Mercedes, who had all the attention. Antonelli was Hadjar's rival in F2 in 2024 and the man (well, boy, really – 18 at the start of the 2025 season) was signed with the onerous task of replacing Hamilton. While Hadjar struggled at race one, Antonelli flourished, finishing an impressive fourth place just a second and half behind teammate George Russell. But undeterred, the French-Algerian Hadjar turned things around, scoring points finishes in five of the next eight races.

From embarrassment to the season's rookie revelation, it has been an admirable turnaround. Ask Marko which of the drivers in Red Bull's junior driver programme he is most excited about and he says quick as a flash, 'I mean definitely Isack Hadjar. He, for me, is the most impressive rookie. He comes to a circuit and doesn't know it and, within three laps, he is competitive. He's a regular Q3 qualifier and it comes very natural. He also proves in his personality. I heard some of his interviews which were really funny. He shows a sense of humour about himself, he can laugh. He is one that will have a great future.'

While Yuki Tsunoda's good sense of humour remains on point, his qualifying and race results have not been. For the past seven Grands Prix he has averaged a 15th-place finish, while Verstappen has finished in the points every time, bar when he was driven into by Antonelli in Austria. Tsunoda has barely warmed the seat vacated by Liam Lawson when talk begins of his own removal. Hadjar is asked about the possibility of moving up early in the season and says he's flattered but he's focusing on the job in hand. But the reality is that behind the scenes, he is nervous to step up to Red Bull, having seen Sergio Pérez, Lawson and now Tsunoda struggle so much against Verstappen. His initial feeling is to be granted another season to settle into the rhythm of F1 at a less pressurised team, and there is sense to that argument, one shared by some at Red Bull. On the other hand, the new regulations for 2026 are a fresh start for everyone, a level playing field in which to go head to head with the best on the grid.

When he picks up a podium at race 15 in Zandvoort, just a place behind Verstappen, Hadjar can no longer ignore the clamour or the advances of Marko, who has made it clear he wants him over Tsunoda for 2026. As for Tsunoda, who finally stops the run of non-points finishes with ninth in the Netherlands, he can't help but hear the rumours despite assurances from the team. Is the change of team boss aiding or dampening his future chances? Having got used to Horner's way of doing things and, in his own words, increasingly feeling the Briton's support, he has had to shift to the Mekies approach. That is less marked for him than for some within the team, having worked with him at Racing Bulls for a season and a half and earned plaudits from the Frenchman.

Speaking about the change in the early days of the Mekies era, Tsunoda says: 'It's really hard to say. I'm not expecting immediate change but I think he will influence things with fresh eyes. One of his strengths is he has an engineering mind so, when drivers talk about limitation, when they go into small details and those small details are hard to understand, someone like Laurent who really understands engines knows what we're talking about, so he can apply his knowledge. He will decide what the priorities are and he's showed really good performance from the last two years in VCARB [Racing Bulls].' The impact on Tsunoda started with a new floor in Spa at Mekies' insistence, which might not have been forthcoming under Horner's watch.

Does it shift his own future and prospects of staying at the team? Already, rumours have been circulating he could be replaced even before 2025 is over. He has been assured his seat is safe until the end of the season, thanks predominantly to the support of Honda, the team's engine supplier, who is financially backing the Japanese driver to the tune of a £10 million discount on the engine deal. Red Bull also reiterate to him no decision has been made on 2026 beyond Verstappen at this stage.

'I've sort of got used to it,' Tsunoda says of the never-ending stories. 'It's just rumours. The only thing you have is performance and you have to show it on the track. In the end, I just focus on what I can control. Sure, sometimes it can be hard. In my first year, everything comes very new and, in my fifth year, I know what to do. If I say I'm not worried about my future, it's not true. But at the same time, it's not a thing I can control. It's up to them what they decide. If I show my performance, things will naturally come. I can't sit back, chill and not worry about anything, that won't be happening, but at the same time I'm always looking at the things I can control. I'm only focused on the driving.'

With the 24/7 nature of Formula 1, the news stories come thick and fast, some with less credence than others. On the day we're talking another report has emerged that Red Bull are axing Tsunoda. A vehement denial follows from the team but the story is picked up by other outlets. Off the back of it, Tsunoda says the one thing he most dislikes about F1 is, 'Rumours. Rumours can be a very dangerous thing. As a driver, the one thing you want to focus on is performance and sometimes rumours distract you.'

Currently he is in something of a vicious circle. The harder he pushes, the more on the edge he is and the less capable he is of producing the required results. For the most part, his race pace is pretty good but he has usually been undone by qualifying and failing to get up to speed in quite the same rapid manner as his teammate in the RB21. He knows the only way he can silence the critics and put an end to the grinding nature of the rumour mill is by getting results, which means consistently scoring points and being within touching distance of Verstappen. For that, he has been pleading for the same upgrades as his more heralded teammate. 'In terms of how I feel in the car, it's getting better and better,' he says. 'It's more comfortable. But in the end I have to perform with the things I have. The last few races I had a couple of packages different between me and Max. I'm not at the level that I want to be but, at the same time, I didn't lose much speed. In terms of speed, it's still there. But confidence is not one of those things that you can have immediately in Formula 1. It's just building and I have to trust the car more.'

In the gap between Silverstone and Spa, he takes himself on a training camp in Majorca to improve his fitness. A boost to his physique, he says, has been immediately visible. There is also a padel match against Paul Monaghan with Tsunoda coming out on top back at base. Tsunoda may live and breathe speed but he relishes the slow stuff too. His ideal morning away from a race weekend involves leisurely making coffee and doing some cooking. He loves being in the kitchen, his ideal cuisine understandably being Japanese but he likes fusion food, too, even a crossover with Italian food, his other culinary love in the country he calls home. As well as his passion for cooking, he also has a love of nature, choosing to be in the wild when away from the rigours of a Grand Prix.

'Having time to prepare more with my body's physical shape, feeling stronger and feeling more mentally prepared, confidence is very important these days when you're fighting with milliseconds,' he says. 'Nature helps a lot. If you see a nice view, mountains, the sea, you feel just deep down more naturally relaxed. I think these things will help, plus biking, walking, driving.' The F1 paddock could barely be more in contrast to the peace, quiet and solitude he craves. But in his day job, speed is of the essence and he's not been showing enough of it.

Another break comes after Budapest but he delays a trip back to see family and friends so he can get straight into the simulator back at Red Bull's factory before the summer shutdown. It is a far cry from the days when his former boss at the sister team, Franz Tost, whom Mekies replaced, accused him of being lazy. He also spends time training in Greece, where he bumps into his idol. Tsunoda readily admits he didn't have any particular motorsport heroes growing up, although his dad loved Fernando Alonso, so he did too. Instead, his idol is well away from the racing world in the form of ex-British national diver turned action hero Jason Statham. The diminutive Tsunoda has struck up an unlikely relationship with the 58-year-old Hollywood hardman after the pair first met in Abu Dhabi two years ago. At the time, Tsunoda posted on social media: 'Best. Day. Ever.' He remains in awe of the actor. 'He's my hero actually and certainly not in bad shape,' he says. 'I can't believe how he is compared to his age, maybe better than me. He's someone I met in person who exceeded expectations of how good a guy he is. He's super-fun to be with.' Being in an action movie is on the Tsunoda bucket list; he aspires to be in the latest outing of the Fast and Furious franchise in which Statham has also featured.

As well as Greece, he uses the summer break to return home to Japan, see family and friends, and enjoy the food. It also takes him back to where his motorsport journey began. It involves him getting behind the wheel of an F4 car too. 'I remember that moment of trying to compete and beat other drivers around me,' he says. 'And it reminds me that whatever I'm now doing at the track, it's always the same as then – to be quick.' He is adamant the mental reset has put him on course for a strong second part of the season. He has had lengthy conversations with friends, family, his manager and team around him. The conclusion is simple – 'Score points as much as possible and be closer to Max.' But it's easier said than done.

Helping in that cause is the fact that where previously he had felt a bit like an outsider in the team, now he says he feels more part of the family despite the persistent rumours that he could be replaced for the season ahead. He is adamant he deserves to stay on with Red Bull for another season, despite the naysayers. 'That's what my priority is – to stay with Red Bull as long as possible. This team is who I want to be racing for; to get that, I obviously need to show my performance. I'll have to do that. You can say I'm fighting for my future but I'm just fighting to prove myself. I know what I can do and I know what I deserve. That's what I've been doing for the last four years. I went through a lot of things every year, different kind of difficulties. And I have good confidence because I went through those and became stronger, so I'm just going to do exactly the same thing. This is a pressure moment, so it's quite tough, but it's an opportunity to be in the next level, so I'm going to enjoy it.'

The message from Mekies is simple but supportive: find better speed. Quick enough and he will earn a future on the grid, be that at Red Bull or Racing Bulls. His team boss says: 'It's always about speed in Formula 1. It is where it's nice sometimes to keep things simple. Max wants a fast car and teams want fast drivers, so you want Yuki's speed. We don't think it's disappeared but he has had a very unique path with such a steep step forwards last year and the beginning of this year. We know that speed didn't disappear. Our job is to try to make sure that he's able to express that speed and, if he does, he'll get the right results. If he does get the right results, that's what we're looking for.'

Hadjar is not Tsunoda's sole cause of concern for the future. The options open to Red Bull are that Tsunoda could stay put, go back to Racing Bulls or else be discarded altogether. He faces a challenge from a resurgent Lawson too. Marko seems to be backing Hadjar. But even if he's not the next big thing, there's always another next big thing, a young driver perpetually breathing down the necks of the current incumbents. Currently, the primary candidate is Arvid Lindblad, the son of a Swedish father and a British mother of Indian heritage. And there is genuine excitement at the teenager being the real deal, particularly from the talent-spotting Marko. He is quick, handsome and hence marketable, good company and an eloquent talker – more mature than his 17 years would suggest. There have been waves of excitement at different stages in the junior programme under Marko's watch, first with Sebastian Vettel, who went on to exceed the expectations with four world titles, so too Verstappen. Lindblad is the next. Marko recalls the meeting before he signed the Briton to the programme at the age of 12. Joined by his parents, Marko recalls: 'It was him who made all the decisions and he was asking all the right questions. At that stage he was just 12. He's been very impressive but the results haven't always shown it. Also, it is his mental strength, his commitment and his very professional approach.' It has echoes of that first sit-down with Verstappen.

Lindblad has the perfect people to guide him, not just Marko but Guillaume Rocquelin, or Rocky, the long-time race engineer of Vettel and now head of the team's driver academy. Lindblad has heard the comments about his maturity before. 'I think some of that is even more related to my upbringing,' he explains. 'From the age of seven I was going away with my team, staying away from my parents for a few days at a time when I went racing. And that forced me to mature very quickly, and then that combined with the fact that I've always been racing in the next category as early as possible. As soon as I was old enough I'd move up. I've always been pushed, you could say, to the next category a bit beyond my years. I'm racing in Formula 2, two years ago I was in F4 and two-and-a-half years ago I was doing my last race in karting. I've come through the ranks very quickly. Both of those have pushed me, forced me to mature very quickly.'

Much like Verstappen he has always been one step

ahead, although it remains to be seen if he is quite the same generational talent. There have been stand-out moments in 2025: wins in the Jeddah sprint and feature race in Barcelona, but there have been mistakes too. Those errors beg the question whether he is ready for F1 or if it is too soon. That is up to Marko to decide and then make his recommendation to Mekies, Mintzlaff and co. There is also the small matter of money. Honda may be parting company with Red Bull but will still supply engines to the team's TPC (testing of previous cars) programme, so crucial in aiding young drivers in their stable with the use of past F1 cars. Honda have made no secret of their desire to keep a Japanese driver on the grid and could yet attempt to put pressure on Red Bull to keep Tsunoda.

Lindblad's paternal grandfather had a passion for racing which was passed down to his son and then his grandson, ignited by karting from the age of five. The goal has never shifted: 'I want to be a Formula 1 world champion. I started this journey when I was five and that was the goal then and it's been the same ever since. I'm very fortunate to be part of the Red Bull programme. Obviously, the chronological path would be to go into the race team. My goal is to be world champion, I want to be a multiple world champion, that's what I want to do. We'll see what happens. I don't like to think too far ahead. I want to stay in the moment and keep focused on F2 and performing well as that gives the best chance for a seat next year.'

He sheepishly admits it was not Red Bull drivers that were his inspiration growing up. Instead, it was Hamilton who he aspired to be, seeing more similarities in his background than others on the grid at the time. 'When I started to get into the sport he was the one winning more, and then obviously me being of colour and him being of colour, I felt some form of link. It's a bit weird but his first year in F1 was the year I was born, so I felt some form of affiliation to him in the beginning when I was seven or eight. We'll see what happens but that will be a very cool moment [racing Lewis].'

Talk of his place on the F1 grid won't go away. Red Bull have a decision to make, whether he is mature enough at 17 – he turns 18 the week after the Hungarian Grand Prix – to deal with the rigours of F1 on and off the grid or whether to keep him back in F2 to build him up. He is all too aware of the conversations and conjecture going on around him about the 2026 season. 'It's good and positive that there is that talk but I'm aware in this sport that things can change quickly,' he admits. 'I don't really feel any pressure. We'll see what happens. I think I've proved in categories so far I've always been forced to make a step up debatable whether I've been ready or not. I've always been pushed very hard. So if the opportunity were to come, I have full faith that I'd be able to make it work.'

As it stands, Lindblad is one of four drivers vying for three seats, and four into three simply won't go.

25

THE TURNAROUND

Ping an email to a member of Red Bull staff – or any other team for that matter – during the summer break and an automated message almost instantaneously bounces back. Its wording is short and concise, explaining it won't be seen until the summer shutdown is at an end. It is a two-week period strongly enforced by F1's authorities since 2014, stipulating that a team's factory must be fully shut for 14 days straight at some point between the end of the Hungarian Grand Prix on 3rd August and the final week of the month leading up to the Dutch Grand Prix. During that time, no design or development work, build of car parts or use of the wind tunnel can take place, and any transgressions are heavily penalised by the FIA.

First introduced in 2009 before the full factory shutdown was added five years later, it was done in a bid to ensure staff have a proper break around the midway point of a monstrous season now spanning 24 Grands Prix, beginning with testing in Bahrain in February and ending with the season finale in Abu Dhabi just two-and-a-half weeks before Christmas.

Since the nadir of Budapest, therefore, there has been little to no time for Red Bull to close the gap. For team bosses, technical directors, engineers and mechanics, some are able to switch off better than others, taking the time to unwind with their families, while others allow the gnawing sensation of a Hungarian Grand Prix weekend gone wrong to creep in and slowly eat away at them.

The team may have come back refreshed from the time off but it is hardly a mood of optimism as the paddock relocates to Zandvoort for Max Verstappen's home race. It appears that the bullishness of seasons past in Red Bull has evaporated.

In his last four Grands Prix, Verstappen has retired once, finished ninth, fifth and fourth. Not since the 2019 season has he driven four races consecutively without a podium finish. The usual Friday ritual of firing all manner of solutions at the imbalance, the understeer, the oversteer and the rest means hopes are not high going into qualifying and the race, the driver himself predicting it is going to be 'hard to be in the top five'.

Circuit Zandvoort has its origins, in part, in Nazi Germany and the Second World War. Its mayor, H. Van Alphen, persuaded the invading forces to build what would, in effect, become the circuit's main straight as a parade/communications route. Following the end of the war it would transform into a fully-fledged racetrack started with rubble from destroyed neighbouring hotels, hosting a first race in the August of 1948 and then a first Grand Prix four years later. Like many circuits in F1's history, it endured periods of glory and depreciation before its resurgence in 2021 when, following negotiations with Liberty Media, it returned to the calendar coinciding with

Verstappen's first championship-winning season. Renowned for some of the steepest banked corners on the calendar, the most notorious is Tazzanbocht (Tarzan corner). A story – quite possibly apocryphal but one the locals like to share – is that said corner was named after a resident with the nickname Tarzan, who only gave up his vegetable garden in the dunes for the circuit's rebuild after the war if a corner was named after him. It is also one of the few places where overtaking is possible and the turn where Verstappen will begin his audacious and eventually successful attempt to pass Lando Norris for P2 in his home race.

Zandvoort the town is a popular holiday destination with its sandy beaches and the cooling waters of the North Sea. Anne Frank and her family were among those who would holiday at the location prior to the war. Today, tourism accounts for about half of its income. Just a 45-minute train ride from Amsterdam's central station, the circuit has the unlikely backdrop of a beach and sand dunes. It's not uncommon for sand to find its way onto the track as Verstappen, weaving furiously to pass Norris in the race, will later find out. At what is his penultimate home race before its departure from the calendar, the Dutch Grand Prix is quintessentially the Verstappen show, immaterial of the fact that McLaren will likely dominate the race.

Take that train from Amsterdam to Zandvoort aan Zee and each carriage is full to the brim with orange-clad fans or else those bedecked in Red Bull merchandise. In the capital itself, tourists can remain acutely unaware of the Grand Prix taking place outside of the major train stations, with little advertising about the race. With up to 100,000 people through the turnstiles at the circuit each day, the Dutch clearly don't need reminding. Arriving at Zandvoort train station, the first street exiting to the right is the perfect gateway, a combination of chequered flags and orange bunting bedecked around it. Max Verstappen posters adorn balconies, a huge container proudly sells the Dutchman's official merchandise. Music blares out from morning till long into the night, Verstappen tribute songs on high rotation: the 2016 song 'Super Max!' by the Pit Stop Boys or '33 Max Verstappen' created by Dutch duo Carte Blanq & Maxx Power, which came into being in 2023. All are unavoidably catchy while, in the grandstands at the circuit, DJ Admin Jansen plays a never-ending conveyer belt of Europop for all four days of the Grand Prix weekend. On race day, thousands of flags depicting the orange, white and blue of the Dutch flag adorn the top of each seat in the grandstand, waiting to be waved later in the day.

Not all the orange jerseys in the stands are for Verstappen. There has been an increasing number of Dutch McLaren fans in recent years, partly influenced by some of the unease within Red Bull in the past season and a half, but also the growing popularity of Lando Norris with the *Drive to Survive* generation.

By the Dutch Grand Prix weekend, it is notable that the pace of Mekies trying to be ubiquitous at a race weekend has been dialled down a little. And he has grown increasingly comfortable in the role, laughing and joking at every opportunity in front of his staff and the hierarchy above him too. Guests of the team, at one point, ask to pose for a selfie with the Frenchman just at the moment that Oliver Mintzlaff arrives for the race weekend at the Energy Station. Mintzlaff jokes as if to follow up with a posed photo of his own with his employee. But behind the laughter, smiles, the clapping of hands in greeting, there is a serious edge to Mekies as he tries to mould the team for the future. He is mindful that some staff who have only ever known the Horner era will look to move elsewhere, while other staff will need to be brought into key areas alongside the team he now heads up. After the summer reset, his target is to turn around Red Bull's fortunes . . . and fast.

Zandvoort will be remembered as a pivotal moment. Up to that point, the team had pushed the car in a certain direction; sometimes it worked, sometimes it didn't, causing frustration for driver and engineers alike. Just before qualifying in the Netherlands, the team decide to go for broke and trust their racer's instinct instead, rather than follow what the simulation and modelling is telling them. Already, it has been a week of frustration and they decide to alter course entirely. How so? For now, the team remains tight-lipped. After that shift, Verstappen doesn't quite pull off one of his Houdini acts in time for qualifying. It is not quite a wonder lap but the P3 he seals is realistically the best the team can hope for and it is enough to turn the mood more buoyant inside the Energy Station and the garage where the music once more blares at top volume. The louder the music, the better the mood.

Reflecting on the moment of change much further into 2025, GP says: 'I wouldn't say it was a throwaway direction but we'd struggled up until then. Max wasn't particularly happy with the car and we went against most simulations. It ended up [that] the outcome was quite positive through qualifying and the race. While our overall level of competitiveness wasn't quite up to matching the McLarens that day we felt we'd made a step forwards and uncovered a few stones that we hadn't been near until that point in the year. From then on we were able to build. Max had been fairly consistent on his feedback on the general behaviour and characteristics of the car. We had tried what we had felt was operating at the extremes and acceptable boundaries. But when you've got nothing to lose, you end up putting that in the bin, *let's move this boundary as it's not getting us anywhere, let's expand it*, and actually we've uncovered something even greater. Ultimately that's what's happened.' Was it a quick fix that is easy to explain? 'It's relatively easy to explain but I won't,' he says, almost with an apologetic shrug and tilt of the head, not wanting to give a sniff of information to his rivals.

At the time, the turnaround may not have immediately been fully relayed to Verstappen or his dad Jos, who shrugs his shoulders and produces a blank expression when I ask him to explain the current issues with the car. The reality is that third is the best the team can expect in the race behind the two McLarens unless Norris and Piastri have a coming together or else are beset by reliability issues of sorts. Exactly that happens to Lando Norris, a mechanical failure leading to his race exit and, with that DNF, Verstappen is back on the podium once more after his barren spell, in second – a spot higher than he'd had ambitions for. And there is good news from the other side of the garage with Tsunoda finally back in the points for the first time since Imola. In the interim, results of P17, 13, 12, 16, 15, 13 and 17 have put his seat under severe pressure. Any celebration of P9 in Zandvoort is muted by the fact that the rival for his seat next season, Hadjar, is once again a star on the rise with that remarkable first career podium finish just two seconds behind Verstappen. The deployment of the safety car masks the true gap to McLaren but, as Red Bull pack up to relocate to the next race at Monza, there is a belief of a proper shift. It feels as if this car, once so hard for its greatest brains to fully comprehend, has finally become one they can start to understand. Is it the Mekies effect? The Frenchman says not. But is it all too late? Verstappen is now 104 points behind leader Piastri – the equivalent of more than four race wins with a string of DNFs needed from the Australian.

And yet behind the scenes, both with the engineers at the track and the boffins back at the factory, there is a sense that a turnaround might be coming, despite the past travails with the RB21. What they see in the wind tunnel in Bedford or running through their various simulations and mathematical models has not always proved translatable to the track. And yet there is the growing realisation that small tweaks to balance out the aerodynamic load more evenly and remedy some of the chronic understeer – a feature at virtually every race weekend – could be a thing of the past before too long.

Suzuka and Imola have been the anomalies of 2025 for Red Bull, albeit very bright ones. After Japan came a sixth place in Bahrain and then, the race after the Emilia-Romagna Grand Prix, Verstappen could only finish fourth. The days of stringing back-to-back race wins have long since disappeared from the Red Bull playbook. To highlight the lack of consistency, a quirk of Verstappen's results is that for eight race weekends straight from race one he had alternated between a top-three finish and finishing off the podium. But leading up to race 15 in Zandvoort, it was four races without a finish in the top three.

Mention Monza 2024 within Red Bull and you're met with a grimace as minds are cast back to what is universally seen as the team's lowest point of that season. Verstappen qualified in seventh place and finished the race in sixth, 38 seconds behind winner Charles Leclerc, and had, at best, the fourth-fastest car on the grid. Looking back, Horner said it was that moment when it felt that a fourth drivers' title was slipping away, with Norris and McLaren looking too strong. Verstappen described the race as a disaster and called the car a monster. But like some sort of phoenix from the flames, Monza would also go on to act as a catalyst for the rest of the season, giving Red Bull the learning tools to avoid a repeat at the same circuit a year on. It was at that point that the team began to finally understand the balance issues with the RB20 that had dogged Verstappen and Pérez, and set about how to fix them to get the championship defence back on track. It was reflected in the two more race wins Verstappen would achieve before the season's end following a barren spell of 10 Grands Prix without a victory, a run that had previously seemed an impossibility the year before and even in the early races of 2024.

This year's Italian Grand Prix has been 12 months in the planning. In 2024, Red Bull had got it entirely wrong, its rear wing not correctly configured to deal with the fastest circuit on the calendar. In the immediate aftermath the team's top brass put their heads together in order to avoid a repeat. There is a nervousness whether all the calculations and conversations will deliver the goods. The biggest shift is on a new floor, which numbers suggest could give them their biggest boost of the season, so too a front wing. But with previous issues of simulation models being wildly different to actual reality, there are no guarantees.

The first indications Monza might be a more positive

weekend in 2025 came back in July at Silverstone, Horner's last race in charge. A new skinny rear wing was placed on Verstappen's car and he duly took pole. Had the rain not come down, the outcome would have been an entirely different matter. In all likelihood he would have gone on to win, and Horner may have hung on for a little longer.

The rear wing in Monza is roughly a repeat of that Silverstone version, the philosophy being it will be quick in both qualifying and the race, with rain not forecast to scupper the team's chances this time. But on Friday Verstappen complains once again of oversteer and understeer. It is clear there is pace to be unlocked but they can't extract it fully, there are constant huddled conversations and sideways glances in an attempt to extricate it. As the clock ticks down to qualifying, time is running out to find a fully functioning solution. One positive aside is that, for once, McLaren are not running away with the sessions and Verstappen is not a million miles off the pace, although Ferrari and Mercedes appear to be in contention, too, with the potential for a rare four-way team thriller for pole. Red Bull, as a team, have not won since May in Imola – a run that now looks set to continue. Is there any chance of that changing?

The team has to balance going for one-lap pace in qualifying, and hence the potential for pole position, but also not to the detriment of their overall race chances. At the preceding race in Zandvoort Verstappen looked relatively quick over one lap, but over the course of the Grand Prix McLaren were in a league of their own. An additional cut has been put in the upper flag of the rear wing to give better top speed – as much as 8kmh down the start–finish straight – knowing that will be to the detriment of speed in the corner-heavy middle sector of the lap. The set-up they provide him with helps give Verstappen the confidence – not something he typically lacks as a racing driver but an even bigger boost – to attack the corners more aggressively without the past issue of rotations mid-corner. Even before qualifying, Helmut Marko has made the bold prediction that a Red Bull race win is a distinct possibility.

In qualifying, the Red Bull – in the hands of Verstappen – is flying. The decision to opt for the skinny wing approach and hence less downforce is rewarded in the early part of the lap when contrasted with Norris, who proves his closest challenger in Q3. Verstappen is ahead after the opening straight and the higher speed, lower downforce Curva Grande. But in the slower corners that follow, Norris claws back the deficit so that by the Ascari chicane they are level pegging. And yet in the two fast straights that follow, separated by the Parabolica, Verstappen remains ahead, crossing the line less than eight hundredths of a second faster. Cue the hugs, whoops and hollers from his mechanics in the garage and a contented grin on the pit wall from Lambiase, who is the first to congratulate his driver. Verstappen's response is to laugh before adding, 'It worked out', as well as a comment directed Waché's way, 'Relax, Pierre, it's all good.' But Red Bull know they have been flying in qualifying before – take Silverstone – only to suffer a horror race the following day. And yet the celebration is warranted. When all is said and done, Verstappen has just driven the quickest lap in Formula 1 history, just shy of 165mph. No one in 75 years of the sport has ever gone faster. It is but another record for the Dutchman.

Watching from the garage, his chief mechanic Matt Caller has no idea at the time. Later, he reflects: 'I didn't realise the significance of it until one of the engineers said it was the fastest lap ever. That's a pat on the back and a nice accolade to have.' He and his band of mechanics have grown accustomed to Verstappen's brilliance being commonplace.

And yet there is still the unknown of Red Bull's far more unpredictable race pace. Only once this season has Verstappen won a race starting on pole – in Japan – while he was denied in Saudi Arabia, Miami and Silverstone despite having parked his car on the front slot of the grid. But this time there is a growing confidence that what he has produced on a Saturday will be matched on the Sunday. There is a bounce in the step of Red Bull staff. Caller says the garage gets a sense early on in a weekend that it is going to be a good one, although that can be misplaced optimism. 'From the start of the weekend we knew, I think, or else there was a feeling in the garage,' he says. 'You sort of know from the off if you're in with a shout. It boils down to the body language and how Max's feedback is, and how the run plan is. Everything just feels a little more comfortable, a little more confident in terms of the decisions we were making. And certainly Max was feeling more comfortable with the car from the off and able to push it to where it needed to be, really. The last few weeks Max was saying he was shooting left and right a little for set-up to find the speed and confidence in the car. The decisions made from the off this weekend put us straight away in a good window.'

Saturdays can be the most intense of days inside the garage. From FP3 to qualifying is a quick turnaround, particularly if the message comes to make alterations to the car. For Caller, there is direction over the rear wing, beam wing, set-up changes to the front and rear wing, and those decisions have to come rapidly to, as he puts it, 'give us half a chance to have a swing at it and get ready for qualifying'. After that, in many ways, the main work is done, mechanics unable to make changes to the car from qualifying to the race. It is a temporary breather and reprieve but with an anxious wait to see if it pays off come race time.

The whole garage knows the race hangs on turn one. Survive that out front and the Grand Prix isn't quite won but far easier to manage in cleaner air. Verstappen goes wide off the line to hold his advantage, forcing Norris onto the grass. As the pair go side by side into turn one, Verstappen has no option but to cut the corner to avoid a collision. Before the opening lap is over, he is rightly ordered to give the position back by GP at the guidance of Knowles, and duly obliges over the start–finish line of that lap, managing to time it to avoid losing a further place to Piastri. But three laps later at the same corner he cut at the start, he is back in the lead and, from there, there are echoes of 2023 as he dominates the race. In Suzuka and Imola, his other two wins of the season, he had to work for it, this time it looks far easier. He pits for his one stop as late as possible, the two McLarens even later in the hope that a safety car may effectively give them a free stop and, in the process, the prospect of an unlikely race win. When Oliver Bearman and Carlos Sainz come together there are some sharp intakes of breath in the Red Bull garage, on the pit wall and in the engineering office. At the time, Caller is thinking, *Oh no, here we go*. In Spain, the safety car had caused all manner of ructions. This time there is a race win on the line. Remarkably, although both spin the pair are able to return to the racetrack without damage or, more crucially, without the deployment of a safety car. The main danger of denying Verstappen a third win of the season has subsided.

As he crosses the line to start his final lap, his pit crew, safe in the knowledge the prospect of any other pit stop has gone, charge across the pit lane to the metal barriers separating the pits from the racetrack, primed to lean over, whoop and holler at their returning hero. Front and centre as always is Caller. 'I know some guys who've worked in Formula 1 for years and never had a race win,' he says. 'I've been lucky so I still celebrate like it's my first as you never know if you're going to get another one, so you have to celebrate like it's the last one you'll ever get. Who knows? Maybe it will be. I never want to lose that feeling of enjoyment. That's why we do this.'

As Verstappen pulls his car into the pit lane afterwards and goes through the routine of returning the steering wheel to its rightful place, his first port of call when free to do so is to run towards his team of mechanics. Before he's even removed his helmet he flings himself over the barriers hemming in his teammates and landing on Caller, helmet and all. 'Actually, it does hurt like hell when his helmet hits you in the head,' he says, rubbing his head in recollection. 'But it's just one of those things you absolutely love despite that. He's quite heavy for a racing driver so he takes some stopping! But it's nice to see he appreciates it and is excited for those things as well, having already won so many races. He's just still so hungry for it and still really enjoys it. I'll admit my back was a little sore after – I'm clearly getting old. It's worth it for the win but maybe I need to start getting out the way more and let some of the young guys catch him next time.'

On the podium, Verstappen is greeted to a chant of 'du, du, du . . . Max Verstappen' by Ferrari's *tifosi*, who have been known to boo him in Monza in the past. Fervent F1 fans, they are acutely aware of watching his greatness and seeing a comeback to halt the one-sided dominance of McLaren. Verstappen is joined by Waché on the podium, an obvious nod to the work that he has helped oversee with his team of engineers. Marko meanwhile declares: 'The Red Bull spirit is back!' He is quick to heap praise on Mekies and Verstappen while also having a dig at his old foe in Horner by calling the win the result of 'a new philosophy'. Mekies rebuffs it by downplaying his part in all of it. 'The level of my contribution is zero,' he tells reporters post-race. There is an element the success lends itself to a former era, much of the car's ongoing developments having been months in their creation – even a year ago, in fact, with the events of Monza 2024 – and carried out by myriad engineers back at the factory. Shifting the success onto the shoulders of others is clever management on his part whatever he truly believes of his role.

Is this finally a moment that may open the floodgates to more race victories or is it another exception as the team have experienced before? Verstappen takes centre stage for the celebratory team photo with Mekies and Red Bull co-owner Mark Mateschitz. The Dutchman tries to lure Tsunoda front and centre but, having finished nearly a minute and a half behind the race winner, he turns down the offer and remains at the fringes of the photo. The usual cans of Red Bull are flicked open and sprayed left, right and centre, many of the mechanics pouring them over the head of Verstappen as he tries to make his escape. The cans are quickly replaced by stronger drinks. Red Bull never shy away from a celebration.

For Caller and his crew, after the celebrations, it's on to stripping down the car and packing it all up, finally leaving the circuit at 10pm, long after Verstappen and the other paddock bigwigs have left. For Caller and co, they are back at their Italian hotel nearby by 10:30pm and ensure there are a few drinks in celebration, nothing too raucous as they are returning to the factory straight after their arrival into the UK the following morning. He understatedly calls it 'a nice little party'.

The hope, nay, belief is that the improved floor in Monza has in turn improved the RB21's balance as well as widened the operating window – two of the biggest stumbling blocks all season long. Baku will be the proof if Red Bull have finally got some consistent understanding of their car. And yet all sensibilities suggest McLaren will return to the fore despite Verstappen's win in Monza and their own struggles. It's unclear how much is track specific.

26

A NEW POWER

'It's like an exquisite piece of jewellery, like an incredible watch when you see the quality of the components laid out,' said Christian Horner, sounding more like an art critic than the overseer of Red Bull Racing, as he was at the time of this observation. 'The unfortunate thing is that they're all wrapped up in carbon and no one gets to see them. It's quite incredible, the engineering that's gone into these.'

Horner may be gone and Red Bull Racing's track team primarily focused on a late-season title push but, in another corner at campus another race is well underway, years in the planning but with the clock ticking ever more rapidly. In a final major call by Mateschitz before his death and pushed primarily by Horner, Red Bull Powertrains came into being, the first in-house-built engines in Red Bull's history. This 'jewellery' is a new engine that alone requires 20,000 new parts, each one initially hand drawn and then built in-house before the complex operation of marrying it to the chassis of the RB22.

And Red Bull are currently performing a high-speed balancing act. On one side, they want to continue to push for race wins this season, and on the other, ensure they are competitive in 2026. Already many teams, McLaren included, have turned their attention to the next season on the development side, rather than focus on this year's car. Which course of action is the better is the big unknown. McLaren's approach could derail them in the push for this season's drivers' title, which had long seemed assured; Red Bull's may undo them completely come the beginning of 2026, only time will tell. But Mekies is unapologetic in the decision to keep the throttle down development-wise this season. He calls it 'the Red Bull way', to keep on pushing – as unlikely as a title challenge might be – until it is officially snuffed out.

Twenty years ago, Red Bull raised eyebrows when the company announced it was buying Jaguar. There was an expectation that this would be a mere flash in the pan rather than the winning machine it metamorphosed into. Back then, it was unthinkable to expect the level of success that followed. In keeping with that renegade spirit, for the 2026 season, it has ramped up its ability to pull off a shock by building its own engine in-house to take on established manufacturers like Mercedes, Ferrari and Honda, whose engines have powered Red Bull's recent run of success. It was Horner who most strongly pushed for the in-house operation when Honda announced it was quitting Formula 1 in 2021. It later agreed to still supply engines to Red Bull and Racing Bulls from 2022 to 2025 before performing a U-turn on its F1 walkout and announcing itself as an engine supplier for Aston Martin under the new regulations in 2026.

On the surface, the idea that Red Bull – despite no

experience in that field – should build its own power units is unthinkable. Sitting in the Energy Station at a race weekend, Mekies laughs at the thought of it, one suspects both from nerves and excitement. 'It's very much a Red Bull-type crazy challenge,' he says. 'As a Formula 1 fan it is just such a crazy story that 20 years after deciding to do its own team Red Bull says, "you know what we're going to do is our own powertrains". It's such a crazy story, it's such a Red Bull-only story. We have to build the building in what is currently a field, get the dyno in, try to get the people, 400 to 500 people. It's such a crazy story, the task is crazy and I'm sure the guys have lost and will lose a fair amount of nights on it, but of course we are embracing it and of course it's something we are not underestimating. There's such a Red Bull spirit there.'

The project is a headache in many ways. It is a race against time to get up to speed and the hundreds of people working on it have no idea whether it will be a success. Mekies readily admits it is the biggest thing for him to tackle on his never-ending to-do list. 'The challenge of doing a new power unit from scratch in what was a field a couple of years ago is unthinkable,' he says. 'That's the Red Bull way and we feel good about it. I think anybody who expects us to be the best in the pit lane straight away, it would be unreasonable to think that, even if the ramping-up by our people is fairly impressive.' It may be a headache gifted to him by Horner but one the engineer in him loves.

It was back in February, 2021, when Red Bull Powertrains was established and it was two years later when Ford were announced as engine partners. Heading up the Powertrains operation is Ben Hodgkinson, lured from Mercedes and bringing a sizeable number of his colleagues with him for the challenge. Sitting behind his desk, he talks with a charming excitement about what lies ahead. And he fully concurs with Mekies' assessment. 'Crazy's a great word for it really,' he says. 'It's insane. I always knew it was a pretty bold decision to start a power-unit project. As a mere fizzy drinks company, as we say, it was audacious and bold, and that was what made me really want to get involved.'

Ferrari are the only other team who have their chassis and engine operation at the same location. Hodgkinson, starting with an entirely blank canvas, set about a plan not just to emulate Maranello, the home of Ferrari, but better it. For all its inherent risk, it's a decision that makes sense. With their own power train they won't have to rely on an engine partner and the insecurity over whether they might quit the sport from one season to the next. While it will inevitably come with teething problems, the team believe it is the right approach in the long term despite the catch-up required. As Hodgkinson puts it: 'The starting pistol has gone off and everyone else is sprinting but we're digging foundations.'

There are pros and cons to what Red Bull are doing. The major advantage is the blank-canvas element, but also that they do not have to focus on the 2025 engine like their rivals. The disadvantage is that they're starting from scratch and do not have to build just the engine but also the building creating the engine as well bringing in a new workforce. Hodgkinson and Red Bull are in a race to get ready for the first test at the end of January, 2026, but he says it has felt like that since joining in May, 2022, a message he has tried to pass on to his staff – what he calls an 'artificial drum beat' to push them along. 'It's like a 400m race,' he says. 'I choose 400m because it's still a sprint and feels like a sprint but in a stadium on your own you're competing against another runner in another stadium in a different city. You've got to work out who's ahead and we'll only find out in Australia. I know exactly where we are compared to the targets that we set. And if the targets are good enough to make us competitive then we'll be in quite a good place. But whether my targets are aggressive enough, I don't know.' That's where the thrill and the nerves meet.

The engine regulation changes for next year are complicated. The main three areas are how the F1 cars will be powered. From next season, the split is closer to a 50–50 between the internal combustion engine and the energy recovery system. In addition, teams will use 100 per cent sustainable fuels (taken from carbon capture, municipal waste and non-food biomass). The other major issue, says Hodgkinson, is turbo lag, which is essentially the time it takes between a turbocharged engine's throttle response and the resulting power boost. What that will inevitably mean is some cars could be slower off the line of a Grand Prix than others, which could make for some thrilling race starts. While Hodgkinson concurs with the general perception that Mercedes will set the benchmark under new regulations, he points out his former employers may have taken a hit with the 170 staff he brought along with him to Milton Keynes. But the reality is that no one entirely knows for sure how it will all play out. As ever in Formula 1, it is an educated guessing game.

The engine is not the only change. Paul Monaghan, while perhaps exaggerating, suggests the only thing remaining on the current car from 2025 to 2026 is the quick-release catch on the steering wheel. Cars are smaller and lighter in a bid to make them more agile and responsive, there is both reduced drag and reduced downforce, narrower tyres and the scrapping of DRS (drag recovery system) to be replaced by movable front and rear wings to enable higher grip and speed when and where needed. 'It's a huge scale to climb,' he says. 'This makes Everest look like a walk in the park. New chassis, new engine, new integration of an engine partner [in Ford], new software, new electronic control unit, new size of tyre, totally different operation of the car, switch off all wings on the straights, new engine regs.'

It means constant collaboration between the likes of Hodgkinson, Monaghan and Pierre Waché. The Frenchman, like his countryman Mekies, believes continuing to push for 2025 will aid the team's cause next season. 'For sure, we lose some wind-tunnel time for next year's car,' he admits, 'but all the motivation you gain from the people, all the understanding you have on the behaviour of the car, is so beneficial to the future that you never lose that.' So how does he feel going into such gargantuan changes next season? 'I'm not optimistic but, if you are, you are losing. I think I am treating this car as a massive challenge. As you know, the engine is a new challenge that Red Bull is taking [on]. We have a lot to try to maximise the car.'

Hodgkinson is not necessarily optimistic, either, but looks remarkably relaxed as he sits behind his office desk even though he readily admits there is so much he is worried about. Every decision is crucial and made with a large element of the unknown. He likes to follow the approaches of leaders like Steve Jobs and Elon Musk in surrounding himself with brilliant people to do brilliant things, but there can be issues with that too. 'When you do that, the problems they bring to you are the problems that brilliant people can't solve,' he admits. 'And you're expected to be able to solve them and you're doing it with an incomplete data set. Do I worry? Yeah, worry is the permanent feature of this job. I'm definitely not confident. You show me someone that's confident in this sport and I'll show you someone who's about to lose. So, I think confidence is a real mistake because you don't actually know where you are. I'm confident in the support I've got from Red Bull, the support I've got from Ford, the team that I've built and facilities we've got. I'm confident in all that. I think we've made the right decisions. It's just where we are in that race. We'll have to wait and see.'

And yet the enormity of the challenge excites him, so too knowing the team and drivers are relying on an effective power unit above all else for next season. Hodgkinson has shown all manner of people around the factory but perhaps the most key visitor in the wake of the Italian Grand Prix is Verstappen. He is able to see next year's car, the RB22, doing laps on the dyno, and hear what the '26 power unit will sound like, a noise he will grow accustomed to being behind him for next year's race calendar. And Hodgkinson argues that Verstappen will have an advantage over his peers with his technical knowledge as well as his inherent ability to multitask in the cockpit. He adds: 'He has got a great understanding. I'm sure that's part of his advantage, to be honest. He was asking lots of really intelligent questions as we went around. He really wanted to know about certain bits that we were talking about. It was a real pleasure to tell him all about it. He was certainly very keen to point out how important it was to have the performance. He very quickly realised he was walking around with like-minded individuals. We all are aiming to be at the front. Anything else isn't good enough, so that's what we're pushing for.'

Most start-ups in F1 allow themselves some glide time and typically that involves finding their feet in year one, aiming for points in year two and finally battling at the front in year three. In typically bullish fashion, Red Bull are aiming for the top spot from the outset, however ambitious. 'I've got to believe that's possible,' says Hodgkinson. 'Aiming for anything else is just not what you do. If you're playing archery, you aim at the middle of the target. Of course, when you have a change of regulations, the first year is the hardest year to achieve the reliability we hold ourselves to account to. We're aiming at being at the front. I'd love it to be tooth and nail with my old team, that would be incredible.'

So much relies on the 2026 power unit, how competitive the car and team will be and whether it's enough to keep Verstappen at the team beyond next season. Get it wrong in year one of a new set of regulations and it is a long catch-up operation to undertake. At the factory the work is relentless, with the team pushing for both this season's final races and upgrades as well as the entirely new power unit. If, as expected, Verstappen falls short of the Mercedes-powered McLarens, is it a price worth paying to the detriment of 2026? It's all very Red Bull.

27

YOU WIN SOME, YOU LOSE SOME

Once a byword for consistency in F1 seasons past, Red Bull have found 2025 to be the polar opposite. For the opening eight races, Verstappen endured finishing on then off the podium in alternating weekends and, in the seven races from Monaco to Hungary, there was just the one podium, in Canada. Not since June last year have he and the team enjoyed back-to-back race wins. Baku – a track where Verstappen has not always shone, twice beaten to the win by then teammate Sergio Pérez – will further prove if Red Bull have finally got a greater, more consistent understanding of their car and whether the improved floor in Monza has stabilised the RB21's balance and widened its operating window. And yet all signs suggest McLaren will return to the fore at Azerbaijan's street circuit despite Verstappen's win at the Italian Grand Prix. On the eve of race 17, it is unclear how much the pace differential at the preceding race was track specific – was McLaren simply having a one-off dud of a race? Often in F1, it's a hitech guessing game.

The skinny rear wing is revised a little further with tweaks also to the front wing. Combined with further floor upgrades, it continues Verstappen's good feeling in the car from Monza, where he said, 'I didn't feel like a passenger in the car as I have for much of the season.' The first acid test is qualifying where the question will be partially answered: can the car's performance at Baku back up the events at the preceding race weekend?

What ensues is nigh-on chaos, with a record six red flags in the qualifying shoot-out. The hour-long session ends up running for more than two hours, with crashes for Alex Albon, Nico Hülkenberg, Franco Colapinto, Oliver Bearman, Charles Leclerc and – most crucially for Verstappen – Oscar Piastri. In addition, an out-of-sorts Lando Norris can only qualify seventh fastest as Verstappen takes pole by nearly half a second. The question now is how to approach the race? Verstappen pushes for the hard tyre, the only one of the top four to do so. In engineering briefings, he is among those to vehemently argue the case for it.

Mekies is relishing the interaction between driver, engineers, strategist and himself as team boss. 'It's always a collaboration and partnership, not only for the drivers but for the team members,' he says. 'It's about trying to make sure everyone is expressing that talent at their best. It's always about relationships. In Max's case, it's the feeling you have that there is so much to download from him to drive the team well beyond what he's doing just on track.' The selection of the hard comes with a risk, knowing he won't necessarily be the quickest off the line and potentially jeopardise that hard-fought P1, but it will give him the best chance of running long. If a safety car is deployed early in the race, it could prove costly; should it come later, he can effectively run on the durable hards for as long as possible and get a free pit stop. The thinking is all centred on wanting to avoid a repeat of the nervy end to the previous race where the threat of a safety car following Bearman and Sainz's coming together almost robbed him of a deserved race win.

There are tense glances across the pit wall moments before the start but there needn't have been. Verstappen gets away well and is never passed for the entire 51-lap duration of the race. As he weaves down the home straight and across the line he is greeted by fist-bumping celebrations from a delighted team of mechanics whooping and hollering while Steve Knowles applauds with a smiling Will Courtenay atop their high stools on the pit wall. Verstappen could barely have made it look easier but argues later his pace and lack of tyre wear may well have been exaggerated by being able to run in clean air. In contrast, Piastri is into the barriers on lap one while Norris can't find a way past Yuki Tsunoda for sixth place. It is Tsunoda's best finish for Red Bull and a much-needed boost, although the fact he is edged out of the top five by Lawson, the driver he replaced, takes some of the gloss off. Norris argues that Red Bull are 'unbelievably fast', have been for some time and that Verstappen poses a real threat in the drivers' championship. Despite cutting Piastri's championship lead by 25 points and now lying 69 points behind, Verstappen refuses to admit he is remotely back in the championship fight. As the celebrations begin, Verstappen is joined on the podium by Paul Monaghan, a nod to his work in overseeing the upgrades that have worked to such good effect.

But it's hard to know the true pace of the McLarens relative to Verstappen with one of their drivers out on lap one and the other in dirty air all race long, not to mention the Mercedes of George Russell showing it is not a million miles away from the Red Bull. Is the RB21 now the quickest car on the grid? Both Mekies and Marko are quick to credit Verstappen for his input in improving the car. The Frenchman reiterates it was Verstappen who pushed to start on the hard tyres while Marko talks of the team's engineers listening more to their number-one driver. No more, he says, are the team stuck simply on following what the sim is saying, it's now more a combination of man and machine, data and the driver. GP, meanwhile, says the shift hasn't been stark but the impact has. 'I don't think it's night and day in terms of how we've treated Max's feedback,' he says of the driver input. 'What I would say is that he's been fairly vocal and fairly consistent with his feedback and I think that's really focused our energy and resources on the two or three main areas that could have yielded the most opportunity and performance.'

Marko also praises Mekies and the team of engineers for the collaborative nature of the turnaround. A season that was in danger of derailing is rapidly getting itself back on track. 'The engineers are listening more to the driver,' he observes. 'If you have such a fast and experienced driver, I think it's the right way as he has to drive it.' If so much comes from Verstappen, is he at the helm of the team now? Has Team Horner simply become Team Verstappen? Marko makes it clear the decisions rest with Mekies above all else but that he is receptive to input. 'The whole technical team is more open to discussing things and they are not blindly taking what the simulation says,' he adds. 'It's more based on data at the track than whatever the simulation is showing you. It's more about the experience of Max and the engineers to make a car that is predictable and drivable.'

But for all the positives of Monza and Baku, the true test to the new-look car lies in wait in Singapore. While the past two racetracks played to the strengths of the revised RB21, this street circuit is a different matter. Singapore remains the only circuit on the 24-race calendar where Verstappen has never won a Grand Prix, although Red Bull took the chequered flag there in 2022 with Pérez. Verstappen would dearly love to change that anomaly. He has been in contention in the past with three podiums at the Marina Bay Circuit and yet expectations are low going into it. Many within the team expect a hefty drop back from the back-to-back highs of Monza and Baku, and yet there is still a modicum of belief among some that Singapore, unthinkable just a few weeks ago, could prove a catalyst to success for the remainder of the season. Can Red Bull dominate at circuits different to Monza and Baku? Singapore is the ultimate litmus test for the team with its combination of high-downforce demands and searingly hot temperatures. But Verstappen's message to the team has been pretty straightforward: give me a balanced car and I'll win.

While many teams are bringing nothing new to their cars for the rest of the season, Red Bull arrive at the street circuit night race with new revisions to their car. When a team makes a visible alteration to its cars for a race weekend, there is a requirement for it to be put in writing to the FIA. With regards to the front-wing alteration, Red Bull writes that it is, 'taking further research to increase the camber of some wing sections to extract more load whilst maintaining flow stability'. Paul Monaghan is responsible for lodging the specifics with the F1 rules overseers. While the changes are visually minor, he is confident it will unlock greater pace and stability.

He says: 'What [we] came here [with] was a mild revision to the front wing from the make of a previous one, a top body which gave us a different balance between various systems that you need cooling in the side pods and central radiator. While the changes are subtle – you'd struggle to see any great change – the changes don't have to be massive but the effect can be quite rewarding and enjoyable. And it's not one thing in terms of the specific build or operation of the car.' The message is the faster car is the resultant sum of its parts, making it better balanced and quicker than the rest of the grid.

Monaghan's nickname 'Pedals' is a throwback to his first job in F1 with McLaren in their research and development department. His role back then was to draw countless pedal configurations for one of the team's drivers, Gerhard Berger. The Pedals moniker stuck. At times, he portrays himself as cantankerous and lacking in intelligence, but his longevity and popularity in the team would suggest he is anything but lacking a brain.

Every session, Monaghan takes a seat centrally in the garage, equidistant between the two race cars, perpetually with his team headphones on, poring over live data on Red Bull's car but also those of his rivals. Up will pop a close-up of Lando Norris's graining left rear tyre or a piece of George Russell's fractured bodywork or the rear wing of Lewis Hamilton's Ferrari. His is one of the calmest and coolest voices over the radio, and there is a solid authority to everything he says. The 57-year-old even downplays his role as chief engineer of car engineering, explaining, 'I don't know what it means, everything and anything,' he adds with a shrug of the shoulders. Someone once called him the minister without portfolio, which is apt for a hugely capable jack of all trades, who has been a key part of every one of Red Bull's successes. Even two decades on, he still loves the job: 'It's rather fabulous, isn't it?'

His first race with the team was the French Grand Prix in June, 2005, 20 years ago. He jokes: 'I should apply for parole from my life sentence! It's so far been a wonderful journey.' When he arrived at Red Bull from Eddie Jordan's colourful eponymous team, he was acutely aware of the team's reputation as 'a party team or fizzy drinks team or however they liked to label us'. In 2009, the team came agonisingly close to winning both the drivers' and constructors' championships but couldn't quite catch Jenson Button and Brawn GP, the team that would become Mercedes the following year. The rest is history: 'We won four world championships in a row and no one expected that.'

The list of drivers he has worked with is remarkable. There was Ayrton Senna in his McLaren heyday, Mika Häkkinen – both of whom won two drivers' titles in his time there in the 1990s – and two other world champions in Button and Fernando Alonso. There appears to be a particular fondness for 'Mr Alonso' as he likes to call him although he is reluctant to compare drivers. 'Working with Fernando was an absolute pleasure although he was a sod at times,' he says. 'There was never a dull day and never did he give up. Sebastian was a different character, nowhere near as aggressive and he delivered four world championships. I once said to Fernando that makes Seb twice as good as you. The conversation didn't go much further, the second word he said to me was "off", I think! But Max, for me, is very much like Fernando – ruthlessly aggressive when he needs to be.'

No two drivers are the same, but having been a constant on the grid since the start of the 1990 season, Monaghan sees traits that star drivers seem to share. 'The more experience they gain, the better they are at understanding how a car reacts,' he explains. 'They know to ask what they want in terms of car configuration. What's really interesting is the quality of the feedback you get from them – it's the ability to compartmentalise the car's behaviour in numerous types of corners and circuits, and you sometimes think *how are you able to do this?* It's breathtakingly quick. It's hard until you see one of these cars close up to know how rapid they are. Cameras lose that awesome sense of speed. Max is able to tell me about the braking, the turning, the apex, the turning-in detail and the minute human movements changing the car's attitude, and describes it as all in slow motion. That's staggering. It's mightily impressive.'

Monaghan is long enough in the tooth to know that despite the setbacks so far this season there is plenty of time to turn things around. And, in the spirit of Red Bull's philosophy, he believes it's not truly over until the last sliver of hope has evaporated. 'We've 24 races. There have been weekends where we've been shown the tails of our competition and there have been weekends where we have prospered. So, Max is still in it and we will not give up. There are many twists and turns. We won't give up and I know he won't give up. It's far from done.'

Monaghan would make a good schoolteacher, although occasionally an impatient one. He light-heartedly calls me an imbecile when attempting to wrap my brain around under-standing the complexities of an F1 car, but he does better than almost anyone to explain everything that goes into one. As for the car, there is no guarantee the changes he has lodged with the FIA will pay off, but from the outset of the weekend, the signs are positive, the Friday headaches not appearing above the parapet. While not always perfectly indicative of how the race will play out on the Sunday, Verstappen is third in both of the opening two practice sessions and quickest come the Saturday morning. High-downforce head-scratching has been replaced by a frisson of excitement that the team has unlocked something in what Horner had labelled a diva of a car.

In qualifying, Verstappen argues he is denied a shot at pole by a slowing Norris heading into the pits just as he is coming around the final corner of his last flying lap. It's a moot point whether he would have had the pace to catch polesitter Russell, perhaps unlikely. And in any case, Russell disappears off the start line in the subsequent race and wins from lights to chequered flag. Moments before getting in the cockpit for the start, Verstappen is in deep conversations with GP, performance engineer Tom Hart, his father, Mekies and Marko. The body language gives off the distinct impression he is telling them exactly what he wants from the car. Red Bull's strategists take the gamble of starting him on the soft tyres, the thinking being on the dirty side of the track he needs all the help he can get to go past Russell and hold off the McLarens of Norris and Piastri in the two spots behind him on the grid. He can't pull off the former but does the latter to good effect, keeping at bay the faster car of Norris for the entirety of the race. As for McLaren, cracks begin to appear in their team solidity, Norris hitting his teammate on turn three at the start only to recover to finish on the podium a place ahead of the Australian.

For his part, Verstappen barely puts a foot or wheel wrong bar a late lock-up of his front tyres in a staunch defence of P2. 'Who else on the grid would have been able to defend Lando and make it look as consummate as Max did?' asks Monaghan from his Singapore hotel room in the early hours of Monday morning. 'Thank goodness he's in our car when he does it. He's quite the talent. He was telling us what he likes in the car, actually the things he doesn't like in it. And all the time, he looks in his mirrors, he's organising himself and knows where he is each time, and where to defend.'

Rather than a sense of jubilation that might have been expected with the runners-up spot at the sort of circuit where they have had a torrid time to date this season, the celebration is muted. With every point vitally important to keep alive the slimmest of championship challenges, there is a feeling of the one that got away, Verstappen struggling with shifting his gears, as well as the balance of the car, issues Monaghan feels could have been rectified. 'We may have let a potential win slip away,' the Englishman says. 'But if you said from Hungary and Zandvoort we'd win the next two and be on the podium in Singapore there would be a few raised eyebrows and *what are the lottery numbers?!* I'm pleased, yes, as our last time at a high-downforce circuit in Zandvoort we were quite poor. Without the safety car it would have been an awful gap to endure. So to come here and be competitive, challenging for the pole and picking up second having a few issues in the race and defend against Lando, having started on the worse side of the grid, I'm disappointed but satisfied.'

Any sense of disappointment in being runners-up in Singapore shows just how far they've progressed as a team. In the engineering debrief with the drivers there are no raised voices, just a unified attempt to resolve the slight gremlins for the next race in Austin and the remaining six races of 2025. Monaghan says: 'It's really constructive. The aim of the debrief is to identify the issues of the weekend. If we don't address them, we don't improve the car. It becomes our problem to sort out. Today's one was the sense of *did we let one slip?* We can improve our performance from that debrief. The race result is now history, we've got a few things to work on that Max identified in the race for us and a few other things he mentioned in the debrief. On we go.'

Another upturn has been the pit stops. After some early-season struggles bedding in new recruits to a wider pool of pit crew, Red Bull are back to their slick selves. They clock the quickest pit stops in both Baku and Singapore and will record the fastest times at six of the final 13 Grand Prix weekends. While Ferrari will go on to dethrone them with the end-of-season pit stop award for the most consistently quick crew, they will end up third just behind McLaren and with three of the six fastest times all season, two of those under two seconds.

No major car changes are expected to follow from this point but there will be slight track-specific upgrades and the learnings from Singapore mean there is genuine hope of further race wins before the season's end. And what of the title race? McLaren have wrapped up the constructors' championship with six races to go, as Red Bull did in 2023 during Verstappen's most dominant year. Watching them celebrate in Singapore just a few metres away certainly hurts and, to highlight their superiority, their points tally is more than double that of the next two teams in the standings combined. Their celebrations are a reminder of the gulf that has existed between them and Red Bull this season. And yet somehow Verstappen is still in the title race, having cut his deficit to championship leader Piastri to 63 points with six Grands Prix left. The title seems a long shot but Monaghan argues: 'Mathematically, he's still in it. It only takes one thing to break down and suddenly it's wide open. There's still 150 points available. It's going to be an interesting run-in, isn't it? And while it's still mathematically possible for Max to win the drivers' championship, it's still possible for us to be second, I daresay. It won't change how we approach the upcoming races to get the best out of the cars, drivers and ourselves.'

For Mekies, who continues his mantra of taking zero credit for the improvements that have happened on-track under his leadership, he tells reporters afterwards that what the team 'have unlocked is not only low-downforce specific'. And he argues the risk to not focus entirely on the 2026 regulations is worth it as the current development trend enables them to test that the tools and methodology are right for next season as well. 'It's very important that with this year's car we validate that how we are looking at the data is correct, how we are developing the car is correct, what produced that level of development. That will give us confidence over the winter for next year's car.' Singapore remains the one circuit where Verstappen has never won and yet it feels like a technical win in the major strides that have been taken on the engineering side.

And a penny for the thoughts of Christian Horner watching from afar, rumoured to be as much as £80 million richer, having just finalised the official terms of his Red Bull exit. The deal frees him to return to a rival team from April, 2026, the very early part of next season. Rumours in the paddock circulate that could be Ferrari, despite Fréd Vasseur having recently signed a contract extension, or Alpine alongside his close friend Flavio Briatore, or even Aston Martin and a reunion with Adrian Newey. He could be in direct rivalry to his old team as early as next season.

28

THE KING OF GRAZ

A Red Bull Formula 1 car is hanging on a cliff face overlooking the city of Graz, almost like a beacon for tracking down Helmut Marko's place of work. From his office on the other side of the street, he has a constant view of the RB14. The vehicle, hoisted there with some difficulty by Bosnian builders, hugs the rock out the back of the Kai 36, one of four hotels he owns in the city. Another, the original of the quartet, the Schlossberghotel, is just two doors down, separated by a single house in between, which he admits he doesn't own before adding after a pause: 'yet'. As always with Marko, it's hard to know whether he's being serious or not, with his deadpan steely-eyed delivery. For all the seriousness of his look at a race weekend, he has an infectious sense of humour and a penchant for mischief. Put this to him and the negative impact it can sometimes have, he shrugs his shoulders and says that, at the age of 82, he has no plans to change his ways.

Graz itself is the capital of Austria's second-biggest state, Styria, and yet has a small-town, almost sleepy feel to it.

263

Its historic centre is picture-postcard stuff and has been a UNESCO World Heritage Site for more than a quarter of a century. His four hotels dotted around Graz – the other two are Lendhotel and Augarten Art Hotel – are all relatively small in size, what you might call boutique, but stand out for the remarkable collections of art in each and every one of them. In all, he owns 1,600 works of art, a number that is constantly rising. He is in the process of building two other hotels outside of the city and friends joke to him it's only to house the remainder of his art. The artists in question tend to be young and, for the most part, undiscovered. Inside one corridor alone of the Kai 36, there are a mixture of landscapes, a portrait of Marko himself just along from another painting of rats eating each other as watching children walk by.

Inside his office, one particular work of art takes pride of place. It is by the New York-based artist and sculptor Frank Stella, who was inspired by the likes of Jackson Pollock and was also passionate about F1. It was the F1–art crossover that brought Marko into unlikely contact. Ask him to explain what he looks for in art and he taps at his stomach, calling it 'gut instinct' – not something he can easily explain. In short, he simply buys what he likes.

The love of art was not passed on to him by his parents nor is he skilled with brush or pencil in hand. Instead, he brushed shoulders in his youth with those in the Austrian art scene – what he calls his 'wilder days' – an unlikely overlap between a budding racing driver and the rising stars of the Austrian cultural milieu. Peter Handke and Wolfgang Bauer were among the writers he would spend evenings with in Graz and they would bring artists along with them. 'They were in their young and wild days here in Graz. I have to say I admire these people as they lived like they liked to do and didn't care about anything. They were just so into their job, they were on the painting and so didn't look left or right. And they were a different kind of people compared to racing, which is good, so I got to meet some other crazy ones! They'd explain what they were doing and why.' Through that and reading books – a mixture of instinct and some learned knowledge – he slowly shaped his artistic likes and dislikes. What's his ideal form of art? 'That's not an easy thing to answer. Each artist is different. I like colours but I have to see it. If it reflects me then I go for it.'

The crossover between F1 and art is not as unlikely as it might seem. Some of the F1 creations are works of art in themselves, hence his decision to put one on a cliff face. He recalls going to the home of the racing driver Jo Bonnier, only to be greeted on arrival by a McLaren F1 car stuck to one wall. On the other, there was an original Picasso. Marko admits he preferred the work by the Spanish artist – but not by much. Bonnier would later lose his life to racing. A man who had done so much to push safety dying at the circuit, Le Mans, he had fought so vehemently to improve to diminish the threat of driver deaths.

Just alongside the clifftop RB14 is another artwork, a giant black cucumber, while other sculptures are dotted along the cityscape. His office opposite his original hotel has another artwork that also functions as a gigantic thermometer. Access to his fourth-floor office is by a lift accessible only with a key. Up top, the furnishings are remarkably simple. The artworks aside, his desk has a large iPad on it, along with some papers and two mini Red Bull helmets behind it. He is not a hoarder of F1 paraphernalia, the cliff car aside. He has been gifted a number of helmets from drivers past and present with an inscription across the visor but, rather than keep them at home, instead they populate his hotels. At the entrance to Schlossberghotel sits helmets from Red Bull's two four-time world champions Sebastian Vettel and Max Verstappen, while there is a display of helmets at the Lendhotel, much to the delight of F1 fans that pass through. There are windows around all four sides of his office that overlook the Mur river and give a 360-degree view of the city where he was born and has lived his entire life. It is a view that allows him to oversee his fiefdom (one journalist in the F1 paddock calls him the King of Graz). He likes to be at his desk by 7am, by which time he says he's already had messages from Laurent Mekies. Not a coffee drinker, he has a morning Red Bull – very on-brand – the sugar-free variety.

Despite being an octogenarian, he firmly believes in youth, not just in his passion for art but in his choice of driver. He has spent nearly a quarter of a century overseeing Red Bull's junior driver programme. He has no plans to retire. His contract with Red Bull lasts until the end of 2026 and he clearly has an eye on extending it if Red Bull Austria see value in keeping him. As long as he stays healthy and the mind still works, he plans to keep up his business and motorsport interests for as long as possible. He is buoyed up by having spoken to Bernie Ecclestone over the phone earlier that week; Ecclestone, still working in his mid-nineties, is as sharp as ever, despite having long since given up control of F1. In Ecclestone, he sees a kindred spirit with a wicked sense of humour. Marko's only complaint is that Ecclestone speaks too quietly for his liking, his own hearing diminished, no doubt on account of decades spent around fast cars.

Marko loves to reminisce about his wild days in Graz, the majority of which were spent with Jochen Rindt, his fellow Austrian, who remains the only driver in history to have won the F1 drivers' title posthumously following his crash at the 1970 Italian Grand Prix. Schoolmates at the Pestalozzi School in their home town, the pair were both expelled before being sent to a boarding school together. The first initiation into motorsport was on two wheels, which then branched to four, including driving Marko's father's Chevrolet without his permission. Rindt's death understandably deeply affected his friend. 'Me and most of the other drivers, we thought if something happens it's bad luck,' says Marko. 'But then there was the opposite: if nothing happens it was luck. You had to make your own philosophy, but when Jochen died it was an especially tough moment.'

Marko had his first chance in F1 with some initial forays with BRM in 1971, which led to a full deal in 1972 after impressively winning the previous year's 24 Hours of Le Mans. In round six of that year's championship, he had been impressing at Clermont-Ferrand when a rock was kicked up from the March of Ronnie Peterson that pierced his visor and struck his left eye. 'I think I was lucky to escape alive,' he says more than five decades on. 'The car was full of fuel, there were a lot of cars on the grid, maybe 20 cars going downhill at Clermont-Ferrand, which is quite a tight circuit. It was so difficult to open my eye, I didn't know exactly what had happened but I lifted my arm and managed to park the car. If I'd not managed to stop the car and control it, it could have been a disaster.'

Wearing a patch in hospital with his damaged eye stitched up, he refused to give up on his racing aspirations. 'For a while in hospital, I was still hoping, because it was my life,' he says. 'One night I remember saying, "OK, that's over, you have to do something else." From there, I started a new life, which in the beginning was difficult but I'm looking forwards. It's the only way that you can have an exciting and enjoyable life.'

There were inevitably moments when he thought *what if?* over his unrealised F1 dream but, having seen so many of his peers and fellow Austrians lose their lives in a variety of accidents, he feels like one of the lucky ones. There have been a couple of times when he almost walked away from motorsport altogether when two other Austrians were killed. The first was just two years later in 1974 when Helmuth Koinigg, then just aged 25, was competing at the United States Grand Prix at Watkins Glen when his car suffered suspension failure and he was decapitated when he hit the barriers. And then in 1980, Markus Höttinger was competing in Formula 2 at the Hockenheimring. An early collision involving Andrea de Cesaris and Manfred Winkelhock left sand over the track surface. Derek Warwick spun on it the following lap and hit the barriers. The impact took the rear right tyre off his car and hit Höttinger in the head. It left Marko pondering whether he should instead focus on life as a hotelier. 'I was thinking, *I helped these guys*,' he says. 'Without me maybe they wouldn't have been in this position. But on the other hand they were so enthusiastic, they would have done it in another way. But there really had been a moment where I thought, *should I stay in this sport, is it worth this risk?* But fortunately, the safety – thanks to Max Mosley, for example, and Jean Todt [both ex-FIA presidents] – changed a lot. Since Imola in 1994 with Ayrton Senna and Roland Ratzenberger, who drove for me in a saloon car, now it's different. You need really bad luck if you are seriously hurt.'

After his accident, he spent time away from the sport to focus on creating his hotel and real-estate business before his passion for motorsport lured him back as a manager and then team boss. His motorsport return began with managing Gerhard Berger in F3, before overseeing teams in F3000 and saloon cars. It brought him into contact with Dietrich Mateschitz, who had been born just 100 miles away. The pair met in an unveiling of Karl Wendlinger in an F3 car and, in time, Marko proposed some Red Bull sponsorship. The company was then in its infancy so Mateschitz – or Didi, as Marko calls him – rebuffed him, saying it was too soon. But it began a friendship and what would become a working partnership when Mateschitz got behind Marko's idea of a Red Bull junior driver programme. Marko misses the Mateschitz days.

Reflecting on the past glories, he says: 'It was not always easy but Dietrich was a man who made decisions very quickly and clearly, and sometimes the money we needed was quite a lot but he trusted us and he saw the potential. Sometimes, in the beginning when we hadn't been so successful, he was critical, but in the end he supported us. It was a one-man show. There may be 10,000 people employed by Red Bull but the man in the front was him and he had a very slim organisation with quick decisions.'

Marko still likes to go skiing when he can. He chooses to do so on non-holiday days when the slopes are likely to be quieter. Having broken his hip a couple of years ago he is conscious of avoiding further injury from the out-of-control people he shares the mountain with. He still walks with a slight limp, a nod to that hip break, but his mood is good.

Later this week, he will fly out to Austin for the United States Grand Prix on the back of the remarkable turnaround in Verstappen and the team's fortunes. And yet he is not optimistic. It isn't just the points deficit to the McLarens but the fact that Mercedes appear to be in the mix due to George Russell's Singapore win and he still feels Ferrari will wake up, as he puts it. And yet his general outlook is of one of positivity. He credits it two-fold: to Verstappen and to Mekies. 'The main difference is that Laurent is a technician and a very good one,' he says. 'There is a different approach now. He's modest, of course; on the technical side his influence is zero because all these parts were already in the planning and so on, but it's how he approaches things, it's more open cooperation between driver and engineers. And Max is more involved. He's asked about his opinion. He's experienced quite a lot of Grands Prix, and he's enthusiastic again and smiling and enjoying it. If he's in a good mood it's worth another two- or three-tenths.'

His praise for the new regime can also come across in a dig at the old one. He still credits Horner with the success he had at the team but also insists it is a happier camp without him. Of his own relationship with him, he says: 'Unfortunately, we drifted away from each other. I wouldn't say it's anyone's fault, it just happened. It's like a football coach – if you change there comes a different approach.'

In Austin, growing belief within the wider Red Bull team is warranted. Where once McLaren had looked invincible, now the cracks start to appear. In the wake of Norris and Piastri's collision at the start of the preceding Singapore Grand Prix, Norris reveals that he has been told there have been minor repercussions for his part in that brief turn-one clash. It is believed they entail Piastri getting first call on when he goes out for each qualifying session from now until the end of the season. Are McLaren in danger of throwing away their own stranglehold on the season with such a diktat and using their own Papaya Rules methodology? The essence of it is admirable: to allow their drivers to race fairly and evenly on track, and to put the good of the team above all else. In their aim to do the right thing by both drivers and the team, the censure for Norris seems a pointless one with Verstappen breathing down both drivers' necks. It's music to the ears of everyone at Red Bull. Despite this slight wobble, in 18 race weekends prior to the Circuit of the Americas, with their two drivers vying for an inaugural world title, McLaren have remarkably avoided a double DNF. Norris may have crashed out in Canada and Piastri found his way into the barriers in Baku but neither have failed to make it to the chequered flag. The McLaren hierarchy believe it is an indicator their approach to racing and favouring both drivers equally is the right one.

Needing a good start in the sprint race in Texas to get a jump on polesitter Verstappen, Norris has a slightly sluggish beginning but is ahead of his teammate going into turn one. But sensing an opportunity, Piastri darts up the inside only to be collected by Nico Hülkenberg, flip in the air and hit his teammate, taking out both McLarens in the process. As Verstappen romps to a comfortable win, it remains to be seen if Piastri faces his own censure behind closed doors despite McLaren initially laying the blame at the door of Hülkenberg. It does not simply deny them valuable points in the drivers' championship but also any sensible track time. While Verstappen and co have a 19-lap sprint race to understand the behaviour of their car, the tricky and changeable wind conditions and the tyre selections, McLaren have just one practice session, which has already been and gone, with which to formulate their strategy.

In the Grand Prix that follows, the pair evade a second coming together, in part by Piastri's lowly grid position of fifth, but Norris's hopes of further closing the gap on his younger teammate are denied when Charles Leclerc, on the soft tyres, gets the jump on Norris at the start. It leaves the Briton spending the rest of the race trying to force his way past the Monégasque driver. His start denies the chance of taking the challenge to Verstappen, who is unassailable to the chequered flag. Bar conceding the extra point for fastest lap to Kimi Antonelli it is otherwise a perfect weekend – sprint pole, a sprint win, pole for the Grand Prix and a deserved victory in the full race. As long ago as Baku, Andrea Stella has said Verstappen is a very real threat in the drivers' championship, a claim swatted away by Verstappen, Mekies and Marko. After Austin comes the admission that a fifth straight world title, which would surely be his most remarkable yet, is now a very real prospect, with the caveat that he and the team need to be perfect for the final four races. Out of nowhere, Red Bull have turned the RB21 into the quickest car on the grid.

For the first time Verstappen has a real chance of turning a two-way fight for the title into three. Verstappen's deficit is now down to 40 points.

29

BACK IN THE FIGHT

The paddock at a race weekend is Formula 1's inner sanctum. Laid out on a strip of tarmac to the side of a race circuit, it is packed up and relocated around the world each weekend. Be it Spa or Silverstone, Montreal or Mexico, this remarkable travelling circus is home from home for the few days of a race weekend. Most arrive at track on a Thursday and leave after the Sunday but teams have workers who set up from the preceding Monday and don't leave until the following Monday when everything is boxed up, accounted for and despatched to the next race on the never-ending conveyor belt of Grands Prix. Access is via a paddock pass, a golden ticket for an F1 fan, where drivers rub shoulders with team bosses, celebrities, engineers, mechanics and those lucky enough to have got access for a weekend.

McLaren are housed just a metre away from Ferrari, Red Bull just a few steps further along the paddock from the Prancing Horse. It is like Liverpool, Arsenal and Manchester City all being parked up next to each other ahead of a big

Premier League weekend. For the most part, teams just go about their business but there are always curious glances at their neighbours, trying to second-guess them, ascertain their upgrades and whether whispers of a latest innovation might be pushing the legal boundaries. It's not uncommon to see team members pop into rival team's trackside headquarters; Jonathan Wheatley, for example, is a regular visitor to his former team Red Bull. And it is similarly not rare for fierce rivals from opposing teams to talk – many are friends, many have been employed by different teams during their time in the sport. The working paddock is a family of sorts, albeit an occasionally dysfunctional one.

Big trucks turn into makeshift engineering offices, hubs of telemetry and high tech, all branded to the hilt. As well as prize money for each team – graded depending on their place in the constructors' championship at the end of the season – they are financially propped up by their sponsors and partners. In the case of Red Bull, they have numerous partners and the deals vary. The one with title sponsor Oracle is worth something in the region of $100 million a year. And understandably these sponsors want a return for the sums paid out, often equating to the drivers' time, the team's most sellable commodity – particularly Verstappen. Most major brands appear to be represented in the paddock and not just the car manufacturers like Mercedes and Ferrari. Barely a week goes by without Formula 1 announcing a new partner, the latest front-line list including LVMH, Aramco, Heineken, DHL, Qatar Airways . . . the list goes on.

The standard paddock is split in two halves. On one side are the trucks with the engineering offices above them, and from there it's just a few short steps into the team garages that, in turn, lead to the pit lane. The garages can be cramped — fewer more so than the tight confines of Monaco — and yet the travelling workforce find a way to dance around each other. Below the engineering office where additional staff to the pit wall and garage are plugged into the on-track operation — focusing on the likes of the power units and the controls of the two Red Bulls — sit stacks of tyres. In Verstappen's case, they are overseen by Greg Reeson, a ball of positive energy known to teammates as the tyre whisperer. Electronic doors access the front and back, the dual bulls locking together each time it shuts.

On the other side of the paddock are the hospitality suites for each team where staff will eat, meetings are held, and sponsors and celebrities are entertained. Each team's hospitality is different and acts as an outwards reflection of their identity. Aston Martin, with soft furnishings and pretty girls in tight green dresses, is a throwback to Formula 1's older days. At McLaren, its doors are emblazoned with the words FOREVER FORWARD, while Formula 1's base has a pop-up ice cream parlour out front. In fact, the sport's owners Liberty Media have their own branded hospitality suite. The biggest and boldest of them all — only a feature of the European races and not what are called the 'flyaways' like Mexico — is Red Bull's Energy Station. Double the size of anyone else's, its bulk is a necessity as it's a shared home to two teams in Red Bull and Racing Bulls. It is a hustle and bustle of energy and movement accessed by a ramp to a set of electric double doors that remain wide open for the duration of the weekend. Standing at the entrance as its gatekeeper is Jurgen. He wears a warm smile and is always there with a gentle nod of the head and a courteous greeting for those allowed in but one imagines he could give off a less friendly greeting to the uninvited. He is in charge of erecting the Energy Station as well as the motorhome where Verstappen stays at the European races to ensure a home from home rather than checking into one hotel after another. Typically, there will be a hub of driver motorhomes set up in a secure hub not too far away from any given circuit. Also, at races he acts as an occasional bodyguard to Verstappen within the paddock when he needs chaperoning past the hordes of fans wanting a selfie or an autograph.

Right in front of you on entering the Energy Station is a large coffee bar manned by servers – mostly hailing from Austria – to supply staff and guests alike. To the left and right are a series of tables and chairs. In one corner is a coffee machine and another a pop-up hatch from which staff of both teams will be fed their meals by their travelling chef. In an off-shoot to that floor is a side door to offices – left for Racing Bulls, right for Red Bull. The Energy Station can be laid out in different formats as required for a given race weekend but at full stretch it has three floors. The first floor has more seating. The higher you're allowed to go, the more important you are. On the second floor, partners and celebrities are entertained and meetings held away from prying eyes. Meanwhile, on the first floor are the marketing offices, usually full to the brim with staff, media officers, videographers, cameramen and social media personnel, all tasked with getting Red Bull Racing out to the wider world, whatever the platform. At mealtimes, across the ground and first floors engineers sit together, likewise mechanics or the marketing group: teams within a team.

The paddock is always 24/7, people flitting in and out

of the garage, mechanics busy working, the roar of engines, wheel guns fired up and almost always loud music playing. Charles Leclerc at neighbouring Ferrari will be among those to complain of the volume in the latter stages of the season. The smell of fuel and oil hangs in the air. Most have an earpiece in, some are mic'd up, and many of the mechanics are heavily adorned with tattoos.

No paddock is entirely the same. In Mexico, there is a festival feel. At one end, a DJ plays loud feel-good music flitting from eighties classics to electronic beats, free tacos are on offer, there's a mocktail stall, a booth where you can get your face painted or body temporarily tattooed. On either side of the paddock, teams are crammed into smaller hospitality suites with just a few tables inside and on a balcony out front with staff crammed into small tented rooms behind it. As the weekend builds so does the nervous energy, people racing around the closer it gets to a session, engineers often looking pensive, huddled conversations taking place.

Running the gauntlet poses more of a challenge for drivers in Mexico than other places. It is often just a short run from exiting the garage to head back to their own room in the team's makeshift headquarters at a racetrack and vice versa. Lewis Hamilton is the driver mobbed the most while Verstappen, as a four-time world champion, is also a popular commodity. Mexican fans can be demanding, shouting out the drivers' names from the balconies, often running alongside, cap, helmet, photo or paper in hand, desperate for an autograph or a selfie. Into the TV pen the drivers are sent on their Thursday media day or herded there like cattle after qualifying, with each outlet limited to just a couple of questions before they move on to the next. The drivers are remarkably compliant with it, appreciating it is a big part of their pay packet.

In Mexico, the positive energy emanating from Red Bull is almost tangible. Just a few days earlier, Verstappen has admitted for the first time this season that he is finally in a championship fight he thought had disappeared. The mood in the garage, while usually good, is even more upbeat, the mechanics loving the fact they have new upgrades – albeit minor ones – to implement on the car for this weekend, in this case an adaptation to the floor first brought in for Monza, which has had such an impact on the RB21's pace. In addition, the team have had to adapt their cooling for a race taking place at 2,200 metres, higher than any European ski resort. As a result, the air is thinner so changes have to be made to allow more air to aid cooling in the car or else compress the air coming in. Opening further inlets on the side of the car can impact its aerodynamics. On the Red Bull it is particularly noticeable and, with how tight the grid is, the team are well aware that even a slight misstep will catapult them well down the field.

On the opening day of the weekend, the Thursday, Mekies gathers the team of mechanics into the garage and stands in the middle, rubbing his hands together nervously before addressing his troops. His short address, a feature of his reign, begins with congratulations. 'Hats off for last weekend,' he says. 'I think it would be wrong to forget how hard it is to win, and you guys know it very well. It was a masterclass what you guys have done in Austin. I don't think we should change anything to what we are doing. We press the reset button again. It's maximum focus again. People ask us if we are thinking about the championship; no, we don't think about the championship. We think race by race and we think session by session. So that's what we do. So let's get a super-important FP1 tomorrow; it will be key to getting this data between the two cars.' Spoken like a true engineer, the approach has to be methodical, step by step, in the quest to finish ahead of the McLarens.

Verstappen has not always been universally loved here, seen by locals as the vanquisher of home favourite Sergio Pérez, and the team is uncertain how he and Red Bull will be received after Checo was axed at the end of last season. Despite the fears, the response is universally warm, in part because, for once, Verstappen arrives here as the underdog with a 40-point deficit to make up on championship leader Piastri.

If he is feeling the pressure of a championship fight then he is not showing it. A small crowd gathers around the seating area snapping photographs of the Dutchman as we sit down to chat. Sipping from a can of Red Bull – a genuine fan of the drink, not just because of the millions it has given him – he has one leg on top of the other, the upper leg occasionally bouncing up and down in conversation; his hands and fingers are interlocked, at times opening up as if to add greater emphasis to the point he's making. He is bedecked in a Red Bull top, denim jeans and a branded cap with the number one on it, a reminder of his position in the sport and a number that he is aiming to hold on to for another season. He talks of matching Michael Schumacher as the only man in history to win a fifth straight world title as though little more than contemplating a morning walk in Mexico City's old quarter. 'I always said if we win it, great, it's always great to add another title but, at the same time, I don't need to in a sense. That takes a lot of pressure away. I also know from myself when I sit in the car, I will always maximise everything that I have.'

And yet despite the apparent nonchalance, he comes to Mexico reinvigorated following his title fight admission. After the Hungarian Grand Prix back in August, Verstappen publicly predicted he would not win another race and, after his home race in Zandvoort, had he given up on a title push? 'When you start going to 80, 90 points, 100 points four, five races ago, you think that's a big ask and also, with the way the performances were going, it was not looking very likely,' he admits. 'It's not like giving up as you're still trying to maximise the results that you get and if that's P3 or five or six, you just try and do the best you can.' Verstappen has been nigh-on perfect for the past four races. The problem is he knows he needs to continue in that vein to have even an outside chance of the title. 'Lately with the results we have it looks like we're back into it but, at the same time, I also know everything needs to go perfect to the end,' he says of the prospect of catching the two McLarens. 'But why not? It's a good task, we have fun, the pressure is not on us, we're enjoying what we're doing and we will give everything we have until the end. If it's enough that will be a brilliant story, if not we will still be proud. The upswing of performance is quite remarkable. And we will be very happy with what we have delivered.'

If he and the team were to pull it off it would surely be the greatest achievement of his career, eclipsing both the drama of the first title win over Lewis Hamilton in 2021 and the subsequent three titles to have followed in quick succession. He concedes it would be his biggest achievement in terms of a comeback but, regardless of what happens in the last four races, it won't be his number one accomplishment. Before answering, he takes another sip of Red Bull. 'I would still go for '23, winning that many races is always better than winning a few less. But at the end of the day, you have to appreciate every single year that you do if you win it or not.'

Verstappen is well aware he is taking all the plaudits for the race wins but also tries to deflect some of that adulation, explaining that the real secret to the upswing is the power of the collective. Asking him about the secret to his turnaround, he says: 'Teamwork. As you know for yourself from the beginning of the season, I would say the first half had some nice moments but mainly difficult moments with some tough races, and it was difficult to understand what was going on. To now have a bit of an upswing in performance and be a lot more competitive and finally be able to challenge again at the top is of course very important for the whole team, for our confidence as well. It just shows that what the whole team was working on is definitely paying off now.' He scoffs at the suggestion from Mekies that the Frenchman has had zero impact on the volte-face. The pair have created a good bond, spending 20 to 30 minutes each Thursday before a race weekend to talk in detail, and Verstappen, who loves the technical side of F1, relishes having an engineer's brain to pick. 'I disagree with the zero per cent,' he says, laughing. 'What's very nice to see with Laurent, he's one of the team and has an engineering background . . . it's good to have someone like that also asking questions to the engineering group and just sitting together and having more meetings and really going over things a bit more about how we can improve the situation or the car.'

Helmut Marko likes to say that a happy Max is a fast Max. While it's clear Verstappen is in a good place, he doesn't agree with Marko's take on his upswing in mood being aligned with track fortunes: 'I know from myself it doesn't matter if I'm first or fifth or whatever, I know when I sit in the car I will always give it everything I have. But naturally, yes, it's more enjoyable coming to a weekend and knowing you can fight for a win or not. So maybe the happiness in terms of coming to a weekend was not the same but I know that I was always giving it everything I had. It wasn't like I was slacking in the car while driving.'

Like Verstappen, Piastri may look relaxed on the surface and yet his results would suggest he is feeling the pressure of being the championship leader. Like teammate Norris, who admittedly pushed Verstappen at points last season, Piastri has never properly been in the title fight before. For his part, Verstappen remembers well the pressure of pushing for a first title win in 2021, thrillingly going down to the season finale. Can he harness that to his advantage, knowing what the McLaren pair might be feeling? 'I don't really think about what others feel or think,' he says. 'I know what I felt in '21 but, at the same time, I just need to focus on what we can control and that's the performance here of everyone and the car. I think then your hands are already quite full. I just live my life. I do my job, go home, come back and I know that I'll give it everything. I'm just very focused on my side of the garage.'

In contrast to Red Bull, McLaren have given their drivers equal billing and allowed them to fully race on track under their so-called Papaya Rules. And yet it is a ploy critics argue might derail both drivers' title ambitions. Put that to Verstappen and, with a mischievous smile, he says, 'I would hope so. That would be perfect for me. But time will tell, right? McLaren do things the way they want to do it. You can agree with it or not but that's not up to us. They are the boss. They do what they want and you have to appreciate that.'

Far more the diplomat than he was in his younger, more direct days, he is not about to have a dig at either driver. Who poses the bigger threat, Piastri as the points leader or Norris as the form driver of the McLaren pair? Verstappen won't bite: 'At the end of the day, it's in my own hands – if we're competitive enough and we keep winning, that should be enough,' he concludes. He is reluctant to pick the best driver on the grid beyond himself: 'If I name one driver, maybe another will get pissed off.' So what would he take from certain individuals to create the perfect driver? Fidgeting with the can next to him, he insists, 'I don't really admire anything specifically,' he says, before more generously observing all are potential world champions of the future.

There are five race weekends remaining to decide the identity of the 2025 world champion. So what if anything will derail his bid for the title? Intriguingly, it is neither of the McLaren drivers that spring to mind but, instead, 'bad luck'. He adds: 'I mean you can have a crash, you can get hit, you can have a puncture, you can have an untimely safety car, you can get sick, you can slip in the shower and break your leg, anything can happen, right? I don't know. I don't want to think about it too much. I just come here and I hope that we can have a strong weekend again, which of course will help for the championship.' And will he make it title number five? He shrugs his shoulders as if to back up his point and says, 'It's not about if I will win it or not. I know that when I jump in the car, I will give it everything I have and that's the only thing I can do.'

30

MEXICO MAYHEM

Ricardo Rodríguez was the youngest man in Formula 1 history to compete in a Grand Prix when Ferrari gave the Mexican teenager a guest drive for them in 1961. Rodríguez qualified a surprise second for the race, making him the youngest driver to start on the front row of the grid until Verstappen beat him to that particular accolade at the 2016 Belgian Grand Prix. A year after that Ferrari drive, Rodríguez, earmarked by many as a future world champion, tragically lost his life at his home race during practice for the first ever Mexican Grand Prix at the new Magdalena Mixhuca circuit while driving a Lotus-24 Climax. 'Little Ricky' as he was known was tearing towards Peraltada corner, failed to brake sufficiently and crashed into the wall. The impact of the accident threw him out of the car and he died on his way to hospital, having suffered a fractured neck and skull.

His brother Pedro immediately announced his retirement from racing, although went back on that decision in due course, and the circuit was named in his sibling's honour before changing to Autodromo Hermanos Rodríguez after a double family tragedy when Pedro died racing in Germany in 1971. On lap 12 of a non-F1 race in Norisring, West Germany, he lost control of his car, careened into a concrete wall and the car burst into flames. He was resuscitated three times before eventually being declared dead. With no Mexican drivers for the fans to cheer, that year's Mexican Grand Prix was cancelled and it did not return to the calendar until 1986 when Gerhard Berger won. Its stint on the calendar was short-lived, removed after 1992 with the track in an increasing state of disrepair. Following a lengthy and costly upgrade including a new pit building, VIP area, a total resurfacing of the track and the iconic stadium section Foro Sol (literally sun forum) being incorporated into the track, F1 returned there in 2015 when Nico Rosberg, starting the trend of the race winner, wore a giant, black sombrero on the podium.

Built to host concerts, where the likes of Paul McCartney and Madonna have performed, Foro Sol also doubled up as a baseball stadium from 2000 until it morphed into becoming the most iconic part of this particular F1 circuit. Mexican fans, despite having no home driver to support this season, still flock here in their thousands and, if not in the colours of their favourite team, adorned in masks and makeshift marigold necklaces purchased from the countless vendors dotted around the circuit's perimeter. Collectively, they make a noise that even the drivers can hear inside their noisy cockpits. It is at Foro Sol where the drivers are serenaded post-race in one of the most visually spectacular sites on the calendar. Needing perfection, as he puts it, between now and the season's end, Verstappen envisages himself lapping up the applause for the fourth time in five seasons.

At a point in the season where every second on the car is vital, it is not ideal that Verstappen is left to sit out FP1 in Mexico, part of the deal teams have with the sport's rule-makers to run younger drivers in certain practice sessions over the course of the season. For Red Bull, though, it is vital, as Arvid Lindblad, a candidate for a race seat at Racing Bulls next season, needs to be assessed behind the wheel of an F1 car. This is effectively his final audition for a seat at the sister team. Verstappen opts to watch the hour-long session from the pit wall, plugged into the team radio to see if he can ascertain anything from how the car is working. After the hour, Verstappen is clearly sufficiently content before getting in the car for FP2. Finally, the car is working to his liking. The secret is the upgrades that have enabled him to run the car in a different configuration meaning he can push the tyres more thoroughly, giving him more faith in the car and greater pace.

Inside the garage for the session, clear pots arrive with high-vis paint which is applied to two main parts of the car: the rear wing and the side to test the aerodynamic efficiency of the new tweaks. After each run, either Paul Monaghan or the team's chief mechanic Phil Turner then take videos of the paint, which are shared on team WhatsApp groups for others back at the factory to investigate and see whether proposed upgrades are working on the car as they should. They are not, the simulation model not in line with the reality on track.

For the first race since the Monza rebirth, Verstappen finds he is struggling for grip, repeatedly complaining over the radio that it feels like he is driving on ice. He complains of the car jumping at turns three and five, and stepping out at turn six. 'Don't get heated,' comes the reply from GP over the radio, while Verstappen says, 'It's literally driving on ice.' It ends with GP telling Max, 'OK, jump out' and the engineer is gone from the garage before a confab between Verstappen, Mekies and Marko begins at the back of the garage. It is the first sign of negativity within the camp for weeks. Is there a fear that the title battle they have fought so hard to be a part of is once more slipping away from them?

FP2 starts with him showing quick pace over one lap but, over the longer runs, the rear tyres in particular are losing grip and a balance needs to be found. By FP3 the following day, no solution is found. Verstappen qualifies in fifth place, his lowest starting position for six races, while Lando Norris is half a second faster on pole. The only saving grace is that championship leader Piastri sits two places behind Verstappen on the grid after struggling to match his pace of earlier in the season.

The championship aside, the other buzzword of the weekend beyond the drivers' championship is 'tape-gate', a rivalry of an altogether different kind with McLaren. For a few Grands Prix now, McLaren have put silver masking tape on the pit wall to act as an additional marker for Norris to align his car for a Grand Prix start. Having clocked this, Red Bull have set out to sabotage that tape. The first time in Monza they successfully removed it but other attempts have since been foiled. On one occasion, a member of Red Bull staff pulled up the tape only to find another bit of tape with the words BETTER LUCK NEXT TIME on it. Other McLaren efforts to foil the sabotage have included putting someone there to guard the tape – the rear jack-man from their pit crew – or else placing tape down that only partially tears off in its removal.

At the preceding race in Austin, it finally reaches a head as Red Bull fall foul of the FIA when an offending arm belonging to a Red Bull team member reaches over to remove the tape just as a gate from the pit wall to the track is shut on said arm. The motorsport governing body don't take safety lightly, nor the potential for the race to be delayed. With the team's head of sporting Steve Knowles having already left for the airport following the race, Mekies is summoned by the FIA to answer their charge, the result being the team is hit with a €50,000 fine, half of it suspended. The FIA take it seriously while there are members of both the McLaren and Red Bull hierarchy who don't take kindly to the tongue-in-cheek incidents that most of the paddock see as amusing. It is all part of F1's gamesmanship between two teams fighting for the championship and, what has become a more common lexicon in sport, 'shithousery' on the part of Red Bull. Following the latest twist in the rivalry between the two teams, there are jokes within the Red Bull garage of putting up posters, one with WANTED with the face of the tape-gate accused or else another of one of the McLaren drivers with the words LANDO PARK HERE. But the message is clear from the FIA not to repeat it, ending a fun interaction between two teams trying to seek any advantage possible as they enter the business end of the season.

If Mekies is feeling the pressure of the championship fight, he is not showing it. Even in conversation over a coffee pre-race it's like he's multitasking, his great brain whirring over. A walk down the paddock is a long one with him, flitting from French to English to Italian as he greets everyone with a warm smile. He wears two watches and a series of cotton bracelets. One watch tells the time, the other a smart watch marking his step count and heart rate, both of which must be formidable, bearing in mind the manner in which he works. In conversation, he fidgets a bit with his watches or his wedding ring, which he takes off and plays with nervously. He's quick to stroke his beard and moustache, and he's quick in the way he thinks and talks. There is a less combative feel to the team with Mekies at the helm – the Frenchman is a hugger not a fighter. Was the former boss's pugnacious nature a strength or a weakness for the team? Probably both. Horner had a remarkable ability to work a room at a Grand Prix weekend. Be it an interview or sponsor meet-and-greet, he would need no briefing beforehand, partly down to 20 years of experience in the role. Mekies, every bit the engineer, is a details man. He likes everything spelled out for him, a document of who he is meeting and key points to mention. He has a remarkable ability to retain all the information, never forgets a face and he appears to be universally liked, not always a common feature in the F1 paddock.

The team is aware the reason for the fallback is down to a wrong set-up, but it is not one that can be rectified between qualifying and the race, with the cars in parc fermé and therefore the mechanics not able to work on them unless they choose to start at the back of the pack from the pit lane. Within moments of the race start, Verstappen finds himself four abreast going down the home straight against the two Ferraris of Charles Leclerc and Lewis Hamilton and the Mercedes of George Russell. As the quartet approach turn one Verstappen has no choice but to take evasive action, leave the track and rejoin it. Russell, who later describes the race as akin to lawnmower racing, repeatedly remonstrates over the team radio over the advantage Verstappen has gained. Under the current rules, teams now have a lap to decide whether they need to give a place back if an advantage is unfairly gained. With the Autodromo Hermanos Rodríguez being one of the shorter tracks on the calendar Knowles has about 80 seconds in which to watch footage and make a call to his team about what to do, with all manner of voices in his ear during those few seconds. His thinking is that Verstappen entered the corner in third and rejoined the race in fourth and, while Russell may have been the unlucky recipient in that quarter, he argues to keep position as nothing has been gained. Laps later, the race stewards concur. It is the same as Verstappen and Hamilton later bang wheels – echoes of their 2021 title battle in that moment – again Knowles concluding no wrongdoing on the part of his driver. In this case, neither man is penalised.

The on-track bumper cars aside, Verstappen is on the back foot. He has started the race on the medium tyres, unlike most of the grid. There is a fear by some at Red Bull that they may have made the wrong call but Hannah Schmitz on the pit wall and Will Courtenay back in the ops room in the UK are confident in their call. It is only when Verstappen begins his stint on the soft tyres that that becomes clear.

Scything his way through the field, he picks off rivals on the mediums with ease and his pace – lap after lap – leaves his Red Bull team once again in disbelief. GP occasionally dips into the team radio to give his driver a further lift, describing his pace as 'insane' and later adding 'this is why we go racing' as, having climbed up to third, he begins his efforts to reel in Leclerc in second. GP never pre-plans what he is going to say to his driver, just going for it in the moment, and the positive spins are generally well received, Verstappen not like others on the grid in telling his race engineer to shut up. There is a moment of levity, which highlights his innate ability to multitask at pace, when somehow the team radio falters and GP goes out on two different channels. The Briton is heard as saying, 'Yes, so are we on a one-stop or two-stop? Right, OK,' before his driver quips, 'I can hear everything.' With two laps remaining, Verstappen is within DRS range of Leclerc only for a virtual safety car (VSC) to be implemented following Carlos Sainz's late off. It is universally seen as a conservative call by the team and one that potentially denies P2, which the team is highly confident Verstappen would have sealed, such was the charge. And despite the what-might-have-been, there is a general sense of positivity of a podium finish that had perhaps looked unachievable at one stage of what has been a difficult weekend.

The only despondent figure is GP, who traipses from the garage to the team's makeshift base deflated and defeated. His argument is that, while Verstappen has cut the championship lead by four points, he now has sizeable gaps to make up on two drivers rather than just one. A week ago, Verstappen had pointed out Red Bull needed to be perfect, and the weekend has been far from that. For GP, the title fight feels over. 'We'd been on a relatively positive run before that weekend,' he says. 'In all honesty, we were demolished on Sunday. Lando was well over 20 seconds ahead at the end of the race. Bearing in mind we're self-critical and particularly hard on ourselves when we win a race, when we have an outcome like that, it's no time to smile, in my eyes at least. Maybe that was a bit of a setback, the end of race VSC which cost us three points to Charles Leclerc, who ended up finishing second ahead of us.' For others on the ground, and for GP when given time to reflect on the flight back home that night, it is anything but.

In the aftermath, Verstappen is cheered at Foro Sol while

race winner and new championship leader Norris is booed, a contrast to times past where the Dutchman was often seen as the villain. As the hunter combined with the team's never-give-up mentality, there appears to be a greater appreciation from fans of the sport towards him. Verstappen's manager Raymond Vermeulen, fiercely protective of his driver, has noticed the change in outlook. 'I think he's getting more respect now by what he's doing on the track with a car that limits performance now and then,' he says. 'He takes everything out of the car. I think people are getting to understand him. Max is the boy next door, what you see is what you get. He's a pure racer and he will defend every inch on track and, if he sees a gap, he will go for it. I think people understand a little bit more about Max the racer.'

31

ENGINEERING
A MOVE

The eyes, ears and brains of Max Verstappen's race operation are his four trackside engineers, headed by Gianpiero Lambiase, each one a very different character and each with different roles for car number one. Soon, of that quartet, only GP will remain. In the final throes of the 2025 season it emerges that Verstappen's performance engineer Tom Hart will be leaving to join Williams. Of the others, Michael Manning had already announced at the end of the previous year he was leaving to seek a new challenge while David Mart is heading to Aston Martin for their first season with Honda, whose engines have powered Red Bull to such good effect. Restructuring a team of trackside engineers with the necessary knowledge is no mean feat, unsettling for Verstappen already at a time of major change going into 2026.

Manning has been in the role since 2011, having guided Sebastian Vettel previously; Hart became performance engineer for the 2020 season while Mart rejoined Red Bull in

March, 2022, having had a stint with engine supplier Honda. Red Bull are victims of the joint success of Verstappen and his engineers but also by the fact that there is not an obvious step-up for many of them in the team. Of the band being broken up, Lambiase says: 'Being in a team like this with the level of success we've had over recent years, you have to expect that. And our planning is not about looking 12 months into the future, it's about ensuring stability and security three to five years if not more down the line. So, the team is incredibly strong in terms of the support we have back at the factory, we have great strength in depth and, while it wasn't a particular surprise that there's going to be one or two leavers, I think we're well covered and well placed to make this a seamless transition.'

Hart, a West Ham season-ticket holder who goes to Premier League games when the crowded F1 calendar allows, typically stands in the garage throughout each session to the left of a seated Helmut Marko. A mechanical engineering student, he joined the team as a graduate and steadily climbed up the ranks. The softly spoken, occasionally bespectacled Englishman is effectively GP's right-hand man on the engineering side, looking at everything and anything performance-related on Verstappen's car. He will pore over the telemetry throughout the entire Grand Prix weekend. Away from the track, he forms a formidable padel doubles partnership with Steve Knowles.

Sitting in the engineering office for a race are Verstappen's other two trackside engineers: Manning and Mart. Formerly of Jordan, Midland, Force India and Team Lotus, Manning joined Red Bull 14 years ago and has worked with Verstappen throughout his time at the team. Manning, who hails from a farm in Cork, Ireland, is the senior trackside control engineer, so his remit involves gear-shifts, the complex steering wheel and the vital race starts. Mart is Verstappen's trackside power unit engineer, so everything relating to the engine, engine recovery system and the like. A quirk of Mart is that he cycles to and from the racetrack on almost every Grand Prix weekend. His role is different to some engineers in that he has to be in constant contact with a string of engineers at power-unit supplier Honda in Tokyo, the communication done via WhatsApp as the Japanese engineers' English is often better written rather than spoken. A key part of his job is to ascertain if there are any issues with the unit and how Verstappen can best harness power out on track. He generally only tends to hear from his driver if something has gone wrong. Hart, Manning and Mart are on a separate channel on the team radio and, in turn, feed into GP, who decides what information is critical to relay to their driver.

No engineering set-up is the same. Each team has their own way of doing things and each driver their preferred approach. Verstappen is the kind of driver who wants as much data in the cockpit as possible, such is his ability to multitask. But he is less bothered about his driving compared to those of his rivals at particular sections of the track, as he has an innate confidence in his own ability. In contrast, Vettel would like sheets of paper laying out what his rival drivers were doing and where at specific corners of a Grand Prix track to ascertain if there was any way in which he could improve. Quite what the impact will be on Verstappen losing three of his four engineer musketeers will become clearer through the course of next season. Any effect is aided by the fact Hart will see out the 2026 season with the team as he works out his notice. Throughout it all, the key, constant figure in GP remains.

Ferrari driver Charles Leclerc has a journal he calls 'Words of Wisdom' detailing some of the quirkier exchanges with his race engineer Bryan Bozzi. At the season start when he complained his racing seat was full of water, Bozzi replied, 'It must be the water.' It went straight into the book. Exchanges between drivers and their engineers are a feature of each televised Grand Prix weekend. The conversations can be tetchy, humorous and sometimes downright bizarre. They can reveal a lot about both personalities and, to some degree, the inner workings of that pairing but also the wider team. The role of a race engineer is effectively to get the best possible performance from both the driver and the car. They should, in theory, be the only voice a driver hears from lights to chequered flag, although occasionally a team principal might chime in. Engineers have to be concise with their information and decide in the heat of battle what is critical for their charge to hear. In turn, the feedback they'll get from their driver over the course of a race weekend they then have to translate into potential set-up decisions.

Few pairings have entertained more over the years than Verstappen and Lambiase, now into their 10th season working together. Lambiase's face will be familiar to many F1 fans, his voice even more so with the usual request of 'box, box' in order for his driver to pit. Race engineers often need a rhino-like skin to deal with some of the invective that comes their way from Formula 1 drivers. GP has had his fair share of abuse down the team radio in his decade working with Verstappen but is both experienced and feisty enough to hit back. There's no shortage of greatest hits between them. At the 2023 Qatar Grand Prix, Verstappen defied GP's wishes to do a second push lap. After doing so came the question, 'Did you learn anything?', 'Not really' came the reply to which GP curtly said, 'Well done.' Belgium of that year was another stand-out. After Verstappen just snuck into Q3 in qualifying, he moaned he should have done two push laps as he'd recommended, with GP essentially observing no harm done as he'd qualified. A frustrated Verstappen responded: 'I don't give a fuck, I'm through in P10. It's just shit execution.' He later apologised once he'd calmed down, to which GP said, 'Slowly getting used to it, Max.' Theirs historically has been less words of wisdom, more often a war of words. Christian Horner once said they were like an old married couple who occasionally needed counselling and once had to step in as a peacekeeper with ice lollies after one particularly heated exchange.

GP began his career in Germany for a Formula 3 team before its owner was part of the buyout of Eddie Jordan's eponymous team, and his F1 career began in 2005 as a data engineer. He was brought in by Red Bull to become Vettel's engineer but then Vettel left for Ferrari, so instead he did the role for Daniil Kvyat. When the Russian was replaced by Verstappen, he began working with the then 18-year-old and the odd couple have been inseparable ever since. GP remembers being blown away by his young charge in the simulator with how quickly he could pick things up. He wasn't confident that would translate to the racetrack but it resulted in a first F1 win for both of them in their first race together. Verstappen has grown up and matured massively in the intervening decade. The tetchy exchanges have become less but neither pay any attention to them when they do happen, knowing from both sides it is just frustration spilling over from their combined competitiveness and perfectionism. They are remarkably similar characters in many ways and, for whatever reason, the partnership works to an extent that Verstappen has said his F1 career would end if he didn't have GP as his race engineer. And that competitiveness translates to the padel court, too, where they make another formidable doubles pairing, although GP is the more skilled of the pair, much to his driver's annoyance.

In 2022, Lambiase was promoted to the role of head of race engineering, and this season he is now head of racing to partially fill the void left by the exit of former sporting director and team manager Jonathan Wheatley. Lambiase remains Verstappen's race engineer in 2025 but is also responsible for the race team, the car build team and the heritage team that does show runs across the globe in former Red Bull Racing cars.

Of the secret to his partnership with Verstappen, he says: 'Trust is absolutely paramount. You need to be able to be completely open and honest with each other. From a human side there is that aspect, then trust in the capability of the engineer that a driver has in him. Fortunately for me, we kind of hit it off on both fronts and built a really good dynamic. I think we work really well together. We're pretty straightforward. There's no holding back in any of our work.' As for any abuse, it's water off a duck's back: 'As an engineer, you need to understand it's the driver that's in the hot seat, the pressure cooker. His adrenaline is running a lot higher than yours. Normally an engineer is that little bit older and experienced and mature. It's down to the engineer to try to bite his or her lip and keep a calm head. You just cannot make it evident that you want to throttle him in real time. It's not just in terms of professionalism but it doesn't get anything out of that driver in that moment. You save that for behind closed doors. We thrash it out in the office or away from the track and then regroup for the next race. And as a race engineer you have to be calm because there are high-pressure decisions to be made. If you're letting your thoughts run away with you or your anger or frustration sets in then you don't make the right decisions.'

As for what it entails to be a good racing engineer, Lambiase says it's getting into the driver's head and seeing a situation from their point of view. He adds: 'We look at all these weird and wonderful squiggly lines on our computers and we can optimise it to the last thousandth of a second or beyond and you can be a real scientist about it, but I think what makes a good race engineer is to put yourself in the driver's shoes: what does this one thousandth of a second mean to him, is it even conceivable that he can try to extract it or could you be putting yourself in a position by trying to achieve this you're knocking him back by half a tenth?'

As the race engineer, GP has a far more layered role than it might seem on the surface: psychologist, counsellor, cheerleader. And in his new role as head of racing overseeing race operations and logistics in 2025, he is more directly in contact with the other race engineer Richard Wood, who carries out the same role for Yuki Tsunoda.

The Scot has the sort of calming voice you'd imagine would be perfect in the heat of a tense race although he admits Tsunoda had a hard time understanding him initially. 'With the driver you have to be calm as they're reacting to your energy,' he says. 'If you're animated, they'll become panicked.

I try to slow my speech down. If you can control that situation even if things go wrong, staying calm is the biggest thing.'

Like Verstappen, Tsunoda can be emotive in the cockpit and Woody, as he's known in the team, has had a few choice words thrown at him. Despite Tsunoda's reputation for bad language, the Scot says: 'I think he's worked really hard to control himself. You have to remember English is not his first language and he learned that language at the racetrack from mechanics and engineers. And anyway, drivers say what they mean and they don't have time to consider it under the helmet.'

Like the other engineer–driver duo in the garage, the pair are a strong padel team, which has helped them bond. He says: 'Compared to GP and Max – they're 10 years into their relationship – you've got a high bar to work against. We're always learning, you're growing, you learn something every weekend, what he likes, what he doesn't like, what he needs what he doesn't need, what I need. There's an initial rapport and there's got to be a relationship at the start. You don't have to have common interests or be best buddies but you need to have a mutual understanding, kind of know how their minds are working and what they're thinking. Pre-empting what they're thinking comes in time. If you can pre-empt what they think, you can answer more easily.' As for the driver change after a winter spent working with Lawson, he has adapted quickly. Going back to early in the season, he remembers: 'After China, hearing the news later that week, it was like, *here we go starting from scratch*. Normally, you have a couple of months in the off-season to work with a driver, settling in – we had four days. So that was quite a quick turnaround. It was just another race event with the pressure of time.

I enjoyed it in a masochistic kind of way. You can't just say "please delay the race by one weekend". It's a lot of learning as you go.'

There are some within Red Bull who suggest its engineers are as competitive as the drivers, be that on the racetrack or the padel court. Lambiase readily admits he is super-competitive: 'I'm probably not the best loser, but upon reflection, I am then able to accept not winning and appreciate the efforts of others. We are just passionate about what we do and set ourselves an extremely high level of expectation, and the challenge is to try to operate at that level at all times.' While GP very much wears his heart on his sleeve in defeat, he says there is nothing better than when working in symmetry with his driver. 'When everything's working perfectly, everything is in sync, Max is driving his socks off, we're on top of the tyres, the balance, giving each other information about where we should be going with strategy, keeping on top of the situation with our competitors, keeping the situation open in terms of the overall race, it just comes so naturally,' he says. 'The race is an hour and a half but it seems to last like 10 or 15 minutes. Come the chequered flag you really don't want it to be over. So those days are really, really enjoyable. But sadly they're too few and far between.'

32

THE WONDER DRIVE

Last year's São Paulo Grand Prix and the great escape is still fresh in the minds of Red Bull staff. All have their own recollections of Max Verstappen's miraculous drive from 17th on the grid to take the win. The hope is he won't need such a Houdini act on the return to Interlagos. He won't be drawn on whether it ranks as his best race ever but, heading into the weekend, he at least concedes it's 'one of my best', and yet the perfectionist behind the steering wheel is always aspiring for more. Perfection is still the quest in the championship fight, not quite attained in Mexico but captured at some of the preceding races. Mexico City felt like damage limitation, now Brazil feels like a must-win – both the sprint and Sunday's race. But alarmingly, FP1 is a return to engineers needing to find solutions to fix the car and mechanics having to tinker to make the relevant corrections in a race against time. In a season of occasional guesswork, sometimes it has worked, sometimes it hasn't.

The headaches aren't immediate, initially the team seem

relatively at ease with the way the car is behaving in FP1 but still make a couple of set-up changes for sprint qualifying, which is when things start to go wrong – and fast. Verstappen is immediately unhappy with the car. In sectors one and three of the circuit he is a match for McLaren's pace but, in the middle of the three sectors, he loses nearly half a second. Extracting everything he can from the car he is only able to qualify a paltry sixth for the sprint race. A repeat of leading every lap of the sprint race, as achieved in the last two shortened versions, is now an impossibility. Verstappen complains of vibrations in the car and ride problems, a lack of grip, and the 'middle sector is terrible' to the extent he says he can't even turn the car. And he has no faith in the rear. The one blessing is a cyclone is predicted with an estimated 30 to 60 millimetres of rain in an hour combined with high winds. Could it scupper the race altogether or negate the advantage of the others and enable him to pull off a comeback akin to last year's main race? 'I don't know,' he confesses to gathered reporters. 'We'll find out. It's quite clear we are lacking something and I'm not expecting that suddenly to be miles better in the wet, but we'll see tomorrow.' As for Tsunoda, he crashes into the barriers in FP1, leading to a hefty workload by his mechanics to repair it.

Red Bull would dearly love two more practice sessions in which to rectify their issues rather than sprint qualifying and the sprint race. Pierre Waché, whose responsibility it is to find a solution, is at a loss. 'We are looking into a lot of things overnight to see if we need to change something,' he says. 'It was a difficult day today. To be honest, the sprint format always throws up challenges across the weekend. The car isn't behaving as we expected here, especially on the soft tyre.

On that compound, the car feels like something is wrong with it and is not performing properly. We are looking into many things to see if we need to make changes. We're investigating what the issue is – it's affecting both cars – and we're aiming to have the car in a better window for the rest of the weekend.'

In what proves to be a cyclone-free race, Verstappen pushes up to fourth, in part helped by Oscar Piastri crashing out early on. It brings out a red flag during which there is a terse exchange between Verstappen and GP when the driver is advised on how to improve the car. The frustration of a title fight ebbing away is being felt by everyone. Verstappen needs to recapture that winning sequence he strung together in the wake of the summer break or else see the McLarens disappear into the distance.

If the sprint feels bad, qualifying for the main Grand Prix is diabolical. Further changes to the car have a catastrophic effect and the best intentions by the likes of Waché and GP backfire spectacularly. The unthinkable happens as Verstappen is out in Q1. Seconds after watching from the team garage, his father Jos turns away in disgust. It is the only time on pace terms alone that Verstappen has failed to get out of Q1 in his F1 career. With Tsunoda also not making it through, it is the first time no Red Bull has made it out of Q1 since the Japanese Grand Prix in 2006. Verstappen complains of having to under-drive the car, an approach that understandably doesn't work when trying to extricate maximum pace over a single qualifying lap. 'I don't really understand how it can be this bad,' he says, at a total loss for any form of solution. As for his championship challenge, he waves the white flag: 'We don't need to talk about the championship anymore. That's done. We had to be perfect until the end and today was, of course, far from that.' Perhaps most striking is the fact Verstappen cannot come up with any solution, such is his usual technical understanding and ability to adapt in the car. When asked in qualifying by GP how they can help from the pit wall, almost admitting defeat, Verstappen says simply that he doesn't know what to do.

Laurent Mekies holds his hands up to admit defeat. 'We have been unhappy with the car pretty much since we got here,' says the Frenchman. 'Nonetheless, we were at the point where we could not fight for the win. It's fair to say we took some risks before qualifying to try to see if we could put the car in a better place and it obviously went in the opposite direction. It's sometimes the price you pay when you take a risk.'

What can be done between now and the race? Verstappen says: 'There's so many things we need to get right. So we'll look overnight again, I guess to try something or understand something.' And yet it is the Red Bull way to take a risk even if it can occasionally blow up in their faces, as it has on this occasion.

The swagger with which Red Bull arrived at the track with a title shot still alive has totally evaporated. However, they have another attempt to get things right for the race. Will it be third time lucky? Rather than play it safe, they decide to throw the kitchen sink at it. As a result they break parc fermé rules and have to start from the pit lane, where Verstappen will be joined by Esteban Ocon – an irony that the top two from last year's race are the backmarkers from the start. The mechanics work tirelessly to install a new power unit and to revert the car to the pre-Mexico floor. They finally finish work on the overhaul at 10:30pm on Saturday night, a 15-and-a-half-hour day in all to get the new power unit installed and sort out the floor. All it leaves is the usual pre-race tinkering in the morning. No one knows for sure if it will have the desired effect but the engineers and mechanics feel confident. The Verstappen rebuild is the final throw of the dice. It could be worse than previously, it could be better – only time will tell.

Amid it all, the strategists, who shield themselves away from the problems of the car, have no idea how it might fare in the race. The plan is for a two-stop strategy, although the starting tyre choices of some rivals suggest a one-stop might also be a possibility. A three-stopper certainly isn't on the cards. From the pit lane, Verstappen charges up to 13th place only to be undone by a front-right puncture from debris on the track. The virtual safety car limits the damage of needing to pit – halving the pit-stop time lost to his rivals – and enables him to get rid of the hard tyres which are not working for Verstappen.

When Norris pits for the second time, somehow Verstappen is in the race lead but on medium tyres that are beginning to wear. In case it goes unnoticed by the driver, GP says over the radio: 'Something I didn't think I'd say, Max, at the end of the pit lane earlier, you are now race leader,' to which Verstappen replies, 'Not bad.' Can he make the tyres last to the end or will he need to pit again? GP tells him on lap 49 that pitting for a third time on the softs is a possibility but says the team are still 'monitoring to see the fastest way to the end of the race'. Courtenay vacillates, such are the fine margins between the two decisions, first suggesting coming in, then recommending staying out before making the final call to pit. He and the team decide – a move later backed up by McLaren team principal Andrea Stella in his post-race interviews –

that they won't last. If Verstappen stays out, he could hold on to P2 if fortunate but the doomsday scenario is he might drop to fifth or sixth if the tyres fall away dramatically late in the race, an unthinkable and underserving outcome after such a remarkable drive. Verstappen comes in for soft tyres and the car again comes alive before he is warned the rubber will be vulnerable. His response is simply, 'We've got nothing to lose.' On lap 59, he is told P2 is on and he quickly eats into George Russell's lead before getting past him rapidly. Now the chase is on for the impressive Kimi Antonelli, himself targeting the highest finish of his nascent F1 career, and GP counts down each and every lap to his driver. Antonelli defends well in turns two and three to counter Verstappen's superior pace in turn four and, while he endures a late wobble to negate his advantage, it is too little too late to get past. Verstappen has to make do with third place, still no mean achievement. Speaking over his radio afterwards, Oliver Bearman, after a strong race himself in the Haas, says, 'Max, back to P3 that is fucking impressive.' It is just that.

In the immediate aftermath, there is much pondering on whether the late pit stop was the right call – was it too conservative and did it deny a better shot at P2? The team will never know. Differences of opinion are exchanged but, while some might be down – GP again – others are not, Verstappen included. 'I can only apologise for yesterday, mate,' says GP immediately after the chequered flag. 'That was a race-winning drive. Sorry.' But Verstappen responds: 'No, don't be. Really good race for us. We at least try. Thank you for today. I think that went really well, so thank you, everyone.' Mekies then chimes in: 'It may not be the win of last year but it looked as impressive from here. Well done. Never give up.' Verstappen has the final word over the radio: 'We keep pushing', and enters the subsequent engineering briefing upbeat and declaring to Courtenay the strategy call had been the right one.

For the McLarens, it is like their two drivers have switched cars. Where once Piastri didn't put a foot wrong, now the previously error-prone Norris is faultless once more to take the win. Red Bull aren't quite waving the white flag just yet – they won't until it's mathematically impossible – but now that they are the equivalent of two race wins behind they are preparing to hoist it. Norris is now 49 points clear of Verstappen and 24 ahead of teammate Piastri. It is his title to lose and yet there is a glimmer of hope: Verstappen and Red Bull have been the quickest car on the track.

Despite his win and the perfect weekend, Norris says: 'Seeing how quick Max was today, I'm pretty disappointed we weren't quicker. I need to go to the team now and see where we weren't quick enough. If Max had started a bit further up, he'd have won. They were quicker than us today.'

Verstappen and Red Bull are still in the heads of Norris and McLaren but just three races remain in the chase: Las Vegas, Qatar and Abu Dhabi.

33

WINNING BIG IN VEGAS

Under the bright lights of Las Vegas, Max Verstappen is desperately clinging to his world-title hopes. At the racetrack where a year ago he was crowned world champion for a fourth time the numbers say the opportunity still exists, although he has told team members behind closed doors his chance is over, with 49 points to make up to championship leader Lando Norris with just three races remaining. But he is not downhearted – far from it – instead buoyed by the team's remarkable change in fortunes, from a season fizzling out to one instead sparking back into life. He has been reinvigorated by the impact, something that feeds down to the rest of the track-team operation.

At Red Bull, the missed opportunities in Mexico and Brazil have not extinguished the desire, although one senior team member effectively concedes the title by saying, 'It's the hope that kills you.' The push is still there but, in reality, more for race wins than anything greater before the season reaches its conclusion. Of the three remaining races, Vegas is arguably Red Bull's best shot for a victory, potentially the last chance to put some gloss on a challenging year. The high-speed track should play to the team's strengths, but ask any team member on the Thursday before a wheel is turned how they'll fare and you get the same shrug, downturn of the mouth and look of uncertainty. No one can quite predict – the big unknown being how the Pirelli tyres will behave. A year ago in Vegas it was Mercedes who mastered that best and they've shown that at cooler tracks this season already. Therein lies the potential for old foe George Russell to further disrupt Verstappen in his bid to contemplate victory and the added bonus of clawing a few points back off the McLarens.

Norris looks to be disappearing into the distance in the drivers' championship following the last two race weekends, what Mekies looks back on as 'complicated races'. He adds: 'After Mexico, there's nothing we could have done to match Lando's pace,' before admitting Verstappen's race pace amid a difficult Brazil suggests he could well be a match for the McLarens in Sin City. Of Vegas, he says: 'The weekend's unique in many respects: a unique track layout, uniquely cold, it needs mastering tyres. It's a track where last year we struggled.'

The Las Vegas weekend begins with the emergence of Zak Brown's autobiography, *Seven Tenths of a Second*. The McLaren CEO's relationship with Red Bull and Christian Horner, in particular, is storied. The pair, once friends, have repeatedly clashed. Horner has always loved sparring with his rivals and getting a rise from them. Brown, along with perhaps Mercedes' Toto Wolff, have been perhaps the most outspoken rivals. Brown has not been afraid to stick the boot in since

Horner's exit in the week following the British Grand Prix and does so again on the pages of *Seven Tenths of a Second* in which he says Max Verstappen rather than Horner was the one calling the shots at Red Bull and had effectively become the de facto team boss. The American suggests everyone is subservient to Verstappen, people are fearful of him, the car is tailored to suit its star driver in a manner in which no one else can get a handle on it and that they tiptoe around him for fear he will take his obvious talents to a rival team. He accuses Red Bull of being a one-man team, an approach he says he will never follow.

He also accuses Horner of making unfounded allegations against McLaren during his tenure. Likening him and Horner to the racers they were in their younger days, he talks of drivers who would push rivals two wheels off the track and those that would go for the four-wheel shove. He concludes, 'Christian is a four-wheels-off guy,' and effectively says the same about Verstappen, calling him a 'bruiser, too aggressive on track'. But he later backtracks in his Vegas media sessions, instead remarking it was meant as a compliment and likening him to his idol, Ayrton Senna. He seeks out Verstappen to explain as much. Brown's words have little effect on either driver or Red Bull staff. They are aware of them but they don't rattle or rile, if anything they like that they can still get in his head even without Horner at the helm and Brown enjoying a good relationship with Mekies. In any case, the attention is instead on the racing rather than getting caught up in any sort of war of words.

Las Vegas is a bizarre place and a bizarre race. A manufactured city in the Nevada desert, this is every bit the manufactured racetrack but, when filmed overhead, it is visually spectacular. During each day of a race weekend, regular cars drive around much of the track, which is mostly open roads. By night, the place is closed off and comes alive. Central to it is the Sphere, usually a music venue but lit up in an array of dazzling colours. One minute it is a racing helmet, the next a WELCOME TO LAS VEGAS sign or else a giant advertising hoarding. Like Monaco, it is a must-see, must-be-seen event. The MGM Grand and other hotels that hug the outside of the racetrack fill towards capacity over the course of the weekend and there is a lively buzz in the city that never sleeps. At all times of day the casinos are busy, but this weekend its users are often bedecked in a McLaren top or a Red Bull cap. For visitors and residents alike, it is the weekend's talking point.

This paddock is particularly bizarre compared to others on the calendar. At one end just after Gordon Ramsay's restaurant – a cooking opportunity with Yuki Tsunoda is called off when Ramsay is held up in a monster passport queue – sits the Little Neon Chapel. It is a bright pink makeshift place of worship with three rows of seats, and outside stands an Elvis Presley lookalike. Here, couples are encouraged to renew their wedding vows in front of 'Elvis' and then have their photo taken holding a fake bouquet before climbing into a giant pink car made entirely out of Lego. That will later be driven by the actor Terry Crews with the race's one-two-three looking a little bemused sitting in the back. Ex-F1 world champion Jacques Villeneuve was among those to tie the knot here on a previous year. Mickey Mouse occasionally walks up and down the paddock with his Disney friends and he too will have a later role to play in the post-race celebrations outside the Bellagio Hotel. Members of the Blue Man Group

– faces painted to match the name – pop up suddenly on the shoulders of unsuspecting racegoers, there are two women dressed head to toe as disco balls, dancers on stilts and more Elvises. Being Vegas, no one bats an eyelid. This is a city and race weekend where anything goes and the celebrities lap it up. Beyoncé is among those in attendance, being driven by Lewis Hamilton for a hot lap of the circuit, so too the musician Travis Scott, the tennis player Taylor Fritz and more high-profile DJs than seems possible for one venue.

There is a buzz about Red Bull. Hordes gather outside their hospitality suite constantly, the Netflix cameras are in with their focus on Mekies all weekend, and it is a bizarre sight to see him have this film crew shadow him all weekend long. He does not enjoy the constant spotlight as Horner did before him, although that may come in time, but he barely pays it attention. His main focus is on a car that is not requiring quite the same dramatic overhaul as in Brazil.

We are in the heart of the desert and locals tell visitors it never rains here but that it has been pouring recently. Had the race been scheduled for earlier in the week it would likely have been called off, such were the dire conditions and resulting flooding. And it starts with a modicum of doubt whether the action could be curtailed at any point. A called-off race would be dire for Verstappen and Red Bull in the quest to claw back points. There is rain just before FP2, meaning teams are reluctant to initially send out their drivers, and then delays over a loose manhole cover resulting in drivers being unable to get any clear information on their tyre wear on the high-fuel runs that emulate that of the race. As Mekies puts it, 'It's frustrating not to have a reference point to our competitors.' And no information is garnered from a qualifying session which is wet throughout. First, drivers are on the extreme wets and then the inters and, in the mêlée of it all, it is Norris who comes out on top with a breathlessly quick lap to best Verstappen. But there are races where P2 can sometimes be better than P1 for the start, as odd as that sounds. It puts Verstappen on the left side of the racetrack for the Sunday, and advantage as he has the inside line. The mood is good in the Red Bull camp. As Mekies reflects later, despite sitting in P2, he, Verstappen and the rest of the team feel comforted by the car at their disposal going into the race.

Race day dawns with high expectations at Red Bull but still with much unknown. How will the tyres fare, will there be graining in the colder temperatures, can McLaren carry over their pace in the damp to the dry, and will Russell's race pace be better than he showed in qualifying? The unanswerable make for a potentially thrilling race and a three-way battle between Verstappen, Norris and Russell. Red Bull pore over all manner of possibilities. They run numerous simulations for a race weekend to work out the best approach. When it comes down to it, their pre-race selection is for a one-stop strategy for Verstappen, starting on the medium tyres and changing to the hard when required. For Tsunoda, the approach chops and changes until the day of the race when the likes of Hannah Schmitz, Tsunoda himself, his engineers and Mekies meet to talk about possible options. Talk turns to what level of risk they are willing to take and the decision is to pit Tsunoda on lap one and effectively leave him to do the entire race on a single set of tyres, which the team are confident is possible. Plus, there is the back-up option of another set of hard tyres should that go awry.

Going into the race, there is still a strategy unknown for

Verstappen. Speaking just an hour beforehand, Schmitz says: 'I think we're going to one-stop, but one thing we don't know is when the graining will occur. If that starts on, say, lap eight, we know we're more likely to be two-stopping. We're very open to both strategies here. Max has still got an outside chance in the drivers' championship, so it's about the risk we're willing to take at this stage to try and basically win the race. As underdog, we have a slight advantage as we're the ones who can take more risk and the person leading should be more conservative.'

Further up the field, no one quite knows for sure what Norris will do at the start. A sensible approach with his 24-point lead over Piastri would perhaps be conservative, knowing Verstappen, with nothing to lose, will be all-out attack at the start. But the Briton rips up any pre-race predictions of that ilk, takes a leaf out of Verstappen's aggressive driving approach and cuts across him, the pair nearly colliding. But Norris then loses grip into turn one and drops behind not just Verstappen but Russell too. Mekies calls it 'defending very aggressively on Max in a way he normally doesn't'. He adds: 'He missed the braking point and the rest is history.' Russell challenges Verstappen in the dirty air, much to the surprise of Mekies and his team, and GP constantly tells his driver the gap to his chaser. By lap 22, Verstappen loses patience and asks for no more information about his rivals. Two laps later, Verstappen is told he doesn't even need to conserve his first set of tyres. 'Maximum pace now, Max,' comes the request, and he doesn't need a second invitation. At the halfway point, he pits and only comes out on track 1.3 seconds clear of Russell, but the challenge only lasts a few laps longer. There is another similar call to reduce all tyre management towards the end while Norris and Russell are struggling, the former with fuel usage and the latter with his steering. At the chequered flag, GP says simply: 'Too good, far too good,' to which the predictable response of 'simply lovely' comes, as well as congratulations all round. Even Mekies pipes up, telling his driver it is a 'masterclass of tyre management. A big well done.' Verstappen has been superb in managing his tyres, the conditions and his race pace.

Impressive as the win is, in the entertainment capital of the world, it is a dull race, but it just about keeps alive the championship with Verstappen now 42 points behind Norris, who finishes the race second, with two Grands Prix left. There's pats on the back all round at Red Bull and a brief celebration in front of the WELCOME TO LAS VEGAS sign just outside the paddock. As the pack-up operation begins, Red Bull aren't able to dismantle their car as it is held by race officials. Whispers quickly start to emerge in the Red Bull garage there might be a possible issue with Norris's car. The top three cars aren't released until the race result is made official and those whispers turn to reality as the FIA confirms it is investigating the legality of Norris's McLaren. Initially, Red Bull assume it is to do with fuel – drivers must have a minimum level of fuel left in their car at the end of a race in order for it to be measured for its legality by officials and, during the race, Norris had been told to lift and coast. But it transpires in an FIA announcement the skid block under Norris's car has been eroded by more than is allowed in the race. Such a rule is in place so that teams can only run so low. The lower the car goes, the quicker, but also it can reduce downforce and thereby put drivers at risk. When watching F1 on TV, when you see the sparks fly under the car that is the skid block hitting the track. It happens but it is effectively only allowed to happen so often. McLaren's error is unintentional, the FIA declares, and yet a line has still been crossed. The sanction for such a wrongdoing is a disqualification. And yet the minutes then hours pass and still no decision comes. When it is eventually delivered past one o'clock in the morning, it is a DQ for both Norris and Piastri. Red Bull have won big in Vegas and Verstappen, already aboard his private jet heading home, is level in the championship with Piastri and just 24 points behind Norris. A title race that had been in danger of being a Norris procession is very much back on.

Many of the track team relocate to Qatar the following day while Mekies heads back to the factory to share in the glory of the win with his wider staff and encourage one final push of an extraordinary season. After most Grand Prix weekends, Mekies, as Horner did before him, will host a debrief for staff. The sun is setting on a cold late-November afternoon just two days after Verstappen's victory on the Vegas street circuit as Mekies walks into a room at the back of MK-7, staff gradually entering the concrete-floored room behind him. At the entrance stands a table laden with opened bottles of Heineken as well as Rauch fruit juices – a nod to two of the team's key sponsors – for a celebration of Verstappen's latest success and win number six of 2025. Footage on screens to either side plays back the victory and the team boss arrives at a similar time to many of the early arrivals. Christian Horner liked to arrive last and stride up to the stage, in contrast Mekies, wearing a blue suit, mingles in short conversations with various members of staff inside a packed room where most are head to toe in their Red Bull outfits. After those clips of a winning weekend are played back, he takes to a small platform to address hundreds of his workforce.

'Very, very special win, a big well done, guys,' he opens with, which is greeted with warm applause around the room before hailing a dominant win. He talks about the struggles of Mexico and Brazil, the complexities of Vegas as a racetrack with its slippery surface and cold temperatures, and the great unknown going into the race, with running having been curtailed in practice and qualifying. 'Every time Max needed to push more he was able,' says the Frenchman, reflecting on the race. 'I think at some stage GP relayed to Max the message that McLaren had told Lando "let's go and get Max now". GP fired him up and Max made another statement. It's a proper sign of domination. We had two complicated races in Mexico and Brazil, and we're back here.'

After working his way through the entire race weekend from FP1, focus turns to the race itself when he and the team got an inkling it could be Verstappen's race, as much by what polesitter Norris was saying on his radio rather than anything else. 'Lando has spent half of the formation lap talking about Max,' he says. 'That last half of the formation lap he kept complaining about Max . . . and whatever imaginary rule,' cue laughter from those gathered in the room. But as if conscious of not wanting to put a rival down, he adds, 'Unlimited respect for the competition.' The chase from Russell followed, after which Verstappen made it look easy. A win was cause for celebration enough before, but as Mekies puts it exactly a month to the day, 'Christmas came a bit early', in the wake of the double DQ, which is followed by more chuckles around him. The effect of that has closed Verstappen to within a race win of Norris and, with McLaren no doubt fearful of a repeat,

Mekies argues they could be conservative going into the last race in Qatar. 'Maybe it will cost them a little more lap time,' he suggests.

Concluding, he adds: 'We are heading towards one of the most sensational final championships ever. Whatever happens next, it will remain an historic comeback. When it comes to the final word, I'm sure that despite the tiredness, you guys being stretched between the '25 and '26 programme as much as ever, I know we can count on everyone. We will reset again in Qatar. Qatar cannot be more different to Vegas. We'll give it our best shot on Sunday night.'

34

CALL ME CHUCKY

It's lap seven of the Qatar Grand Prix and Max Verstappen's championship hopes are once again dangling by a thread. Currently 25 points adrift following the sprint race, he knows he needs to finish ahead of Lando Norris to keep any title ambitions alive. Norris is perched behind him on track in a McLaren that has been quick all weekend, although polesitter Oscar Piastri, in the race lead, has been a class apart from first practice on the Friday and winning the earlier sprint race, a return to his form of earlier in the season. Verstappen has been saying he needs to be both error-free and have a little luck for title number five, and McLaren delivered just that in Vegas with their double disqualification.

Seven laps into this race, Nico Hülkenberg and Pierre Gasly go wheel to wheel in a battle for ninth place, as the German tries to go around the outside at turn two. They touch, causing Hülkenberg to spin off into the gravel trap, losing his right-rear tyre and bowing out of the race. Crucially, it brings out the safety car. Like other teams, Red Bull have already pored over the possibility of a pit stop and the earliest point they might pull the trigger. With a decree from tyre supplier Pirelli that tyres can only be used for a maximum of 25 laps over safety concerns, lap seven is the exact earliest moment where teams can stop – pitting under the safety car is quicker than in full race mode – and then pit again 25 laps later.

Hannah Schmitz makes her recommendation to pit and there is just enough time for a difference of opinion among the team's hierarchy before her colleagues on the wall nod their approval. 'We were happy as a team that it was the right thing to do,' she says in the race's aftermath. But when the leading McLaren of Piastri doesn't pit, nor the following Norris, Schmitz has a moment of doubt. 'We were quite clear that our safety-car window was going to open on lap seven,' she says. 'There's just such an advantage to pitting under the safety car. For us to make one of those stops at a much shorter pit-loss time it made sense, also given our position in the race and the fact we were between both McLarens. I thought maybe they'd not pit the tail car or something if they were open to splitting strategies. I didn't expect them to keep Piastri out.' So, when both McLarens stay out, she questions herself. Moments later, the rest of the grid bar Esteban Ocon come in to change their tyres leading to a collective sigh of relief among the Red Bulls, even more so when it becomes abundantly clear McLaren have made a costly mistake. It denies Piastri a much-needed race win, guides Verstappen to a seventh Grand Prix victory of 2025 and assures the championship battle will indeed go down to the 24th and final race of the season.

F1 strategists are few and far between so, despite the competition between them, there is also an element of sympathy for her opposite number at McLaren. 'It's always extremely easy with hindsight to say people made the wrong decision and messed up,' she says. 'But there will have been reasons why they made that decision at the time, I just don't know what they are.'

The crash, the safety car and the resulting pit stops create a bizarre situation in that everyone knows the McLarens will pit by lap 25 and those who pitted early will come in together en masse on lap 32. For Verstappen, who ends up out front after the McLarens' eventual opening stop, it puts him clear and away from a hectic pit lane. Schmitz's call wins Red Bull and Verstappen the race and, moments after the chequered flag, she gets a tap on the shoulder from Laurent Mekies and GP to tell her she will join Verstappen on the podium, which comes as a surprise as she didn't feel her involvement in the race merited it. 'There wasn't a lot of strategy in the race,' she says, laughing. 'But I guess at the end of the day strategy did impact the outcome of the race so it was really nice to go on the podium. It's such an honour.'

Back home, her two daughters, aged six and four, are watching Mummy get sprayed with rosewater. 'I was fortunate enough to go up in 2019 when my eldest was just a baby, so this time they could both watch and appreciate what was happening, and they were really proud of Mummy,' she says. 'They were really excited. It was a really nice moment.' On her return home they want to see the trophy, not understanding the winner's prize isn't hers to keep. 'My younger daughter was also concerned I didn't get a medal like Max does. "You should get a medal, you won too."'

The win leaves Verstappen 12 points behind Norris, with Piastri four points further back going into the season finale.

The deficit could have been even less had an error from Kimi Antonelli not allowed Norris to grab fourth place late in the race and thereby gain himself two more championship points. The reaction from GP in the moment is an incredulous one – did Antonelli let the McLaren by intentionally? Watching the footage back later, GP realises the error of his ways in the heat of battle and seeks him out as well as Mercedes team principal Toto Wolff to pass on an apology. Speaking a few days on from the race, he admits: 'Sometimes I'm a little bit disappointed in myself with how I can get carried away with that, because I've been doing this long enough to know better on some occasions with respect to some of the broadcasts, referring to last week in particular.' Helmut Marko is more scathing in his post-race interviews about Antonelli, leading to a swathe of abuse towards the Italian on social media. Red Bull go on to issue a public apology from Marko too.

Before the weekend, Zak Brown, in an interview on the *News Agents* podcast, likens Verstappen to a film character. 'He's like that guy in that horror movie that right as you think he's not coming back, he's back.' Following his Qatar win, Phil Duncan of the Press Association asks Verstappen in the press conference if he feels title number five is for the taking. 'You can call me Chucky,' he replies, referencing the character in the Child's Play film franchise. He continues: 'I thought it was quite funny. I just focus on myself. I know that when I go in the car, I just try to do my best like everyone does. That's the only thing that I can control and the only thing I can focus on.' Chucky could yet grab this title.

Qatar is also when Verstappen's teammate will officially be announced by Marko post-race. Mexico was meant to be decision time. After round 21 of the 2025 Formula 1 World

Championship it had been scheduled that Red Bull would reveal the identity of its number two alongside Verstappen and also the Racing Bulls duo. Isack Hadjar is the front-runner to be second seat to Verstappen on the strength of his performances despite some pushing for him to have a second season at the junior team. But the identity of the remaining two drivers is harder to call. It's essentially a three-way tussle between Yuki Tsunoda, Liam Lawson and Arvid Lindblad, although Formula 2 driver Alex Dunne may be in the mix after splitting with McLaren and there are whispers of a more established figure outside of the Red Bull family joining the team.

In Mexico, Laurent Mekies opted to delay the decision. The official reason was that the team wanted to focus on the title fight after Verstappen finally put himself forward as a contender. To avoid constant questioning, Mekies said the plan was to put off any decision for two or three races. By Las Vegas, he was adamant no decision had been made but they were 90 per cent there and the official call would come after the penultimate race in Qatar.

The wait also highlights how tight the decision is. Marko, with his faith in youth, has long been pushing the case for Lindblad to make the step up from F2. There are the drives in places like Jeddah and Barcelona but there have also been moments where his inexperience has showed. Errors, argues Marko, are to be excused. One only needs to look at Hadjar's 'embarrassing' first F1 outing for Racing Bulls to see that. He argues that something in the 18-year-old Lindblad reminds him of Verstappen and, before him, Sebastian Vettel. With neither Lawson nor Tsunoda having set the grid alight this season, Lindblad is his primary pick, but his is just a recommendation, the final decision being made by Mekies, Oliver Mintzlaff and Ahmet Mercan.

For weeks, the rumours are swirling. At one point, it seems Lawson and Tsunoda will be paired together, Red Bull thereby trusting in experience – and perhaps on the fact that Tsunoda is backed by Honda. A spring in the step of Tsunoda and his manager in Vegas suggests he might have been given a lifeline in his F1 career. And his cause is further helped by an impressive drive in Qatar in which he out-qualifies Verstappen for the first time this season in the sprint race. But is it too little too late? And has Lawson, deemed not good enough by Red Bull and replaced by Tsunoda, done enough to avoid a second demotion in one calendar year? The decision is tantalisingly close.

At 9:15pm following the race in Qatar, Marko sits down with Tsunoda and his manager to inform them that he will be dropped from the grid altogether. The official line is that Racing Bulls is a junior team with the aim of blooding youngsters from the academy programme. Tsunoda, as a veteran of five seasons on the grid, no longer fits that bracket. Instead, Marko asks him to be the team's test and reserve driver next season. In the brutal world of F1, it is not beyond the realms of possibility that he might get another shot on the grid before 2026 is out. And tellingly he has the support of the sport's overall puppet master. When the news breaks, Formula 1 CEO and president Stefano Domenicali seeks out a meeting with Tsunoda's manager to talk about his future. In the *Drive to Survive* generation, the sport is crying out for its characters and Tsunoda is one of those.

There is sadness in the team for a driver who is hugely popular and brings his own unique energy. Mekies' official statement announcing the final decision allocates two-thirds of it to the departing driver, thanking Tsunoda for his exceptional race starts and excellent race craft as well. As for Hadjar, he praises his raw speed and predicts he can thrive alongside Verstappen in a manner that others have so far failed to do. Hadjar, meanwhile, disbelieving that Mekies would be working alongside Verstappen when he took over as team boss, will need to get over that awestruck feeling to have any chance in 2026. Excitedly, he says: 'It's an awesome move, to work with the best and learn from Max is something I can't wait for.'

To unpick the decision to axe Tsunoda goes all the way back to Imola when, after a promising start with the team, he had that hugely damaging crash, both for his RB21 and also for his confidence. The half-dozen races that followed highlighted the accident's impact enormously: an average finishing spot of 16th and failing to get out of the first stage of qualifying on three of six occasions. Any momentum that had been built was eradicated almost immediately and it always felt like he was on the back foot from that point onwards.

In Baku with more of a revamp to his car he managed to put in a good run in qualifying and Mekies was quick to praise his qualifying and race pace, but the reality was he could rarely string together a strong race weekend in its entirety. Only once all season was he quicker in qualifying than Verstappen – admittedly a hard ask – and never once was he above his teammate at the chequered flag in a Grand Prix bar Austria when Verstappen was driven into and out of the race by Antonelli. It was a backwards step from that of Pérez, who had provided 25 per cent of the team's points in his final season. In contrast, at the point of his axing,

Tsunoda has managed less than 7 per cent. Red Bull made it clear they needed both consistent points finishes from him to reinvigorate their hopes in the constructors' championship as well as be in a position on track where he might be more of a help to Verstappen rather than just an occasional guinea pig to test out tyres and strategy in a race.

Is Hadjar the right call, though? Only time will tell but he has been quick even at tracks he doesn't have previous knowledge of and he has been a regular points finisher. Sure, there have been mistakes, but Red Bull think he's worth the risk. Marko especially thinks he's the best asset since Verstappen first stepped up to the A team. As for Hadjar, he appears to have cracked part one of being Verstappen's teammate: putting his ego to bed and not thinking he can beat him from the outset. Following his promotion, he says: 'Everyone thinks they're special. You come in, you're like, "he's human, I'm going to beat him". And then you get stomped, then the snowball effect starts. If anything, the goal is to accept that I'm going to be slower the first few months. And I think that if you go into that mindset you accept it's going to be very tough. Looking at the data and seeing things you can't achieve yet, it's going to be very frustrating. If you know, then you're more prepared.'

That Lawson survives is no small miracle, his career looking very much on a downward spiral with his Red Bull axing after just two races. Horner had promised the chance to rebuild his career and he has done so impressively.

35

THE TITLE SHOWDOWN

Laurent Mekies stands outside villa number seven, Red Bull's home in the F1 paddock for the season finale in Abu Dhabi. There's every reason for positivity. At his first race in charge in Belgium more than four months ago, Red Bull Racing were in disarray. The team had lost the only leader it had ever known in Christian Horner, the car wasn't consistent, going from race winner one weekend to an also-ran the next, and morale was dwindling. Under Mekies' watch, the renaissance has been nothing short of astonishing and, at the season finale, Max Verstappen is in a title fight he had once given up on. Mekies' broad grin sums up the mood in camp: optimistic but laser-focused on the task ahead. Of his star driver's title chances, he says, 'we shall see' with a shrug of the shoulders. The Frenchman is all too aware the title fight is out of his hands with a 12-point deficit to make up on Lando Norris. The sole focus is on trying to win the race – nothing more and nothing less. It isn't that Mekies' attitude is laissez-faire, it is just the reality of what his team faces.

It is the Thursday of the final Grand Prix weekend of this monstrosity of a season. Normally at this stage teams look utterly exhausted, particularly at what is part three of a triple-header (three Grands Prix over consecutive weekends) and yet there is renewed vigour within the four walls of Red Bull's home. Regardless of the result on Sunday, the latter part of the season will be seen as a success: Verstappen, at one stage 104 points off the championship lead, has taken it to the wire. That is down not just to his skill but also that of the multiple personnel around him.

He has won the title before in Abu Dhabi back in 2021 in a thriller with Lewis Hamilton. And then, the permutations were simpler. Effectively, whoever won the final race was world champion. On his subsequent visits to Yas Marina in 2022, 2023 and 2024, titles two, three and four had already long been sewn up. This time, Verstappen has to hope, if he wins the race, that Norris finishes fourth or lower at the chequered flag.

At Red Bull they know that they have got in the heads of McLaren, for whom this is a far nervier weekend. Even Pierre Waché is in relaxed mood. He needs enormous credit for having overseen the U-turn in performance. His message to the team is simple – 'make sure that we are the quickest, that we are winning the race' – but to have no regrets should that prove insufficient. Matt Caller is in relaxed form as he walks into the garage with a hot drink in hand, having had a day's wakeboarding with his fellow mechanics in between Qatar and Abu Dhabi. For him, this is potentially his last race for Red Bull before he makes the move to Audi for next season. His place as Verstappen's number-one mechanic will be taken next season by twin brother Jon. He jokes that the driver might not even notice the difference.

Abu Dhabi has hosted the F1 season finale since 2009 and there has been no shortage of drama, 2021 being a case in point. But this title fight has greater echoes of 2010 with what was effectively a three-way fight for the title. Back then, Fernando Alonso led Mark Webber by seven points, with Sebastian Vettel eight points further back. Ole Schack, who has been at 400-plus races for Red Bull, remembers being on the grid for that race, working on Vettel's car. At the time, no one was paying Vettel or his car any attention, with all eyes on Alonso and Webber. In the end, Vettel pulled off a massive surprise to win the race and, with it, the first of what would be four straight world championships. In echoes of that, Piastri is in the Vettel position with Webber acting as his manager and mentor. The Australian seems the least likely protagonist to win the championship and yet, in a season awash with twists and turns, it still remains a distinct possibility.

Helmut Marko stands with his hands in his pockets looking grim-faced. He has more experience than most of being at the business end of a championship fight. He remembers the stress and pressure of 2021; this in contrast, he argues, is almost carefree. He knows Verstappen can win the race and still lose the championship. He points out that McLaren have often been strong here but Red Bull have gone on to find a way to win. Steve Knowles, meanwhile, has already been called in by the FIA, along with his opposite number at McLaren, to warn him pre-race that the stewards and the sport's officials have carte blanche on all sanctions if there is any foul play in deciding the championship. The message is they want a clean fight at all costs.

*

The paddock backs on to Yas Marina. On one side is the W Hotel, held together by a steel and glass-shelled bridge, where most of the F1 family are staying and from which music is pumping to the extent that guests staying there are given earplugs on check-in. On the hotel side of the harbour sit the superyachts, on the paddock side the smaller vessels just a few metres away from the paddock itself, each one hosting parties of their own throughout the weekend. As the wind comes in, there is the constant tinkling of metal from ropes on the boat's masts. Inside villa number seven is the engineering office on the left, to the right the catering facilities, while upstairs are located driver rooms, physio and marketing offices. Verstappen flits from his personal space to the shared quarters, spending his time away from driving or media duties watching racing and football. For much of the time he simply sits alone and could not be more at ease with the situation he is facing.

Verstappen's pre-race build-up begins with him walking from Red Bull's base in the paddock to the media centre for the press conference, guided in by his press attaché, Anna Webster. When he arrives, Norris and Piastri are already sitting awkwardly side by side on sofas outside the room, scrolling through their phones while trying to act non-plussed but with cameras hovering above them. As the packed press conference starts, Verstappen enters in relaxed mood, sipping a can of Red Bull. He shakes hands with both his title rivals and takes his position next to Norris who, as championship leader, is sitting centrally. As if a reminder was needed of what's at stake, the drivers' trophy stands gleaming over the left shoulder of Piastri.

All three sit leaning back to exude an air of nonchalance

but only Verstappen's is properly convincing. It's not that he doesn't care – you'd be hard-pressed to find a more competitive driver – it's just that he's aware he simply has nothing to lose and that the pressure is squarely on the shoulders of Norris. In one breath, the Briton insists his life won't change as a world champion, in the next he says he's been working his whole life towards this moment.

As for Verstappen himself, he has stuck to the same line that he has nothing to lose, and you believe him. 'I'm enjoying being here,' he says. 'I've been enjoying the second half of the season, working with the team, how we've been able to turn it around from difficult times, having a debrief after the race, being very disappointed and frustrated with the performances to just enjoying, smiling. Having these wins again is fantastic. So, I just take it – everything here is just a bonus, sitting here fighting for the title. So, that's also what makes it very straightforward for me. We will just try to have a good weekend. But then it's not really in my control.'

Asked about winning a record-equalling fifth drivers' championship, he adds: 'I mean the trophy looks the same. You know, I have four of those at home, so it'd be nice to add a fifth. I've already achieved everything that I wanted to achieve in F1, and everything after is just a bonus. And I just keep doing it because I love it and I enjoy it. And that's also how I go into this weekend – have a good time out there, try to maximise the result.'

Seeing it all play out for half an hour is a psychologist's dream. Roger Federer used to say he used his tennis press conferences to dissect his own performance but to also gain a psychological advantage over his rivals. Verstappen is doing the same, knowing all too well the level of pressure and stress he felt at the same venue four years previously, then without a single world title to his name. That ensuing night, the title protagonists all go out at Zuma Abu Dhabi, one of the city's top restaurants, for a drivers' dinner organised by Lewis Hamilton. It is agreed Verstappen, who happily sips gin and tonics at one end of the table, will pick up the tab, but in the end, Pierre Gasly sneaks off and beats him to it. Verstappen has already pencilled himself in to pay in 12 months' time. Despite what is at stake, Norris later tells fans on stage the following day there were, 'no dramas, no food fights, no beef'.

The team principal's press conference the following day echoes that of the drivers', with all the pressure on McLaren CEO Zak Brown and little on Mekies. The Frenchman uses it to single out Verstappen for praise but also share the plaudits of the team's turnaround with his 2,000 colleagues. On Verstappen, he says: 'Look, this guy never gets it wrong. Max just never does a mistake. The world discovered an even more extraordinary Max this season after his fourth world title. It gives a lot of confidence to the whole team. If you think back to the 2,000 people in Milton Keynes that have been doing the magic in the shadows, trying to get that car back to life in the second part of the year – obviously that creates a great connection and it gives great confidence. The credit for the turnaround is very simple – it's down to 2,000 people that you never see back in Milton Keynes, who simply didn't want to give up. It didn't matter how hard the first part of the season was, how hard the changes that were made in the middle of the season for them to digest – it didn't matter. They just didn't give up. That's what they have managed to achieve – a historic turnaround. That's where the secret is – a united group that doesn't want to give up.'

Verstappen needs to win but is also hoping for the McLarens to slip up. From the outset on track, Norris sets the standard. He nearly tops the time sheets in all three practice sessions, denied by just four thousandths of a second by George Russell in FP3. Verstappen, who has a revision to his floor and reverts back to an engine first used in Brazil, is complaining through practice but no one is concerned. It has been a familiar refrain when seeking perfection.

Driver and team are confident in the build-up to qualifying until a broken valve is spotted on one of Verstappen's tyres for Q3. From a distance, it initially looks like Greg Reeson, Verstappen's 'tyre whisperer', and Monaghan are performing CPR on a stricken colleague. Monaghan orders the tyre to be deflated just 40 minutes before the session. It is treated and he stops it being taken back up to full pressure until it's cured. There are panicked looks all around. If not remedied, it will leave Verstappen with one fewer set of softs for the finale to the biggest qualifying session of the season. With less than half an hour to spare, it is remedied and the grimaces turn to smiles of relief. With the tyres in question, Verstappen is once again a qualifying class apart. With the help of teammate Yuki Tsunoda, he gets a tow down the straight to clock the quickest opening flying lap in Q3 and backs that up on his second Q3 lap. The problem is Norris is second-quickest and Piastri third-fastest, the former needing to be well placed to finish in the top four and seal a maiden title.

That night, the team assemble en masse on their villa rooftop for a team BBQ. Mekies' message is simple: win or lose, everyone should take immense pride in what they've achieved, both those at the racetrack and back at the factory. There are thanks for the sponsors but not for predecessor,

Horner. The oversight doesn't sit entirely comfortably with allies of his who remain at the team. He has stayed in contact with many, Verstappen included, messaging him regularly throughout a Grand Prix weekend to give him his support.

On the day of the race, Marko is sitting outside in the Abu Dhabi sunshine. With six decades of experience in F1, he insists there are no nerves. As for his prediction, he says the 1–2–3 will not finish in their starting order. What will the order be? 'Ask me again after turn 1,' he says with a smile. This is night and day to the 2021 climax when lawyers were called and, as he puts it, poisoned darts were being fired in a tumultuous finale. This season, there has been the occasional squabble with McLaren but it has been a title battle, for the most part, lacking in acrimony. Having been alive for every single F1 season, he cannot think of a comeback quite like Verstappen's and he credits both driver and Mekies for the metamorphosis, arguing the same wouldn't have been achieved with Horner still at the helm.

Just a few hours before the season finale, the team pose for a photo. As Verstappen leaves his room in Red Bull's villa, he faux karate kicks his trainer Rupert Manwaring, who jokes the kung-fu training's been going well. The driver seems virtually devoid of any nerves. It is a relaxed mood shared by the rest of the team, although a few talk of a combination of nerves and excitement as the clock ticks on. Both owners and their families are in attendance and there are warm smiles in particular from Mark Mateschitz, his mother Anita and his girlfriend Victoria Swarovski, an Austrian pop singer, model, TV presenter and a fifth generation of the family jewellery business of the same name. Mateschitz is dressed in a tight, figure-hugging navy blue T-shirt and slacks, looking every bit the billionaire. He and Chalerm Yoovidhya want to see if the comeback can be complete and ponder whether there will be an end-of-season cause for celebration.

Every permutation is being talked over and there are already discussions within the team of the what-ifs and what-could-have-beens before events on the track have even played out in Abu Dhabi, Verstappen driving into Russell in Spain and the resulting penalty or Antonelli crashing into the side of the Dutchman in Austria and ending his race before it had even begun. There is also talk of past dramas in 2010. Then, it had been Fernando Alonso's title to win but an error in the timing of his pit stop proved costly. His race engineer that day was a certain Andrea Stella, who as team principal is overseeing McLaren's bid to guide one of its two stars to the drivers' championship. Can history repeat itself?

The drivers are on split strategies. Hannah Schmitz is among those feeling the nerves, so she comes in early to write up her pre-race report and think of all the various scenarios that may play out. Now she has it clear in her head, there is simply a sense of excitement. Schmitz was not scheduled to be in attendance but a late decision is made to bring her to the race. With Courtenay off to McLaren, it is a sensible approach to avoid any questions, should strategy prove a controversial end to the season. Instead, Courtenay is back in the ops room in Milton Keynes for what is his final day in the office. Conversation between the pair and the team's hierarchy has flitted between a one-stop and a two-stop but they opt for the former. Schmitz argues: 'I don't think from the lead we should be willing to give up track position and assume we'll get that back. If after the start we end up behind both McLarens then we might think about a two-stop in that scenario. Otherwise, a one-stop is what I'm expecting. And McLaren might choose behind us to split strategies so maybe put one on a two-stop and go more aggressively and make us decide if we're covering or not. Our aim today is to win the race. If there's anything we can do to prevent McLaren from coming second and third, we'll think about it.'

With Tsunoda shod with the hard tyres compared to Verstappen on the mediums, the thinking is the second seat can run long and potentially help his teammate's cause. As Schmitz predicts, the McLarens are split too, with Norris on the mediums and Piastri on the hards. Verstappen's potential ploy is to back up the field, as Lewis Hamilton did here in the 2016 title fight to make life difficult for his teammate Nico Rosberg. Off the start line, Verstappen is super-aggressive in cutting across Norris to take the lead and pull out a 1.4-second gap by the time DRS is enabled, with Piastri also getting past Norris on lap one. There are concerns the pit crew can't hear the team radio but that is quickly remedied and all eyes are on Norris as much as Verstappen. On lap 19, Norris produces a stunning double overtake on Lance Stroll and Liam Lawson – next up the road, Tsunoda. Four laps later, he makes his move. Tsunoda twice cuts across to try to block him off, the double move later earning him a five-second penalty. Sparks fly from the underside of Norris's McLaren as he goes off track before getting past. Race control mentions an investigation into Norris for gaining an advantage off track and Steve Knowles is immediately on the radio arguing the case. It falls on deaf ears.

For Norris, the issue remains chasing Charles Leclerc, who is proving quick in the fourth-place Ferrari. The Briton pits on lap 41 to cover Leclerc. Towards the end of the race, the

Red Bull radio begins to fall steadily quieter and quieter. It is akin to a tacit admission of defeat, not in the Grand Prix but in the title fight. It is cagey on the pit walls and in the garages of both McLaren and Red Bull. Verstappen pulls over the line for a dominant victory, Piastri is second and Norris an all-important third. By just two points over the course of a marathon season, Verstappen is denied a fifth world title.

Some point out the costliness of the two points Norris gained for passing Antonelli late in the previous race in Qatar but Piastri could also have let his teammate through in Abu Dhabi, if needed. Inevitably, there are those who pore over the details of the season past, dissecting where things might have gone differently. For Lambiase, there are regrets. Speaking before the race, he casts his mind back to Zandvoort and says, 'I can't help but look back on the season and think, *what if we'd elected to move in this direction even just one or two or three races earlier?* I can't help but think it is an opportunity lost.' Post-race, he bursts into tears in his seat on the pit wall, the rigours of life on and off the track of the past few months having taken their toll. He is consoled by Richard Wolverson and Helmut Marko. And GP finds it harder than most to fully accept defeat in the immediate aftermath, although he tells his driver, 'Max, you have given everything. You can be proud of that, mate. Hold your head up high.' Crucially, Verstappen is arguably the most upbeat, both in and out of the car: 'We did it in style, so thank you very much for that. We showed that one final time in this class. I confess, guys, when we came back in our second half of the season we can be really, really proud of that. So don't be too disappointed. I'm definitely not disappointed. I'm really proud of everyone. We never give up.'

The title race may have come down to just two points but

Verstappen argues it is immaterial whether it's two, 20 or 120, it is still a battle lost. However, it is not one he will dwell on with regret, instead he prefers the message to be of a team that never gives up and that, not having thought about the championship for roughly two-thirds of the season, everything of the past few weeks and months has been a bonus.

Steve Knowles thanks the departing Courtenay over the radio, saying he played a big part in him initially joining Red Bull from Mercedes. In response, Courtenay jokes Knowles has played a role in his exit. Knowles ponders past errors and how they might have swung differently. The response to the race and championship outcome is a mixed one within the team. There is a weird combination of celebration for an eighth race win of the season – one more than each of the McLaren drivers – as well as disappointment at a missed championship, but also utter exhaustion and relief at the end of this high-paced marathon. Key team personnel pore over the race in the debrief before everyone gathers out the front of the garage, Mateschitz too, for the celebratory photograph. On arrival, all are given a can of Red Bull to open and spray in celebration. Verstappen, wearing white shorts and a Red Bull top, arrives with his girlfriend Kelly Piquet and her daughter Penelope. The timing board placed centrally at the back carries the words YES SUPER VES WINS, while the race-winning trophy is central on the floor as photographer Mark 'Thommo' Thompson tries to marshal everyone into the shot. As the cans of sticky liquid are sprayed – there is a delay to allow Kelly and Penelope to get out beforehand – Mateschitz is among those soaked, not that he looks unduly concerned. Not usually afraid to party post-race or post-season, Verstappen prefers a dinner out with family and friends that night.

And then the pack-up begins. There will be testing in Abu Dhabi on Tuesday, with Isack Hadjar in Red Bull colours for the first time. Some are heading straight on holiday, others back to the factory for a team celebration on the Wednesday to take stock of the events of Yas Marina and the 23 races that preceded it. For Verstappen, there is little rest. There are plans for GT Racing in Estoril before racing in Uzbekistan and, before he knows it, testing on the new 2026 cars will begin behind closed doors in Barcelona at the end of January. Meanwhile, Tsunoda is held aloft by his team of mechanics for his farewell. Car parts are signed for some leavers. There are hugs aplenty, the fizz of Heineken bottles being opened and the odd clink of glasses for a first drink at the track. But quickly the party – with Red Bull there's always a party – relocates to the team hotel in the hours afterwards. Some choose to pore over the race and the season as a whole, others prefer to immerse themselves in entirely irreverent and irrelevant chat. The race is run and won, the championship not.

36

ON THE WAY OUT

Amid the celebrations for a race won but commiserations for a title lost, the farewells begin in earnest. For many, the goodbyes will be brief, reunited after a Christmas hiatus; for others, the wrench is infinitely bigger. Will Courtenay will start his new role with McLaren on 2nd January, 2026, after a family holiday in the Maldives, having been released a few months early from his contract. Under his watch, Red Bull have long been masters of perfecting the right strategy calls. Matt Caller, Verstappen's number-one mechanic, is set for a spot of house-hunting in Switzerland ahead of his new post with Audi. It is farewell from Verstappen to half of his trackside engineers, with David Mart off to Aston Martin and Michael Manning also heading for pastures new after a holiday in Oman with his partner. Tom Hart is also leaving for Williams but not until after the 2026 season, while there are even suggestions in the wake of Abu Dhabi that Gianpiero Lambiase might be reducing his trackside responsibilities or else could look for a new venture elsewhere amid talks with

Aston Martin and Williams. A family holiday in Dubai prior to Christmas is a chance to take stock of a season that has been brutal for him. He will turn down those teams' advances before eventually sealing a surprise move to rivals McLaren but not until the 2028 season.

But the biggest exit, for now, is the last to be revealed, a proper end of an era with the news that Helmut Marko, one of the lifers in the team's colours, will be leaving with immediate effect. A great survivor in the cutthroat world of F1, he has faced the axe before – Austrian head office toyed with removing him previously, while Horner also tried to move him aside during his tenure. Amid any talk of 2025 being a finale for the 82-year-old, whenever I ask him he has pushed the message that he has no plans to walk away while both mind and body are willing. But whispers begin in Abu Dhabi that the race might, in fact, be his last. And just 48 hours after the chequered flag comes the news that he will end his association with Red Bull Racing through his own choosing. In an official statement, he says: 'I've been involved in motorsport for six decades now, and the past 20-plus years at Red Bull have been an extraordinary and extremely successful journey. It's been a wonderful time that I have been able to help shape and share with so many talented people. Everything we have built and achieved together fills me with pride. Narrowly missing out on the world championship this season has moved me deeply and made it clear to me that now is the right moment for me personally to end this very long, intense and successful chapter. I wish the entire team continued success and am convinced that they will be fighting for both world championship titles again next year.'

The decision comes after a meeting with Oliver Mintzlaff in Dubai on the Monday after the Grand Prix. The German says: 'Helmut approached me with the wish to end his role as motorsport advisor at the end of the year. I deeply regret this decision, as he has been an influential figure for more than two decades, and his departure marks the end of an extraordinary era. Over more than 20 years, Helmut has earned incomparable merits for our team and the entire Red Bull motorsport family. He played a decisive role in all the key strategic decisions that made Red Bull what it is today, a multiple world champion, an engine of innovation and a cornerstone of international motorsport.

'His instinct for exceptional talent not only shaped our junior programme but also left a lasting impact on Formula 1 as a whole. Names like Sebastian Vettel and Max Verstappen stand for the many drivers who were discovered, supported and guided to the very top under his leadership. His passion, his courage to make decisions, and his ability to spot potential will remain unforgettable. After a long and intensive conversation, I knew I had to respect his wishes, as I gained the impression that the timing felt right for him to take this step. Even though his departure will leave a significant gap, our respect for his decision and our gratitude for everything he has done for Red Bull Racing outweighs it. Helmut Marko will be deeply missed, both personally and professionally. We wish him all the very best for the future and that he will remain closely and warmly connected to the team.'

It is an effusive valedictory from Mintzlaff, far longer than usually comes from GmbH. Verstappen, too, is quick to praise the octogenarian, and it was the Dutchman who effectively stepped in to save him when his head was previously on the chopping block. Is it telling he does not do so publicly this time? What does that say about their relationship or, more crucially, about his own future at the team that such a key ally has gone? It will only add to rumours of his potential exit, should next year's car not prove competitive.

Marko's exit begs the question of whether he was pushed behind the scenes or was it as simple as the fact his influence was waning since his great friend Dietrich Mateschitz's death? It is no secret that Marko has ruffled feathers over the years. More recently it is in his going rogue to snap up Arvid Lindblad to Racing Bulls and then doing something similar with Alex Dunne from the McLaren young driver set-up. Red Bull Austria would accept the former but not the latter. The other facet was his outspoken nature. It did not go down well internally when he was publicly very critical of Kimi Antonelli for what he saw as letting Lando Norris through late in the Qatar Grand Prix. It led to hundreds of messages of abuse online towards the Italian teenager for which Marko later apologised. This is not the first time his blunt outbursts have landed him in hot water, but it will prove to be the last while on Red Bull's books.

It fully marks the end of the old guard. Through the team's entire period of dominance, there were three people at the top: Horner, Adrian Newey and Marko. Now all have gone in very separate ways, Red Bull Racing entering such a seismic season in 2026 without at least one of them for the first time in their richly successful history. Gone are the days of power being in the hands of that anointed few.

Marko needs immense credit for overseeing the most successful junior driver programme in F1. The stand-outs may have been Vettel and Verstappen, and without Marko's fast-tracking Verstappen would never have been the youngest driver in F1 history nor its youngest race winner, but there has been a conveyor belt of talent to have shone at other teams after Red Bull, including the likes of Carlos Sainz, Daniel Ricciardo, Pierre Gasly and Alex Albon. And there are success stories of former Red Bull drivers having gone to different fields of motorsport. Others have tried their own driver programmes, from Ferrari to Mercedes, but without producing quite the talent as Red Bull. His appointing of Lindblad continues his philosophy: 'The whole programme was the philosophy of Mr Mateschitz,' he says. 'We don't buy stars, we make stars.'

Marko clearly had a talent for unearthing young talent but his skill set and his CV have been far more than just unearthing the next big thing. It was he who helped Mateschitz to enable Red Bull Racing to become a reality in the first place and for his good friend to realise his motorsport dreams. He was also the one who took a chance on a young Horner before eventually being one of the architects of his downfall. His voice has always been a refreshing one in the PR spin of F1 in the modern era, and he had fun in raising hackles. Now, it is a return to Graz and his burgeoning hotel empire, property portfolio and ever-growing list of artworks.

It piles the pressure on Mintzlaff, too, having overseen the exit of such key figures at the top of the team and inevitably begs the question of whether he can lead Red Bull with Mekies into a bold new era. The big characters have gone, perhaps a sign of a different era for F1, certainly for the team. But the change is big for Verstappen too. Like the rest of the grid he will have a new car and new engine, but, added to that, half his trackside engineering team is changing, his number-one mechanic is going, and he has another new teammate to get accustomed to. It might be a refreshing boost but it might also be the beginning of the end. Despite publicly reiterating his loyalty to the team, he has a clause in his contract that allows him to move to another team in 2027 if not in the top two at the next summer break. As a new engine manufacturer, it seems unthinkable he will be in such a lofty position come August. Mekies has already warned of a painful transition in this brave new world, and could the infighting of recent times reemerge if results start going downhill? F1 is an unforgiving world and moves on quickly. If the team is faltering, the epic effort of 2025 will quickly be forgotten. But what will be good enough for Verstappen to stay? He has repeated his loyalty to the team – 2026 is his 12th season under the Red Bull banner – but will it be enough for him to buy into the prospect of this project going right and the potential for another period of dominance in the future? Even if a season starts poorly, Red Bull have shown quite how dramatically they can claw it back.

Already, the focus is on 2026, which comes into even sharper focus in the days after Abu Dhabi, even with Christmas and a short break for many to look forward to. When the racing resumes, Verstappen will be front and centre. The team, the grid, the entire paddock have been in awe of what he has achieved this season. His on-track efforts may not have resulted in a driver's title but, taking nothing away from Lando Norris, he has been the driver of the season. And GP has had the best seat: 'Max has just elevated himself to a completely different stratosphere this year. Not only in our eyes but in the world of motorsport's eyes. And I think to see that happen gives me immense pleasure and it's an immense privilege to work with him. He's had to work with a different piece of hardware this year. He hasn't had the most competitive car yet look at him. It's not been the most competitive car at all times this year and for him to be still in with a shout of the drivers' championship is just a reflection on him. He's 28 years old and I honestly don't think he's at his peak just yet, and the main thing is he's still having fun. When he's having fun, you see a smile on his face, that's ultimately when you need to be frightened of him.'

Verstappen, who has not been off the podium since the Hungarian Grand Prix 11 races ago, admits he can still improve and it is an insatiable hunger both for success and perfection that continues to motivate him to elevate his performance even higher. His talent has long been established but he believes he is yet to truly hit his peak. His decision-making is second to none, so too his ability to evade danger while being acutely aggressive, soak up the pressure and not let it affect his on-track performance. The hot-headedness may even be a thing of the past too. It is seven months since his high-speed bumper car trick on George Russell in Barcelona and the red mist has not really ignited since then. While he says becoming a parent hasn't changed him, it certainly hasn't had a negative effect, either; he is more grown up but also has something far more important than driving around in circles . . . his family. Whether he reaches the peak GP talks about at Red Bull or elsewhere remains a moot point.

Next comes the acid test of a new set of engine regulations, the new in-house engine, a new racing number – 3 instead of 1 – and a new teammate, although that aspect is nothing new for Verstappen, having seen three come and go in the last year. For him, it is a first Christmas with daughter Lily and then a holiday with family and friends. He has repeated the mantra of 2025 – at least the latter part – of having fun. But keeping it fun also entails winning. It is just 50 days from the chequered flag being waved in Abu Dhabi to the season's first test in Barcelona and behind the scenes, Red Bull staff are working around the clock to ensure they are up to speed from race one. Will the late-season push for the title in 2025 be to the detriment of the coming year?

Paul Monaghan argues not, saying instead that such an approach allowed Red Bull to understand their simulation tools better and the correlation between those and the on-track reality, thereby aiding any 2026 planning. 'We finished with the quickest car with a driver whose confidence is sky-high, he's intimidated all the others again,' he says in the dark of the Abu Dhabi evening. 'And the nice thing is we can be confident in the way we develop the car that applying the same logic to next year's one is correct and right and rational, reasonable, and the filtration of good and bad can go on with the confidence we are doing the right things. It's huge, isn't it, in that respect?'

Red Bull have shown themselves once more to be a special team, on the back foot for much of 2025 before pulling off a near miracle, and that isn't just down to a driver's brilliance. Trying to pinpoint what makes the team so special is different in its key personnel's eyes. For Monaghan, it is: 'Teamwork. But someone asked me a while back, what is teamwork? I said it's having each other's back without doing their jobs. If you trust the people around you then that's teamwork, and each person doing their little bit.' For Pierre Waché, it is a steadfast refusal to wave the white flag even to the final lap in Abu Dhabi. 'It is the mentality of the people to never give up,' he says. 'We are always thinking about racing, what the driver needs, what our goal is when you participate in a race, not just to take part but to win. You try everything you can to do it. This mentality is a very high strength compared to some others.'

It has been fascinating to watch the team and the season evolve at such close quarters. I'm left to wonder if any other team on the grid would have done it in quite the same fashion. It has been a rollercoaster of a season. It started with such promise and had everything in between: a driver sacked after just two races, a team boss gone just after the midway point of 2025, rumours its star driver could leave, a championship derailed, then remarkably back on track before the title fight was extinguished at the death. Red Bull are a very special group, more loved or at least liked than they think, the fact they were being cheered on by many up and down the paddock and beyond in their unexpected comeback testament to that. It was a reaction that took many in the team by surprise. And yet it is an us-against-them ethos that has held them in good stead for so long. They can still be unapologetically brash and competitive even under new, less combative leadership. It is a collective of brilliant minds with such different and disparate skills that somehow come together to make a winning combination. It is as impressive to watch them trackside as it is inside the various hubs that make up campus, back in Milton Keynes. It can be a team of warring factions – as can happen in any business and any form of competition – and yet this mismatch of a family is just that . . . a family. In a period of massive upheaval and uncertainty, they have remained solidified as one, but what next? They are clearly evolving and the team is being broken up a little with various exits. But Formula 1 has forever been about evolution. Rumours have already begun, that they and Mercedes have found a loophole in the 2026 engine regulations to give them a jump on rivals like Ferrari and Honda. The next chapter promises to be as fascinating and no less thrilling than the last great ending!

ACKNOWLEDGEMENTS

This project originally began with a podcast, the Inside Track, with BBC Studios. So, a big thank you to all the brilliant people who worked on that: James Cook, Rick Edwards, Georgina Revill, India Opie Meres, Nick Thomson, Jon Weeks, Gaelan Davis-Connolly and many more behind the scenes.

Red Bull Racing is a truly remarkable team and I'm hugely grateful to them for opening their doors to me during the 2025 season. Initial thanks go to Paul Smith and Christian Horner for letting me peak behind the curtain in the first place, and to Laurent Mekies and Alice Hedworth for enabling me to continue doing so even after some seismic changes in the team midway through the season. It was a truly privileged position to be in.

The list of other people to thank at Red Bull is long but, in no particular order: Paul Monaghan, Pierre Waché, Steve Knowles, Will Courtenay, Hannah Schmitz, Gianpiero Lambiase, Helmut Marko, Richard Wood, Alice Webster, Mark Thompson, Vladimir Rys, Helen Lawson, Matt and Jon Caller,

Greg Reeson, Ed Hemsworth, Tom Hart, Michael Manning, Madeleine Coe, Ben Hodgkinson, Taylor Toney-Green, Max Verstappen, Yuki Tsunoda and their wider teams.

A big thank you to my literary agent David Luxton for his constant support and all the wonderful people at Blink Publishing: Matt Phillips, Justine Taylor, Charlotte Brown, Eleanor Stammeijer, Holly Milnes and Rosa Picard for making this book far better than it would have otherwise been.

Also, thanks to the F1 journalists for keeping me company on the round-the-world travels: Tom Cary, Jon McEvoy, Phil Duncan, Alan Baldwin, Molly Hudson, Mark Hughes, Edd Straw, Jon Noble, Erik van Haren, Jacky Martens, and many more besides.

And a final mention to my wife and children. This project took me away from home for a big chunk of 2025. Here's to the next project being closer to home.

INDEX

A

Abu Dhabi Grand Prix (2010) 90, 330

Abu Dhabi Grand Prix (2021) 2, 3, 32, 35, 115, 148, 329, 330

Abu Dhabi Grand Prix (2024) 9, 173

Abu Dhabi Grand Prix (2025) 1, 2, 196–8, 328, 337–8

  practice and qualifying 334

  pre-race interviews with drivers and team principals 331–3

Adams, Callum 121

Albon, Alex 39–40, 43–4, 252, 345

Allen, Beverley 194–5

Alonso, Fernando 2, 9, 30, 116, 147, 222, 257, 330

AlphaTauri 140

Alpine 39, 77, 262

America's Cup 54

Antonelli, Kimi 15, 149, 159, 169, 176, 180, 207, 213, 218, 272, 307, 323, 338, 344

Apicella, Marco 77–8

Arden Motorsport 80, 81

Aston Martin 25, 34, 40, 188, 197–8, 262, 275, 293, 341

Audi 35, 341

Australian Grand Prix (2005) 19

Australian Grand Prix (2025) 45, 74–5

  practice and qualifying 67–8, 73–4

Austrian Grand Prix (1985) 104

Austrian Grand Prix (2024) 173

Austrian Grand Prix (2025) 175–6, 185

Autosport 161–2

Azerbaijan Grand Prix (2023) 179

Azerbaijan Grand Prix (2025) 241, 252–4

  qualifying 252

B

Baghetti, Giancarlo 44

Bahrain Grand Prix (2020) 137

Bahrain Grand Prix (2021) 140

Bahrain Grand Prix (2024) 128, 141

Bahrain Grand Prix (2025) 125–6, 142

Bahrain International Circuit 48, 125

BAR Honda 119

Barrichello, Rubens 17, 76

Bearman, Oliver 169, 239, 252, 307

Belgian Grand Prix (2016) 284

Belgian Grand Prix (2022) 106

Belgian Grand Prix (2023) 297

Belgian Grand Prix (2025) 201, 212–15

sprint and qualifying 206–7, 212
Benetton 35, 105, 112, 113
Berger, Gerhard 104–5, 256, 269, 285
Bianchi, Jules 137
Bild newspaper205
BMW Sauber 52–3
Bonnier, Jo 265
Bortoleto, Gabriel 149, 157
Bozzi, Bryan 296
Brailsford, Dave 26
Brawn GP 257
Brawn, Ross 13
Brazilian/São Paulo Grand Prix (2024)
    9–10, 106–7, 110–11, 173, 189, 302
Brazilian/São Paulo Grand Prix (2025)
    305–8
  sprint, practice and qualifying 302–5
Briatore, Flavio 82, 262
Bridgestone 52
British Grand Prix (2022) 137
British Grand Prix (2025) 3, 181, 186–
    92, 207, 236
  practice and qualifying 186–7,
    188–9, 236
BRM 267
Brown, Zak 3–4, 163, 310–11, 323,
    333
Button, Jenson 119, 148, 149, 257

C
Caller, Jon 14, 120–5, 126–7, 329
Caller, Matt 14, 50, 121–5, 127, 150,
    237–9, 240, 241–2, 329, 341
Canadian Grand Prix (2025) 174–5, 271
carbon emissions 30
celebrity F1 fans 145, 222–3, 313
Chalerm Yoovidhya 89, 93, 185, 336
Chinese Grand Prix (2009) 16, 19
Chinese Grand Prix (2024) 76
Chinese Grand Prix (2025) 45, 75–6,
    98, 100
  sprint and qualifying 76
Circuit de Barcelona-Catalunya 161
Colapinto, Franco 10, 252

Combes, Les 206
constructors' championships 17, 30,
    31, 45, 59, 60, 62, 93, 261
cost-caps, F1 35, 95, 144, 165
Coulthard, David 16, 19, 21, 22, 29,
    82, 83
Courtenay, Will 14, 95–6, 97, 99–100,
    101–2, 103, 157, 253, 290, 306, 308,
    336, 339, 341
crash in qualifying Emilia-Romagna
    Grand Prix (2025), Yuki Tsunoda
    135–6, 143, 144
Crews, Terry 1, 312
Cruyff, Johan 147

D
Daily Mail 37
de Armas, Ana 1
De Telegraaf 8–9
Dennis, Ron 13, 84–5
designers *see* Newey, Adrian; Waché,
    Pierre
DHL best pit stop prize 120
DJ Admin Jansen 231
Domenicali, Stefano 325
Donnelly, Martin 161–2
Donohue, Mark 185
DRS (drag reduction system) 169, 248,
    291
Duncan, Phil 323
Dunne, Alex 324, 344
Dutch Grand Prix (1975) 138

E
Ecclestone, Bernie 32, 82, 155, 266
Emilia-Romagna Grand Prix (1994)
    136–7, 268–9
Emilia-Romagna Grand Prix (2022)
    179
Emilia-Romagna Grand Prix (2025)
    138, 143, 156, 189
  qualifying 135–6, 137–8, 144
engine development, in-house 27, 42,
    243–7

engine regulation changes (2026) 180,
250, 350
engineering and driver set-up, Red
Bull Racing 14–15, 293–301
European Grand Prix (1993) 10
European Grand Prix (1999) 17
European Rally Championship 116

F
F1 Academy 42
F1 The Movie (2025) 162
F2 140, 218, 225, 268, 324
F3 140, 269
F4 Championship, Japanese 139–40,
223
F3000 19, 80, 81, 269
Fangio, Juan Manuel 8
fatalities, F1 136–7, 185, 265, 267,
268–9, 284–5
Ferrari 2, 7, 12, 13, 15, 30, 31, 34, 37,
57, 67, 76, 77, 82, 94, 102, 105, 162,
163, 177, 197, 211, 236, 240, 244,
246, 273, 277, 284, 289, 337, 350
see also Hamilton, Lewis; Leclerc,
Charles; individual Grand Prix by
location
FIA (Fédération Internationale de
l'Automobile) 15, 207, 210–11, 228,
255, 287–8, 316–17, 330
regulations 57, 59, 61, 95, 159, 162–
5, 173, 179, 180, 247, 262, 350
Foley, Declan 50–1
Ford 18, 27, 42
Formula 1: Drive to Survive Netflix
documentary 13, 19, 83, 86–7,
231
Formula 3000 80, 105
FP3 152
French Grand Prix (2005) 257
front wing regulation changes (2025),
F1 59, 159, 162–5
Fushida, Hiroshi 138

G
Gasly, Pierre 39–40, 43, 77, 128, 142,
320, 333, 345
gearbox stress test, remote 160–1
German Grand Prix (1953) 77
German Grand Prix (1994) 113
Graz, Austria 263–5
Grosjeans, Romain 137, 152
'ground-effect' era 190
GT Racing 115, 116, 340
Gührs, Dominik 155–6

H
Haas 19, 82, 307
Hadjar, Isack 75, 159, 207, 209–10,
217–18, 219, 224, 233, 324, 326,
327, 340
Häkkinen, Mika 31, 257
Halliwell, Geri 84, 87
halo innovation, cockpit 137
Hamilton, Anthony 217
Hamilton, Lewis 3, 7, 8, 13, 15, 30, 32,
35, 77, 85, 100, 102, 106, 115, 139,
147, 162, 165, 168, 177, 178, 188,
197, 215, 218, 226–7, 277, 280, 289,
290, 313, 321, 333, 337
Hart, Tom 259, 293, 294, 295–6, 341
Head, Patrick 13
Heineken 42
Hemsworth, Ed 121
Herbert, Johnny 17
Heritage team, Red Bull Racing 29–30
Hill, Damon 31
Hodgkinson, Ben 27, 245–7, 248–50
Honda 7, 42, 107, 139–40, 220, 226,
244, 293, 350
Honda Formula Dream Project 139
Horner, Christian 16, 25, 32, 49, 103,
182, 262, 297, 310, 335
and Adrian Newey 21, 31, 34
allegations of coercive/controlling
behaviour 36, 92, 184
axed from Red Bull Racing 3, 192–5,
202–3, 205

conflicts within Red Bull
    management 37, 91, 92, 128,
    179–85, 186, 270
Drive to Survive Netflix
    documentary 13, 83, 86–7
driving career 80–1, 87, 148
on F1 Grand Prix World
    Championship (2025) 76, 78,
    129–30, 134, 157–8, 159, 168
on introduction 2025 front wing
    regulations 59, 159, 164
and Liam Lawson 40, 45, 72–3, 75,
    76, 78
and Max Verstappen 8, 9, 103, 108,
    109, 110, 171, 174, 189, 235
pre-season address 60–3
Red Bull Racing career 13, 18–20,
    21, 22, 27, 31, 35–7, 55, 57, 59,
    69–70, 81–7, 94, 192–5, 202, 243,
    289
wife and children 87–8, 194–5
Horner, Garry 80
Horner, Olivia 87–8, 194
Höttinger, Markus 268
Hughes, Olly 193
Hülkenberg, Nico 252, 271, 320
Hungarian Grand Prix (2025) 151, 208,
    215–16, 229
qualifying 208

I
Italian Grand Prix (1993) 77–8
Italian Grand Prix (2024) 234–5
Italian Grand Prix (2025) 239–41,
    251–2
qualifying 236–9

J
Jaguar Racing 17, 18, 19, 22, 27, 101,
    105, 244
Jamoul, Renaud 116
Japanese Grand Prix (2007) 139
Japanese Grand Prix (2014) 137
Japanese Grand Prix (2022) 7

Japanese Grand Prix (2025) 107, 125,
    129, 141–2, 189
qualifying 107–9
Jenzer Motorsport 140
Johansson, Stefan 185
Jones, Alan 13
Jordan 19, 257
junior programme, Red Bull Racing
    23, 105, 140, 226, 266, 343, 344–5
Jurgen (Red Bull security and
    bodyguard) 276

K
karting 112, 113–14, 115–16, 123, 139,
    148, 166, 225
Katayama, Ukyo 138–9
Kick Sauber 35, 157
Klien, Christian 19, 20, 22, 105
Knowles, Steve 15, 95, 170–1, 172,
    174–6, 215, 239, 253, 288, 290, 294,
    330, 337, 339
Koinigg, Helmuth 268
Komatsu, Ayao 82
Kvyat, Daniil 66, 297

L
Lambiase, Gianpiero 'GP' 14, 56, 66–7,
    95, 103, 109, 116, 157, 168, 169,
    170, 173, 189, 232–3, 239, 254, 259,
    286–7, 290–1, 293, 294, 296–9, 301,
    306, 307–8, 316, 322, 323, 338,
    341–2, 346–7
Las Vegas Grand Prix (2024) 7–8, 27,
    310
Las Vegas Grand Prix (2025) 314–17,
    318–19, 320
practice and qualifying 313–14
Las Vegas vibe 311–13
Lauda, Niki 204
Lawson, Carl 122
Lawson, Craig 121–2
Lawson, Liam 13, 40–1, 43–6, 50–1,
    58, 62, 64–5, 100, 149, 169, 197–8,
    215, 219, 224, 253, 324, 328, 337

Australian Grand Prix (2025) 71–5
axed from Red Bull 3, 77–9, 177
Chinese Grand Prix (2025) 75, 76–7,
    102
interviews 65, 72, 76–7
Monaco Grand Prix (2025) 159
Leclerc, Charles 7, 77, 87–8, 100, 102,
    112, 154, 158, 164–5, 169–70, 177,
    197, 235, 252, 272, 277, 289, 291,
    296, 337
Liberty Media 229–30, 275
Lindblad, Arvid 224–7, 286, 324, 344,
    345
Liuzzi, Vitantonio 81
Loof, Ernst 77
Lotus 138, 152, 162
loyalty, driver 177

M
McLaren 2–4, 8–11, 13, 15, 21, 30, 31,
    37, 39, 57, 59, 60–1, 67, 95, 105,
    107, 109, 120, 129, 134, 163–4, 167,
    174, 186, 188, 196, 207, 231, 233,
    242, 244, 250, 251, 253–4, 257, 261,
    270–2, 273, 275, 310, 321–3, 329,
    337, 341
front wing regulations introduced
    (2025) 163–4
Las Vegas Grand Prix 'DQ' (2025)
    316–17, 318–19
Papaya Rules – driver equal billings
    9, 39, 271, 282
'tape-gate' 287–8
see also Norris, Lando; Piastri,
    Oscar; individual Grand Prix by
    location
Magenta 47
Mallya, Vijay 155
Manning, Michael 293, 294–5, 341
Mansell, Nigel 31, 107, 138
Manwaring, Rupert 2, 335
marginal gains in F1 26
marketing 20–1, 29, 41–3, 44, 46–7
Marko, Helmut 13, 14, 18–19, 22, 40,

49, 67, 75, 81, 130, 183–4, 188, 189,
    192, 193, 204, 211, 215–16, 217–18,
    237, 241, 254–5, 294, 330, 335, 338
choice of Verstappen's team partner
    for 2026 323–5
conflict with Christian Horner 91,
    92, 128, 179, 184, 270, 342
F1 driving career 267–8
home in Graz, Austria 263–6, 267,
    345
and Max Verstappen 91–2, 105–6,
    109–10, 123, 184, 270, 281–2,
    343–4, 345
Red Bull junior drivers programme
    and talent-spotting 105–6, 224–5,
    266, 269, 343, 344–5
retirement from Red Bull Racing
    342–5
Mart, David 293–4, 341
Masi, Michael 35
Mateschitz, Dietrich 13, 14, 17, 18–19,
    20, 21–3, 88–91, 93, 104–5, 128,
    183–4, 185, 210, 269, 339, 344
Mateschitz, Mark 90, 185, 241, 335–6
Mekies, Laurent 4, 82, 142, 159, 195
addressing the team 212–13, 278–9,
    317–19, 334–5
career and engineering background
    208–9, 210–11
as the CEO of Red Bull Racing 201–
    4, 207, 211–13, 214, 216, 219–20,
    231–2, 241, 245, 252, 262, 270,
    278–9, 288–9, 305, 313, 315, 317–
    19, 322, 325–6, 328, 334–5, 346
choice of Verstappen's team partner
    for 2026 season 325–7
and Max Verstappen 209–10, 252,
    254, 259, 315, 318–19, 326, 333
on Powertrains, in-house engine
    development 245
wife and family 213
and Yuki Tsunoda 219–20, 224
Menchaca, Diego 142–3
Mercan, Ahmet 205, 325

Mercedes 12, 13, 15, 37–8, 58, 67, 94, 106, 137, 170, 178–9, 197, 213, 218, 236, 244, 245–6, 250, 254, 257, 270, 289, 310
   see also Antonelli, Kimi; Russell, George; individual Grand Prix by location
Mexican Grand Prix (2022) 126
Mexican Grand Prix (2024) 173
Mexican Grand Prix (2025) 289–92
  practice and qualifying 286–7
Michelin 52
Milewski, Michel 205
Milton Keynes HQ, Red Bull Racing 16–17, 24–30, 100–3, 188
Minardi 23, 105, 113, 210
Mintzlaff, Oliver 90–1, 92, 184, 186, 192, 193, 205, 211, 231–2, 325, 343
MK-7 27–9
Monaco Grand Prix (2005) 20
Monaco Grand Prix (2006) 16
Monaco Grand Prix (2015) 152
Monaco Grand Prix (2021) 153
Monaco Grand Prix (2023) 153
Monaco Grand Prix (2024) 154
Monaco Grand Prix (2025) 145, 154, 157–9, 168
Monaco Grand Prix qualifying 153–4
Monaco, Principality of 145–7, 154–5
Monaghan, Paul 'Pedals' 14, 83–4, 116–17, 122, 123, 144, 157, 168, 189, 190–1, 203, 204, 221, 247–8, 253, 255–8, 259–62, 286, 334, 348
Montoya, Juan Pablo 80
Mosley, Max 268

N
Nakajima, Kazuki 138
Nakajima, Satoru 138, 139
Nasser, Jac 18
net-zero carbon emissions target 30
Netherlands Grand Prix (2025) 219, 229–33
  qualifying 232–3

Newey, Adrian 13, 21–2, 25, 27, 30, 31–5, 36, 51, 53, 85, 262
News Agents 323
Norris, Lando 1, 2, 3, 8, 9–10, 37, 39, 60–1, 69, 100, 109, 120, 133, 148, 154, 157, 158, 164, 167, 168–9, 173, 186, 188, 196, 197–8, 233, 237, 252, 253, 259, 270–2, 282–3, 287, 291–2, 306, 308, 310, 314, 315–17, 320, 321–3, 331–2, 334, 337–8

O
Ocon, Esteban 10, 112, 305, 321
ops room, HQ 100–3
Oracle 274
Österreichring Circuit 185

P
paddock, Red Bull Racing 273–7, 312
Papaya Rules, McLaren 9, 39, 271, 282
Pérez, Sergio 'Checo' 15, 39–41, 43, 44, 123, 126, 219, 235, 251, 255, 279, 326
photo shoots, promotional 41–3, 44, 46–7
Piastri, Oscar 2, 3, 8, 37, 39, 66, 77, 83, 100, 108, 134, 143, 157–8, 164–5, 167, 168, 173, 186, 189, 191, 196, 206, 234, 239, 252, 253, 259, 261, 270–2, 282–3, 287, 304, 315, 317, 320, 321–3, 331–2, 334, 337, 338
Piquet, Nelson 107
Pirelli tyres 52, 123, 310, 321
pit crew and pit stop practice 25, 95, 119–21, 124–5
pit stops, Red Bull Racing 118–19, 125–6, 158, 167, 261
Pitt, Brad 162
Pringle, Stuart 188
Prost, Alain 107, 209
publicity events 28, 64–5
Purnell, Tony 18, 81–2

Q

Qatar Grand Prix (2023) 7, 120, 179, 297

Qatar Grand Prix (2024) 173

Qatar Grand Prix (2025) 320–2

R

RA272 107

Racing Bulls/VCARB 23, 39, 40, 75, 82, 140, 141, 142, 159, 195, 197–8, 203, 211, 215, 217, 220, 224

Racing Point 40

Raikkonen, Kimi 162

rallying 116

ram-raid on HQ 25

Ratzenberger, Roland 136, 268–9

RB3 22

RB6 30

RB7 29

RB8 29

RB14 163

RB17 27, 33

RB18 57–8

RB20 11, 44, 62, 129, 235

RB21 1, 25, 50, 62, 67, 119, 128–33, 153, 154, 215, 221, 234, 242, 254, 272, 278

RB22 243–50

Red Bull Advanced Technologies 27

Red Bull Ford Powertrains 27, 243–7

Red Bull Racing 2, 12–16, 56–7, 61, 163, 244, 348–50

  Christian Horner sacked 192–5, 202–3, 205

  end-of-season BBQ 334–5

  in-house engine development 27, 42, 243–7

  internal unrest 37, 91, 92, 128, 179–85, 202–3

  junior programme 23, 105, 140, 226, 266

  lodge complaint against George Russell after Canadia Grand Prix (2025) 174–5

  Milton Keynes HQ 16–17, 24–30, 100–3, 188

  paddock set-up 273–7

  pit wall line-up 94–5

  'tape-gate' 287–8

  see also Caller, Martin; Courtenay, Will; Horner, Christian; Knowles, Steve; Lambiase, Gianpiero 'GP'; Lawson, Liam; Marko, Helmut; Mekies, Laurent; Monaghan, Paul 'Pedals'; Newey, Adrian; Schmidt, Hannah; Tsunoda, Yuki; Verstappen, Max; Waché, Pierre; individual Grand Prix by location

Red Bull Racing Energy Station, 19–20, 204, 275–6

Reeson, Greg 275, 334

regulations, F1 *see* FIA (Fédération Internationale de l'Automobile)

Renault 19, 20, 30, 35

Ricciardo, Daniel 40, 43, 141, 345

Rindt, Jochen 185, 201, 267

Rocquelin, Guillaume 225

Rodríguez, Pedro 284–5

Rodríguez, Ricardo 284–5

Rosberg, Nico 3, 162, 285, 337

RSM Marko 81, 105

Russell, George 15, 58, 100, 148, 170–1, 172, 173, 174–5, 178–9, 181, 182, 213, 218, 254, 259, 270, 289–90, 307, 310, 314, 315–16

Rys, Vladimir 15

S

safety cars 98–9, 154, 169, 174–5, 233–4, 239, 252–3, 320

safety, F1 136–7, 161, 174, 268–9, 288

Sainz, Carlos 7, 43, 169, 177, 197, 239, 291, 345

Sato, Takuma 138

Sauber 18, 34

Saudi Arabian Grand Prix (2025) 133–4, 142, 271

Schack, Ole 330

Schmitz, Hannah 4, 14, 68–9, 95–100, 101, 167–8, 169, 290, 315, 321–2, 336–7

Schumacher, Michael 8, 9, 49, 112, 147, 162, 166, 279

Schumacher, Mick 140

Scuderia Toro Rosso 177–8

Senna, Ayrton 10, 31, 107, 116, 136, 138, 166, 209, 257, 268–9

Seven Tenths of a Second (Z. Brown) 310–11

shakedowns in Bahrain, pre-season 48–52

Shanghai International Circuit 75–6

Silverstone Racetrack 187–8

sim racing 111, 115

simulator training 45, 51, 222

Singapore Grand Prix (2025) 255, 259–60, 270
  practice and qualifying 259

Sky Germany 128

Sky Sports 76, 170

Smith, Mark 19

Smith, Paul 193

social media 45, 64–5, 145, 149, 150, 171, 193–4, 223

Sony PlayStation driving games 111, 115

Spanish Grand Prix (1990) 161–2

Spanish Grand Prix (2016) 106, 162

Spanish Grand Prix (2025) 61, 139, 160, 164–5, 167–71

Spice Girls 87

Spini, Mattia 140

sponsors/partners 29, 42, 49, 274

spy photographers 58

Star Wars marketing partnership 21

Statham, Jason 222–3

Steiner, Guenther 19

Stella, Andrea 2, 3–4, 9, 164, 272, 306, 336

Stella, Frank 264

Stewart Grand Prix racing team 17–18

Stewart, Sir Jackie 17–18

strategy/strategists 4, 10, 14, 68, 95–103, 157, 167–8, 259, 290, 306–8, 315, 320–2, 336–7

Stroll, Lance 34, 197, 337

summer break/factory shut down 228–9

Super Aguri 138

Suzuka Circuit, Japan 107–8, 128, 129

Suzuka Racing School 139

Suzuki, Aguri 138

swearing rules 59, 173

T

'tape-gate,' McLaren and Red Bull 287–8

Team Redline 115

Ted Kravitz 76

Tennyson, Michaelagh 121

testing and shakedowns in Bahrain, pre-season 48–52, 55–9

Thompson, Mark 'Tommo' 15, 339

tifosi, Ferrari 240

Tilke, Hermann 75–6

Todt, Jean 13, 211, 268

Toro Rosso 23, 105, 106, 210

Tost, Franz 140, 222

TPC programme, Red Bull Racing 226

Tsunoda, Nobuaki and Minako 139, 155, 156, 216, 340

Tsunoda, Yuki 41, 71, 77, 79, 117, 123, 125, 177, 202, 218–24, 226, 233, 299–300, 324, 334
  on Max Verstappen 143
  boat trip in Monaco with author 155–6
  career progression 139–41
  crash in qualifying at Emilia-Romagna Grand Prix
    see Emilia-Romagna Grand Prix entry below
  Grand Prix Races
    Abu Dhabi (2025) 198, 337
    Austrian (2025) 185–6
    Azerbaijan (2025) 253

INDEX

Bahrain (2024) 141
Bahrain (2025) 125–6, 142
Belgian (2025) 206
Brazilian/São Paulo (2025) 303
British (2025) 186
Emilia-Romagna (2025) 135–6, 137–8, 143–4, 156
Japanese (2025) 141–2
Las Vegas (2025) 314
Monaco (2024) 156
Monaco (2025) 155, 158, 159
Spanish (2025) 139, 167, 168
United States – Miami (2025)142–3
relegated to reserve driver for 2026 season 325–7
rumours of removal from Red Bull Racing 219–21, 223–4
Turing, Alan 24
Turner, Phil 125–6, 286

U
United States Grand Prix – Miami (2025) 134, 142–3, 163
United States Grand Prix – Texas (2020) 127
United States Grand Prix – Texas (2021) 106
United States Grand Prix – Texas (2025) 272, 287–8
practice and sprint 271–2

V
V6 engines, hybrid 30, 160
V8 engines 30
Valkyrie sports car 30
Van Alphen, H. 229
van der Garde, Giedo 78, 172
Vasseur, Frédéric 164, 262
Vermeulen, Raymond 46, 179–80, 292
Verstappen, Jos 17, 37, 49, 91, 110–11, 112–16, 133, 148, 166, 184, 205, 214–15, 259, 304
Verstappen, Max 3–4, 23, 26, 37–8, 39, 43–4, 45, 46–7, 61–2, 66–8, 76, 89, 93, 100, 105, 205, 218, 311, 347–8
break-up of engineering team 293–4, 295–6, 341, 345–6
Drive to Survive Netflix documentary 13
drives author in a Ford Mustang Dark Horse in Monaco 151–3
Dutch fans and tribute songs 230–1
family and fatherhood 148–9, 205–6, 339
and Gianpiero Lambiase 14, 66–7, 103, 116, 157, 168, 169, 170, 232–3, 239, 254–5, 286–7, 290, 296–9, 306, 307–8, 346–7
Grand Prix Races
Abu Dhabi (2021) 35, 115, 147, 329
Abu Dhabi (2024) 173
Abu Dhabi (2025) 1, 2, 196–8, 337–9
Australian (2025) 68–9
Austrian (2025) 175–6, 185–6
Azerbaijan (2025) 252–4
Bahrain (2025) 125–6, 128–9, 130
Belgian (2022) 106
Belgian (2025) 205–6, 212
Brazilian/São Paulo (2024) 107, 110–11, 302
Brazilian/São Paulo (2025) 304–8
British (2025) 186–92, 236
Canadian (2025) 174–5
Chinese (2025) 102–3
Emilia-Romagna (2025) 143, 189
Hungarian (2025) 215–16
Italian (2024) 235–41, 252
Japanese (2025) 107–8, 125, 129, 189
Las Vegas (2025) 314–16
Mexican (2020) 127
Mexican (2025) 286–7, 289–92
Monaco (2021) 153
Monaco (2023) 153

Monaco (2024) 154
Monaco (2025) 147, 157–8, 168
Netherlands (2025) 229–31, 232–3
Qatar (2025) 320–1, 322–3
Saudi Arabian (2025) 133–4
Singapore (2025) 259–60, 262
Spanish (2016) 106, 162
Spanish (2025) 160, 165, 167–72
United States – Miami (2025) 134
United States – Texas (2025) 271–2
GT Racing 116, 340
and Helmut Marko 91–2, 105–6, 109–10, 123, 184, 91–2, 105–6, 109–10, 123, 184, 270, 281–2, 343–4, 345
as a junior talent 105–6
karting days 112, 113–14, 115–16, 166
on Liam Lawson's sacking 78–9
non-racing personality 147–50
on-track aggression and penalties 166–7, 169–76, 347
pre-race interview with author at Mexican Grand Prix (2025) 279–83
pre-race media interview Abu Dhabi Grand Prix (2025) 331–3
pre-season shakedown and testing in Bahrain 49–50, 56, 59
and Red Bull publicity/promotion 29, 41–3, 64
relationship with father 112–16
rumours of team change 177–82, 187, 213–14
sim racing and Team Redline 115
skill as a driver 106–11, 114–15, 116–17, 132–3, 150–1, 189, 347
Sony PlayStation driving games 111, 115
technical knowledge 111–12, 115–16, 249, 258

world championship titles 2, 7–11, 16, 28, 29, 32, 35, 49, 93, 115
see also individual Grand Prix by location; Red Bull Racing
Verstappen, Sophie 148, 205–6
Vettel, Sebastian 2, 8, 16, 23, 28, 30, 31, 89, 90, 110, 116, 160, 225, 293, 295, 297, 330, 345
Villeneuve, Jacques 135, 312
virtual safety cars 98–9, 291
Vowles, James 82

W
Waché, Pierre 14, 33–4, 35, 51–5, 57, 59, 94–5, 109, 130–3, 158, 164, 171, 207, 237, 241, 248, 303–4, 329, 348–9
Watkins, Sid 136, 161
Webber, Mark 3, 20, 30, 32–3, 83, 90, 209, 330
Webster, Anna 331
Wendlinger, Karl 269
Wheatley, Jonathan 35, 95, 120, 274, 298
Williams 13, 21, 31, 82, 83, 138, 197, 293
Williams, Frank 13, 32
Wolff, Toto 13, 83, 94, 106, 174, 178, 181–2, 213, 310, 323
Wolverson, Rich 95, 102, 119, 120, 167, 338
Wood, Richard 'Woody' 14–15, 75, 95, 143, 198, 299–301

Z
Zandvoort Racetrack 229–30
Zhou Guanyu 137